Bender Rules

Paul Marsh

Paperback Edition First Published in the United Kingdom
in 2020 by aSys Publishing

eBook Edition First Published in the United Kingdom
in 2020 by aSys Publishing

ISBN: 978-1-913438-26-5

aSys Publishing
http://www.asys-publishing.co.uk

PORTUGAL
Trás -os- Montes
Porto
Espinho
Figueira da Foz
Fatima
Nazaré
Sintra
Lisbon
Cascais
Estoril
Setúbal
Elvas
Badajoz
Alentejo
Algarve
Lagos
Portimão
Albufeira
Quarteira
Almancil
Faro
Olhão
Tavira
Monte Gordo
Vila Real d.S.A
SPAIN

SOME "PORTUGUESE" WORDS THAT YOU MAY ALREADY KNOW

Alley cats = pliers

Beaker = Espresso

Bombed here = Good morning

Camera = Town hall

Cop = A glass

Kent = Hot

Late = Milk

My = Mother

Peru = Turkey (meat)

Pie = Father

Prat = Plate

Push = Pull

Ray = King

Set = Seven

Sink = Five

Trays = Three

STRANGE COINCIDENCES

Jon Smith, who very kindly edited this book, also covered the story and wrote the newspaper article that is featured later on in the book. At that time he was a young trainee reporter working for the Bedfordshire Times.

My first name Paul means Marsh in Portuguese.

ACKNOWLEDGEMENTS

I would like to thank my good friends and family for all the help that they gave me during the long process of getting this book published especially the following.

My **mother** for keeping a lot of my old letters which I found in her possessions after she died.

My brother **David** for his proofreading skills, his memories and his sensible advice.

My two sons, **Rodrigo** for designing the cover and **Leonardo** for offering to compose the music for any future film offers that may come this way.

Anita Randall for coming up with the title by accident after I spent months trying to think of something suitable.

Martin Chambers for the digital imaging and map design.

Jon Smith not just for editing the book but for his encouragement and guidance during the whole process.

Thomas Dolan (Tommy, who still lives in the Algarve) for sharing some of his memories with me.

Guy Charlton (Guy,who has remained my closest friend during all these years - he only lives down the road)for his memories,-photos and putting me straight on a few facts towards the end of the story.

Mark Ayton for sharing some of his knowledge, advice and expertise with me.

DEDICATION

I would like to dedicate this book to my great friend **Dave Broster.** Dave and his wife Jane moved to the Algarve in March 2014 to enjoy their new life in retirement. Very sadly Dave died of a heart attack one morning in July of the same year, he had been constantly encouraging me to write a book-so this is for you Dave!

Foreword

WHEN I began writing this book, I had no idea how poignant the times would make it as I completed it, under lockdown, while the virus known as COVID-19 cast its deadly shadow on the world. There are stories here of loved ones whose lives were tragically cut short over the years, friends whose loss we had to cope with then and, if truth be told, are probably coping with still.

But for all that, these are my memories of more freewheeling days, also full of joy and laughs, of sun, sea, sand and (fill in the blank)... times that gave me lifelong friendships, that taught me a lot that those who were supposed to 'teach' me didn't. And one thing I definitely learned is that if anybody writes you off, they're wrong. Fact.

It's been a heck of a journey and along the way we got into a fair few scrapes, but mostly got out of them. As with anybody looking back on their life, I think they probably seem funnier now than they did at the time!

So without any further ado, and sincere apologies to anybody I may have unintentionally offended... please read on.

Paul Marsh,

Albufeira, March 2020.

Early Days

Bedford Modern School

1

School

I WAS infamous at school for my rebellious attitude. I don't know why I was a troublemaker. Nowadays I would probably be diagnosed with some type of syndrome. One morning, in the final term before O-levels, my past finally caught up with me. My best friend and fellow conspirator Mick Barker and I were summoned to the headmaster's office. This meant that we were to receive a serious reprimand.

The headmaster was the Reverend J.E. Taylor, better known as JET, and his black mood reflected his name. I had only met him face-to-face once before when he had come into our classroom one morning unannounced and began asking each one of us what future career we would be pursuing. After a few doctors, accountants and a couple of don't knows he turned to me and shouted: "You boy, stand up and speak up!" I managed to keep a straight face while I heard myself saying, "A disc jockey sir." He thought for a moment and looked me up and down. "Well I suppose you're small enough. Have you had a lot of experience with horses?"

When we were ushered into his study he was shaking with rage; we were shaking with fear.

He had Denis Healey eyebrows and was wearing his black gown over his black suit. He put his black mortar board on his head, and it crossed my mind that we might get the death penalty.

The only thing that wasn't black was his face – which was purple and red (I thought to myself: heart attack, maybe soon, hopefully before sentencing). He started off quietly informing us that we were a disgrace to the school and that caning was too good for us. (I nearly let out an audible phew!) His voice got louder and louder: "There has been an internal inquiry into a series of unfortunate incidents involving damage to school property and serious misbehaviour on an unprecedented scale in the classrooms and school buildings which apparently has now, according to reports from the public and the local police, spread to the town centre. Both your names are mentioned on almost every occasion, so I am sending you home as of now and, when you get there, tell your parents to come in and see me." He had reached boiling point by now and then exploded, smashing the cane down on his desk. "Get out before I change my mind about the six of the best!!!"

I'd had a beating recently from the physics master which I hadn't recovered from, so another caning would have been too painful to take. Over the years I'd had a lot of caning with varying degrees of brutality; usually on the backside, sometimes on the hands. I'd been smacked around the face and the head, had my ears twisted, knuckles rapped with a ruler. I even had a blackboard cleaner thrown at me – which was a heavy wooden object with a piece of cloth stuck on it. Luckily for me it missed, as that could have caused a serious head injury. Some of the teachers seemed to me to be sadistic vicious bastards and they were allowed to vent their fury on us with impunity.

When I arrived home, my mother greeted me with bewilderment as to why I wasn't still at school. I gave her an abridged version of events, carefully missing out most of the serious accusations for self-preservation purposes. I was ready for a verbal onslaught and maybe a slap around the face – not that either of my parents were violent, but this was serious stuff: unchartered territory even by my standards and it's hard to determine how people will react when in shock. "I knew this would happen! Wait until your father gets home!"

My father was the Head Postmaster of Bedfordshire, a member of the local Rotary Club, a Freemason, a churchwarden, a leading member of the Prisoners of War Association. Mick's dad was the county architect. Two or three days later, when the dust had settled, we heard that Mick was back at school. Apparently, his father had had a meeting with the headmaster and was given a second chance. I'd forgotten to tell my parents the part about going to see the headmaster.

A couple of days later I was re-instated and received a hero's welcome, clapping and cheering in assembly – which didn't go down too well with the teaching staff. My father had negotiated a deal with the headmaster who was also a Freemason and Rotary Club member – friends in high places etc. Apparently, Mick's dad had said that Michael had never been in any trouble before he had met me and from now on would be a model student. So, I was the ringleader and would remain at school until the end of that term so that I could take my O-levels and then leave. No sixth form for you. So, no A-levels. No university. No hope, basically.

With the O-level exams looming I was literally locked in my father's study every day after school and forced to try and catch up with all seven subjects that I didn't really know anything about because of my bad behaviour – and in some cases bad teaching.

The school was very strict and old-fashioned despite its name, Bedford Modern School. A lot of the staff had been there so long they had become institutionalised. They were a strange group of eccentric individuals, most of whom could not control a classroom which had a small group of rebellious teenagers who were permanently engaged in subversive activities, instead of paying attention to what the poor souls were trying in vain to convey. So most of whatever they were teaching us went in one ear and out the other. Especially in my case.

The exams were stretched over a few days, so I studied hard for each one individually the day before – except for French which I knew would be time wasted. My father had told me that if I got maths and English and three other subjects, he would be able to get me a job at the local chartered accountants, thanks to one of his Rotary or masonic mates – who probably owed him a favour, I suspected. Not that this information inspired me to work harder. In fact, I thought, "Out of the frying pan into the fire, being bossed around by another group of old fuddy-duddies." Unlike most of my contemporaries I found maths very easy, so I only had to worry about four of the other five subjects and one by one I managed to just scrape through – three of them with the lowest possible pass mark.

2
Work

AND SO, now the proud owner of six O-levels, I'm thrown into the world of commerce at the tender age of sixteen, mental age about twelve, and I've become an articled clerk to a Mr St. John Buller. He owned me for the next five years basically, for two pounds and ten shillings a week. My parents decided that from now on I would pay them food and lodging at three pounds a week. Now, although my training as an accountant hadn't actually begun, it didn't take long for me to realise that this arrangement wouldn't work. My father kept reminding me how lucky I was to have this opportunity and that I would have to find other sources of income to make ends meet; apparently it was a lesson in life on how to stand on my own two feet and the sooner I grasped the fact the better.

I was employed by a company called Thornton Baker, apparently one of the best in England. I had to wear a suit and tie every day but was allowed to have long hair like my idols The Beatles. I shared an office with another clerk who had already been there a few years and had failed his intermediate exams a few times. I admired him for that, and we got on well. My boss was a Mr Bullock, who had an office down the corridor. He was nearly as scary as my ex-headmaster. I suppose when you're sixteen anyone over the age of forty could come across as aggressive. I don't know if it was my attitude or my manner, but I had a knack of bringing the worst out of people in power. Everyone in high places seemed to be angry with the world, frustrated maybe that some of us weren't taking things very seriously or just not smart enough to be treated as equals. I had a problem with authority but with the constant threat of dismissal I did my best to make a go of becoming an accountant.

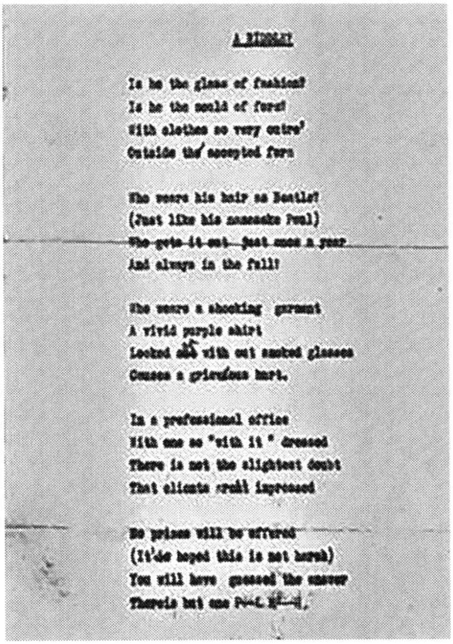

A RIDDLE

Is he the glass of fashion?
Is he the mould of form?
With clothes so very outre'
Outside the accepted form

Who wears his hair as Beatle?
(Just like his namesake Paul)
Who gets it cut just once a year
And always in the fall!

Who wears a shocking garment
A vivid purple shirt
Looked at with out smoked glasses
Causes a grievous hurt.

In a professional office
With one so "with it" dressed
There is not the slightest doubt
That clients would impressed

No prizes will be offered
(It's hoped this is not harsh)
You will have guessed the answer
There is but one P[illegible].

The office was full of odd characters, especially the older qualified accountants. Mr Clinton Bullock, or Clint as they called him (when not within hearing range) had suffered from polio and had lost the use of the muscles in his left leg, so he had a metal leg brace with a hinge in the middle which he unlocked to sit down and clicked back into place when he stood up, rather like reloading a shotgun. When he came down the corridor, he would step normally with his right foot then goose-step with his left which would come crashing down on the floor with a loud thud of metal on wood echoing round the office. As soon as we heard the click bang! click bang! approaching, panic set in; lots of shuffling of papers to hide whatever we weren't supposed to be doing. The door would fly open, usually followed by a lot of abuse, then he would somehow manage a pirouette on his good leg and crash bang his way back up the corridor, sounding to me like half comedy Gestapo, half accountant. We would listen for the click to make sure he'd sat down again before we knew the coast was clear and that we could get back to our game of battleships or whatever we were doing to avoid the daily drudgery.

My other office superior was called Sanderson, who was the go-between for the clerks and the top brass. Although he wore a suit and tie, he had taken scruffiness to a new level. He was one of those eccentric types you see on TV who are experts on subjects you've never heard of (similar to Patrick Moore or Stephen Hawking). He looked like he actually slept in his clothes; some of the local tramps would have offered him their bench for the night. He hadn't discovered personal hygiene. His hair looked like he'd just come out of a one-hour session in a wind tunnel. If he shaved, he probably didn't use a mirror, as there were clumps of stubble dotted all over his face. This was a man in a hurry with whom sometimes I had to spend all day, calling numbers out to me. He used to call them out from his ledger to me and then I would look for the amount in question in my ledger, but I just wasn't quick enough compared to him. It was almost as though he was on speed. Sometimes I swear he answered the phone before it rang, he was so fast, saying "Sarsn." When he first called numbers out to me, he would say, for example, "thur tie pounds seventeen and sixpence", meaning thirty pounds. I thought that on top of all his other problems he'd also got a numerical speech impediment.

After a day of "four ties" and "six ties" I plucked up the courage to ask him why he pronounced the words like that. He explained that it was to distinguish between thirteen and thirty etc which, as we all know, sound very similar, so we would eliminate any errors that can occur during verbal, numerative exchanges. It then occurred to him that I'd never come across this before. "I bet you thought there was something strange about me didn't you?" he bellowed, guffawing loudly. As I had to respect his seniority I politely chuckled back, "It did cross my mind I must admit", while quietly muttering under my breath, "Something strange? Where the hell do you start!"

On the other side of the building, with her own office, was Miss Lesley who was a dwarf. She had recently somehow managed to pass her driving test and owned a specially adapted Mini. (I thought an MG Midget would have been more suitable.) The pedals had blocks of wood attached to them so that she could reach them, and the steering wheel had a knob sticking up out of it to help her manoeuvre with one hand while changing gear with the other, a recipe for disaster basically.

She hadn't been driving long when she brought the town's morning traffic to a halt. There was an empty car going around and around in circles in the town centre using up both sides of the road. This went on for a minute or so until the vehicle reached escape velocity and shot out of orbit crashing into a wall. Onlookers rushed to open the driver's door to find a very dizzy but uninjured dwarf. Apparently, her coat sleeve had got caught on the steering wheel knob and, in her attempts to free herself and because of the G-force, she had fallen onto the accelerator.

After about eighteen months I had my first attempt at the intermediate exam. I had been given seven weeks off work for study leave, I had completed my correspondence course successfully, but instead of studying I spent most of my time in Bedford Park, which was just up the road from where we lived, doing what teenagers do – having fun. By the time the exams arrived I had forgotten most of what I had learnt. The exams were in London. When I saw the other contestants, I was shocked to see how much older they were and how many were Asian students. I'd been informed that it wasn't a question of passing but being in the top fifty percent. I spoke to some of the students who were university-educated or had been training for the exam on intensive courses for years paid for by rich families; people from all over the world were there. I wouldn't have been surprised if I'd been told that I was the youngest person in the exam.

The three accountancy and auditing papers were relatively easy, as that's what I'd been doing for the last year-and-a-half, but unfortunately the fourth paper was a written paper which required some literary skills and some knowledge of the financial world. A few weeks had passed when the results arrived: Passed three, failed one, which meant taking them all again in six months. I'd thought that I could bluff my way through without making any real effort, like my O-levels, but this was A-level standard with only self-tuition. Three-and-a-half more years was looking very unlikely to me.

And so, a year later, at my third attempt, I had a total of fifty pounds bet on me from my work mates that I would pass. If I passed, I would be on a higher pay scale so I would soon be able to repay them. I had already made up my mind that if I failed, I was going to leave the profession and use my winnings to go hitch-hiking in Europe. When I nervously opened the envelope with my results I was secretly hoping that I had passed if only to prove to my friends, colleagues and family that I wasn't an idiot and that I was perfectly capable of going on to take the finals and maybe be a success in life – but the devil in me wanted me to fail and set off into the unknown on an adventure. As you've probably guessed, I collected my winnings and soon after, set off on my first trip.

3

Girls

MY FIRST girlfriend Geraldine was a gorgeous redhead who lived in Turvey, a short bus ride from Bedford. We'd met at Nancy Harding's ballroom dancing classes on my first – and what turned out to be my last – lesson. The first lesson was a free trial, and someone had mentioned that there was 'posh crumpet in abundance'. I'd never heard of a bun dance but the thought of bodily contact with the opposite sex was difficult to resist. I pranced about and trod on a few toes and was told to leave by the snooty instructor; however, some of the young ladies had been amused by my antics, Geraldine in particular. I used to visit her on Sunday afternoons. We would go for country walks to escape from the watchful eyes of her parents. They were strict Catholics and despite trying everything I knew (not that I knew anything as I was a virgin) she always managed to fight off all my attempts to actually "do it". In the evening she would walk me to the bus stop. We always set off far too early so that we had plenty of time for more kissing and groping. When I was finally on the bus, I couldn't stop thinking about her and that it would be another week until I saw her again. I would sit upstairs away from the other passengers with my coat wrapped around me. Still slightly aroused, I was so sad the tears would run down my leg.

We were having dinner with her parents one evening when her older brother John arrived. I'd heard all about him but never met him – or so I thought.

As his face appeared at the door we both took one look at each other and screamed in unison, "Oh my God, not you!"

His bewildered mother asked the obvious question: "Do you two know each other?"

"It's bloody Marsh from the office!" he answered.

How neither of us knew about each other baffled me completely. John was a few years older than me; he was one of the three rogues from the office who were always bragging about their sexual conquests. I was fascinated with their stories and was totally in awe of them – and they were smart too.

After dinner John took me aside.

"So, all this time you've been mouthing-off to all the lads in the office about almost having sex with a girl with big breasts and ginger pubes and it's my fucking sister!" he shouted.

"Well you can talk, out shagging nearly every night with three or four of them on the go!" I replied.

"Never mind about me, I'm not shagging your sister, am I?"

"I haven't got a sister."

"Well I have and from now on you can leave her alone and don't you dare say anything to the lads in the office – and keep your sweaty little hands off her or else!" Like most blokes he was bigger and tougher than me, and he also had the power to give me a hard time at the office, so I had to tread carefully from then on.

While still trying it on with Geraldine every week – to no avail – I was propositioned by another girl, Judy, who made it quite clear that she was up for it as long as I dumped Geraldine. First of all, I asked Judy if she had a brother and if so where he worked! Judy's parents seemed to be quite open-minded and let me listen to records in her bedroom with her and her dog. There was one particular song by Elvis Presley (it wasn't Hound Dog) that as soon as it started, he would stick his nose up in the air and start howling like a wolf.

I'd bought my first 'packet of three' Durex condoms from the local barbers after walking around outside nervously for ages, before finally plucking up the courage to go in and ask. When I arrived at Judy's house we went straight up to her bedroom to 'listen to records' as we got more and more passionate with less and less clothes on. I fumbled to get the condom onto my erection (I'd had a practice run earlier in private) but as is often the case the rehearsal went a lot smoother than the actual event. First of all it took me ages to rip the packet open and as I was in the dark (in more senses than one) I then tried to put it on inside out. She put the Elvis record on "in case my parents hear anything" which set howling wolf off. By this time, as the outgoing Japanese prime minister might have said, I've lost the erection.

"What the hell's going on down there?" she asked, peering under the bed- covers and starting to get annoyed.

"I'm having a few technical problems; normal service will be resumed as soon as possible. And put another record on – this is my first attempt at mating, why do I have to have a werewolf egging me on!"

Finally, that evening I managed to lose my virginity. She'd done it before so she must have been seriously unimpressed by my antics. Like most things, practise makes perfect, so we did a lot of practising over the next few months until eventually we sadly split-up. I missed that dog.

Many years later I went to visit my brother in Canada. Part of the trip involved joining a large group going into the forest at night on a wolf howl. Our guide made a very impressive imitation of a howling wolf and explained that if we could all manage to keep perfectly silent; we would soon hear the howls of the real wolves. The silence seemed to go on forever and I started to think about Judy and her dog. I started giggling to myself, trying desperately to muffle the sound. There was a lot of shushing and evil looks.

The guide came over to me and said that I must keep quiet, otherwise the wolves would be frightened away. The silence returned, but there's no hope for me once I start. The more I tried to control myself the worse it got. I put my hands over my mouth to try to suppress the laughter that was building up inside of me. With my mouth blocked my nose was now the only orifice available to release the pressure. Suddenly I let out this huge snort followed by a fit of uncontrollable hysterical wheezing. I was immediately surrounded by an understandably angry noisy group of fellow nocturnal nature lovers. I'd found Canadians very charming up to that point, but the minute the slightest little thing upsets them you see a completely different side to them.

"I'm sorry, I couldn't help it," I explained.

"You've ruined the whole trip. What the fuck man? We've driven 300 miles to be here and instead of wolves we get a British guy doing donkey impressions!"

Fortunately, the guide stepped in before the lynch mob went any further. Pointing at me he suggested that I sat in the car with the windows closed while the rest of these kind people will have another chance to hear the wolves when the noise had subsided.

4
Travelling

MY FIRST journey of discovery after leaving the accountants was to hitch-hike alone to Italy. I had kissed my mother goodbye at the doorstep of our house. She was always a worrier, but I couldn't really blame her on this occasion, as she genuinely feared that I would never return. My parents had done everything in their power to prevent me from going on a trip that was generally considered quite dangerous at the time. On my first night in Belgium I was picked up (literally) by a middle-aged man who offered me a bed for the night. I was exhausted after my first day on the road and a ferry crossing, so I gladly accepted his offer.

We drove to his apartment in Ostend. He spoke in pidgin English, we had something to eat and some beers and he then showed me my bed in his spare room and said goodnight. I was chuffed with myself that I had already landed on my feet, thinking, "what a kind man", how wrong my parents and their friends had been. I'd been practically brainwashed into the fact that everyone on the continent was either a murderer, rapist, homosexual, prostitute or a thief. I was just nodding off when Michel (or whatever his name was) came into the room wearing only his bulging underpants and, without a word, attempted to get into bed with me. I don't know where it came from, but before he got any nearer, I jumped out of the bed and shouted: "My Mum told me about men like you!" I packed up my stuff and tried to leave but he said it was "très dangereux dans le nuit".

"So are you," I said.

As a peace-offering we went for a beer around the corner, where he introduced me to a very sexy young lady. A few beers later, he said if I wanted her it was only ten francs for the night. I told him I was on a limited budget that certainly didn't cover whores. Not having a lot of choice, I stayed the night at his place with my door locked. First imaginary travel diary entry: "Naive eye-opening evening" – but at least that was two items ticked off my parents' bucket list already. I wondered what the next day would bring. Maybe I'll be murdered, robbed and raped – not necessarily in that order.

That year and the next three summers were spent hitch-hiking all over Europe, visiting famous places, having fun, seeing the world. And when the money dried-up I would somehow make it back to England, get a job for the winter and plan for the next year. I went through a few bad times, had a few scrapes with the law and the locals, but also had some amazing experiences never to be forgotten. (Well, some I have now, but you know what I mean!)

When I went back to my local pub in Bedford after being away for two or three months, it was as though I'd been time-travelling. Nothing had changed, nothing had happened, some people hadn't really noticed my absence. I got a few, 'Ain't seen you around for a while' comments. I became friends with a bloke called Bisto, purely because he was the one of a few people around at that time who had hitch-hiked abroad. People used to nudge each other and point at me, whispering, "That's him, he's the one" – as if I was some kind of pervert. In the summer of 1969, I was unlucky enough to find myself in Morocco. I didn't really fancy going there, but I had no choice. Because my final destination was Gibraltar, I had to fly from Tangiers to get there. The Spanish border was closed, so this meant taking a ferry over to Ceuta, which is basically a Spanish port in Morocco, then take a bus to Tangiers airport. I had never flown before, but I really enjoyed my first flight – which although airborne, barely went above sea level.

The Spanish were threatening to invade Gibraltar. They had a few little boats parked near the airport runway. The Spanish from La Linea, who made up the majority of the workforce, had been kicked out – so there were job opportunities on the Rock. Seeing a gap in the market, three groups of us had decided, one drunken evening, to head, first to Gibraltar and then work our way around the world. I was the only one to make it there. I had had the feeling from the beginning that the others weren't taking it too seriously. I had set off with the aforementioned Bisto. As experienced travellers, we were the first group to leave Blighty and our aim was to set up base camp on the Rock and establish Headquarters. Somewhere near Valencia I lost Bisto. We had split up and he never arrived at the designated campsite. The second team to leave comprised my friend Mick from school and John Daniels. After crossing the channel to France, they actually arrived a few days later in Cardiff. The third team was Vernon and his girlfriend Cherrybank. Vernon and his girlfriend finished up in Switzerland. They had got as far as Spain, but it was too hot, so they gave up.

Vernon had spent some time with me in Italy on my first trip, with another friend Crispin, where we hitch-hiked separately and met up at an agreed campsite. This always went to plan until we went to Yugoslavia, where the agreed campsite had been closed. Plan B was to go to the nearest alternative. When I arrived, I soon met up with Crispin, but there was no sign of Vernon. After two days we had given up on him There was no way we could contact him, so we decided we would have to carry on without him. The next morning, we were walking past an English plated luxury caravan and heard a very posh lady's voice asking, "Any more tea Vernon?"

My beach residence in Gibraltar

I spent a few months on the Rock working as a civilian labourer for the British army. It was a cushy number, but badly paid, and I eventually got sacked and flew back to England.

The next year I was back in Morocco again. I had hitched a ride in the middle of Spain in a VW van with some Canadians. I was travelling with my friend Mick from Ireland, who I had just spent the hardest six months of my life working with at the Vauxhall car factory in Luton, spot-welding Bedford vans. We had been trying to get a lift to Portugal at a crossroads in the middle of Spain, but no one would stop for two long-haired foreigners in the middle of nowhere. So, we were forced to give up on that idea and tried the other direction, which was where the Canadians picked us up.

We travelled all over Morocco with them, and all went well until we visited a place called Sidi Harazem, which was famous for its water, which supposedly had therapeutic powers. When we arrived, the police were smashing their truncheons on women's heads, as they fought to have their turn to suck on what was just a hosepipe. I said to my friends, "They're animals". One of the policemen overheard me, turned to me and said "Animaux? animaux? " I thought he was going to hit me – but instead he grabbed me and frog-marched me over to a police car, threw me inside and told me to wait there. This was my *Midnight Express* moment. I was thinking, "Moroccan prison, here I come." Before I'd even had time to start contemplating my fate, the Canadians had had the presence of mind to drive the van over to the police car, with the engine revving. I opened the car door, jumped into the van and we drove off out of town as fast as we could. I looked back. No police were behind us. They were still beating up the sick and the lame. What a courageous rescue that was; if we'd all been caught, I dread to think what kind of punishment they would have meted out. We drove non-stop to Marrakesh, where Mick and I decided we'd had enough. We bought train tickets to the border and got out of the country the next day before anything else could go wrong.

Bem-Vindo a Portugal

5

Arrival in Albufeira

IN JULY 1970 I finally set foot for the first time in Portugal. After a day in Vila Real and Monte Gordo, we were starting to have regrets. We headed west to Faro and stayed the night on the campsite with the airport on one side and the Atlantic on the other. A fellow traveller informed us that Albufeira was "where it's happening man!" In the morning he pointed west across the sea. "It's over there, that white blob in the distance, you could probably walk there along the beach in a few hours." Stupidly, we took his advice and set off with our heavy rucksacks on our backs. Mick was from Donegal "which is in Southern Ireland in the North of Ireland," he used to tell everybody we met. He pointed out the fact that Faro Island was probably called that because it was surrounded by water and then we would have to come back again.

"We'll cross that bridge when we come to it," I laughed.

"What if there isn't a bridge?" he asked.

"No I meant... never mind."

Two days later we arrived, totally exhausted, in Albufeira. We'd spent the previous night on the beach in Quarteira, where we had dinner in a nearby cafe. We should have taken the soft option and got a bus, but it was as though we felt we were on some kind of pilgrimage to the promised land. For me it had all been worth it. I didn't realise it at the time, but after all those years of aimlessly wandering around I'd found what I was searching for. This was one long journey's end and the start of a new one.

We'd arrived at night, so I had no idea what a charming little fisherman's village Albufeira was until the sun came up. After spending our first morning looking around, we found the tunnel where some foreigners were sitting selling paintings and jewellery. There was John, who was an artist, with his wife June, and David who was making and selling the jewellery. They were English and had been there for about a month. We soon got chatting with them, swapped a few stories and agreed to meet up with them later on.

That evening we sat in the tunnel with our new friends, who were doing a roaring trade with the tourists. After they had packed up all their equipment, they invited us for dinner in a nearby cafe which was known as Arnaldo's.

David, the man making and selling the jewellery, told me that he was planning to leave in a couple of days and wouldn't be coming back. Out of the blue, he asked us if we would like to take over his little business and said that if we were interested, he would teach us how to do it, and show us where to buy the materials. I couldn't believe what I was hearing, and of course jumped at the opportunity. I told him that we were basically skint so we wouldn't be able to pay him anything. He said that – in the unlikely event that we would ever see each other again – a drink or two would be fine.

John and June told us that they would help us buy the tools and materials and drive us around to the suppliers. The jewellery was made of horseshoe nails with galvanised wire for the links. I had no idea what a horseshoe nail looked like until I bought my first box. They are made of steel, flat and tapering to a point in some cases with a lump on the other end. There are different sizes depending on the size of the animal's hooves. The big chunky ones were for the men's bracelets and the smaller ones for the ladies. With a pair of round-nose pliers gripping the point, David showed us how to bend them into a figure of eight which was then linked together with the wire. He used the same pliers to make what looked like a long spring and then cut them one by one to make rings, which, once in position, were closed with a flat pair of pliers. The last bent nail had a little curly bit so that the last link could fit over to open and close the bracelets.

David was driving back to England the next day, and sadly Mick decided to get a lift back with him. He'd been badly sunburnt on the beach walk and was suffering with mild heat stroke. The temperature in the Algarve in July was unbearably hot even at night, so we said our goodbyes and off they went.

My first few attempts at bending the nails were pretty hopeless. I could manage the smaller ones quite easily, but the larger ones were impossible. I just didn't have the strength in my wrists; but as time went on and after investing in a pair of industrial gauntlets, I eventually got the knack of being a bender.

John and June were camping in an old Commer van at the end of town in a sandy car park, where the Marina is today, near two small beaches. I pitched my tent amongst some pine trees, at the top of a very steep hill which overlooked the car park and the two beaches. In the daytime I got into a routine of bending enough nails to make about twenty bracelets per day.

At night we would traipse down to the tunnel and set up shop. All I needed was a black cloth to show my wares. Most evenings I would sell everything that I'd made that day. One bracelet was 25 escudos which wasn't bad, considering 1000 escudos was worth something like four pounds – and chicken, salad, chips and wine was also about 25 escudos. When business was over for the night, we would pack everything up and go to Arnaldo's.

I had soon been able to repay John and June and could now afford to have all my meals in cafes and restaurants, spend a lot of time on the beach and have fun at night after work. I got so good at bending the nails I started doing it while I was selling which attracted more attention and was good for sales. I would let members of the public have a try at bending the nails just to prove how strong and clever I was.

But after a couple of times when nails went flying through the air John quite rightly told me to stop showing off and not to encourage any further audience participation before someone was blinded!

6

For Dog's Sake!

DURING the last few days my life had changed completely, and I was now living like a king by my meagre standards. I was making a good living. I wasn't exactly living in luxury, but it didn't bother me. I was getting on great with John and June – and as things turned out, they were to become two of the best friends that I have ever had. The next day I was about to make another one.

In those days, there were packs of what appeared to be stray dogs strolling around town. It wasn't unusual to see twenty or more dogs together. I'd never owned a dog and knew little about them. They were in packs, so I was told at the time, because they were uncastrated males following a poor bitch on heat. Most of them actually weren't strays. They had probably been sitting at home, minding their own business, when they had picked up the scent which to them is irresistible – and off they went in hot pursuit.

A few days earlier I had seen one of these gangs of canine sex maniacs taking it in turns to jump on the back of quite an attractive blonde number, and from what I could see, most of them were failing miserably (not that I had any voyeuristic or bestiality tendencies, it was just hard to ignore them) . There was one particular nasty-looking character that appeared to be able to successfully do the business while simultaneously keeping the rest of the pack at bay until he had finished his go.

Later that evening that same canine Casanova plonked himself down next to me. It certainly wasn't love at first sight, especially on my part, and when he then got up and decided to sit on my black cloth with all my shiny new bracelets on, I took an instant dislike to him. I had some very strong words with him.

But instead of getting off my now filthy-dirty display he went round and round a few times on the cloth and made himself even more comfortable by lying down and got himself into the curled-up sleeping position simultaneously letting out a huge sigh as if to say, "what a day I've had!" – which made his lips vibrate, blowing dust everywhere.

Obviously, this wasn't good for business. It now looked like I was trying to sell a dog. The tourists were sensibly keeping a wide berth. I tried to pull the cloth from under him, but to no avail. He looked up angrily at me as if to say, "Don't you dare!" Eventually John came over to assist and between us we managed to push him off and shoo him away; but, as I soon learnt, the more you encourage dogs not to do something, the more they do it. It's a game as far as they're concerned. I cleaned all the jewellery, tried to get the dirt off the cloth, and started selling again. I lasted about five minutes, before the dog was back and made a beeline for the cloth. It was at this point where I completely lost it. I'm normally very calm and laid-back about most things – but sometimes something snaps, and all fear and logic go out the window.

"Get off my jewellery you stupid animal." I screamed.

"Don't ever come back again or else!" – as if there was a chance in hell that he would get the message. Not really thinking straight, I then kicked the dog up the arse as he ran off. I was thinking, "Shit, maybe he'll come back and attack me" – but I was so wound up I didn't care anymore.

John and June weren't happy because I'd frightened away some potential clients but eventually things calmed down and all was back to normal.

"Bloody dog's ruined the evening" I said to John.

"Sorry about that. I'll buy dinner tonight."

"Well I doubt if we'll see that mongrel again."

"I have a feeling you might," June laughed.

"Why do you say that?" I asked.

"Turn round!"

Sure enough there he was, sat down by my bag.

"I think he likes you," June suggested.

We packed up and went off for dinner. We sat down looking forward to a reasonably quiet evening for a change. Next minute there's a lot of shouting and screaming, Arnaldo's holding a chair over his head, trying to intervene in what looked like some kind of punch-up going on outside. We went outside to investigate – and there was the same bloody dog on top of Arnaldo's black dog; territorial issues of course. Our new four-legged friend then walked in as if he owned the place and sat down under our table. Arnaldo was pointing at the dog and shouting "Fora!" (Get out!). His wife Joselia was trying to patch-up their poor now-wounded animal. Eventually things calmed down and the dog stayed under the table until we left. There was nearly another dog scuffle on the way out, and then we started on our journey home, with our new companion trotting along behind. We arrived at our destination, I said goodnight to John and June and started the steep climb up to my tent. I had hoped that somewhere en-route we had lost the dog. I certainly hadn't seen him for a while, so I got in my tent and closed the flaps that fastened together with Velcro.

I hadn't been lying there for long when I heard something outside. On my hands and knees in complete darkness I opened the tent flap – to be greeted with a huge wet nose followed by the canine equivalent of a kiss. I'd been hoping for a bit of love action now I was settled into my new home. What more could a young lady wish for? Who would be the first to join me in a night of passion under canvas, I had wondered? Who's my first visitor? Guess who!

It was a two-man tent. I was 5ft 8inches tall, about 9 stone, or 130 pounds as our transatlantic brothers would say, so in theory there was plenty of room inside for me, a few clothes and a rucksack. But add one large dog: instant disaster. I tried to stop him getting inside the tent; then, once he was in, I got out, hoping he might follow. That didn't work, so I climbed back in, turned on my torch to assess the situation, and discovered he'd made himself at home, spread out on my sleeping bag.

"And where do I sleep?" I shouted at him. "This is ridiculous – you'll have to get out!"

I managed to pull the sleeping bag from under him, got in it and, despite everything, fell asleep. The next morning, I woke up struggling to breathe. I had a mouth full of canvas, as the tent had collapsed on top of me. He'd obviously gone off during the night and knocked the front tent pole over as he'd left. When I finally managed to crawl out of the wreckage, there was no sign of him thank goodness.

Later on that day, I caught up with John and June and told them all about my nocturnal visit, which they thought was hilarious of course. They had also heard scratching on the outside of their van during the night.

"I wonder what that could have been?" I enquired sarcastically.

From then on, as soon as we set up to sell, every evening along came the dog, and thanks to him I had to buy a collapsible picnic table and chair to prevent any further cloth incidents. This turned out to be a very sound investment as it gave a more professional appearance to my display at a more convenient viewing height, making it a lot easier, particularly for the older clients to feel the goods as it were. For me, sitting in a chair was a great improvement from being on the pavement. I now had a bit of extra baggage to carry home every night -but, after a few glasses of vinho, who cared?

After a few days, the dog had become part of the gang. He was about seven or eight years old, sandy-coloured, like the majority of the local dog population.

His face was like a mastiff, he had a very thick neck and a big chest like a bulldog. He had a stump for a tail and was covered in scars mainly around the face. His ears had chunks missing out of them, – all that was missing was a gold tooth and a facial tattoo and we would have had a canine Mike Tyson (who wasn't around then but you get the picture). We decided to call him Bender: somehow it felt right. I was bending nails and he was as hard as nails.

Over the next few weeks I gradually got to know and understand his behaviour patterns. Most of the local dogs would steer well clear of him, but he still got into fights almost on a daily basis – some of them quite terrifying. I knew when something was going to kick-off as it would begin with one or sometimes two dogs cocking their legs up, growling at him Then he would cock his leg up and piss on the exact spot where they had pissed, followed by a few circling manoeuvres while glaring at each other showing their teeth. And then suddenly, just when you were hoping that one of them would back down, all hell would break loose. Bender would go straight in, usually knocking his victim over, grabbing their neck as they went over, biting hard into them. That was usually the knock-out blow. He'd release his grip, leaving blood and hair all over the place, people running about screaming, with me trying to pull him back. Total carnage. I tried intervening a couple of times, but it only made things worse – plus there was my own safety to consider: The best thing was to just let him get on with it. He'd been doing it for years, so why bother?

With people he was literally a different animal. He was the type of dog that you would be wary of if you didn't know him but, once you'd been properly introduced, he was very good-natured. He used to sit by people eating in outdoor restaurants and put his begging face on which always seemed to work well, especially with tourists, who would usually throw him a few scraps. I suppose he'd developed a technique over the years, where first he'd get rid of all the other begging dogs, then give the diner the sad look. If that didn't work the paw would come up usually greeted by, "Aah poor dog, must be starving!" If all else failed, which I saw a few times, he would put his front paws on the table and pick up the steak or whatever they were eating and run off with it!

I also heard a report that he was once in a restaurant up on his back legs, with his front paws resting on the terrified customer's back, looking over their shoulder staring at the plate as if to say, "Come on, hurry up I haven't got all day!"

We learned from one of the locals that Bender was actually called 'Leão' (Lion) and belonged to a little girl who was the daughter of the owners of a hotel called Vila Recife almost opposite Arnaldos. One day she came down to the tunnel and called him to come home, but he wouldn't leave us. She pulled him by his collar, but he wouldn't budge. She ran off in tears, which was very sad for us to watch – but there wasn't a lot we could do about it. At least we now knew he had a home, and that's why he had a collar and was probably well fed, despite his begging. Also, it was a great comfort to me, because I knew that when the summer was over, I was going to have to say goodbye to him. There was no way that I could take him with me back to England – although maybe I would have done if it wasn't for the quarantine laws. He'd become my dog, basically, and John and June were the Godparents.

Bender had stopped coming up to the tent at night, but he'd always turn up sooner or later most days, somewhere or another. He knew how to find us by following the scent. There could be hundreds of people on the beach, but he'd always find me – or my towel if I was in the sea or in the cafe. One day, one of the locals came rushing over to me on the beach waving her hands in circles and pointing up at the top of the hill where my tent was. The tent was moving around on its own, at some speed, banging into trees then rolling over down the hill with my clothes falling out all over the place. I ran up the hill trying to understand what on earth was happening. I reached the tent just in time to prevent it falling over a steep rocky drop. And there was Bender inside, looking very guilty and a bit worse for wear! He never got the hang of the Velcro opening. I'd sewn up the front of that tent on quite a few occasions thanks to him crashing through like a bull in a china shop. I re-erected what was left of my tent and gathered up all my belongings that were strewn all over the hill side.

7

John and June

John Coy

JOHN'S surname was Coy, although he was anything but. He was in his early thirties, heavily built, handsome, boisterous and always lived life to the full. He had fallen in love with Spain, where he spent a lot of time in Andalusia in cities such as Seville and Granada, where he made a decent living during the day as a street artist. At night he was enjoying the company of flamenco dancers, bullfighters, Gipsies, all kinds of crazy characters. He reminded me of Oliver Reed (the famous hell-raising swash-buckling actor) and could often become a bit of handful after a few drinks.

His wife June was very attractive, with a slender figure topped off by abnormally large breasts. She regularly received a lot of unwelcome attention from men, especially when she was alone selling the paintings. John said it was good for business and reckoned that she could handle herself.

Sometimes John had to make an appearance just to get rid of all her admirers. He'd give her a kiss and a cuddle to let everyone know who she was married to – which usually had the desired effect.

Once he winked at me and whispered, "I'm a bit of a leg man myself."

Frequently over dinner in Arnaldo's they would have a drunken argument that continued on the walk home: shouting and swearing, dropping paintings and bits of equipment on the way. The stress of living rough and working together, being in each-other's company for 24 hours a day took its toll, and the alcohol would bring out all their frustrations.

In the morning, looking down the hill from my tent through bleary eyes, I would sometimes see their van rocking backwards and forwards. This was a clear indication that they had resolved their problems.

Arnaldo

Most nights over dinner we were joined by people who had either got chatting to us in the tunnel, or customers who had bought our wares. There was a noisy drunken party atmosphere almost every night that often got completely out of control. Arnaldo and his wife never complained. They were glad of the business and tolerated almost anything.

There was a restaurant next door that was more up-market. Some nights they had to ask us to keep the noise down, which we usually managed to do for a while, but one night, as the evening progressed into the normal rowdy early hours of the morning, we had a lock in. Arnaldo had closed the front door because some angry male diners from the restaurant next door were outside and were refusing to leave until we came outside. We weren't bothered and hoped that they would eventually go away.

They then started banging on the door, so Arnaldo suggested calling the police. We didn't really want to get involved with the authorities, as we had already been warned about our late-night bad behaviour. John then decided that he would go out alone and have a word with them; thankfully he told the rest of us to stay behind and he took Bender with him for back-up. June was screaming at him, telling him not to be so stupid – but he wasn't listening. Arnaldo opened the door to let John and Bender out. A minute or so went by, John walked nonchalantly back in, sat down and said, "Don't worry they've gone."

"What did you do?" I asked him.

"There's a metal road sign outside so I bent it over and pulled it out of the ground and waved it in their faces."

"So, then what happened?"

"They took one look at me and another at Bender and, after quickly assessing the situation, ran off down the road!"

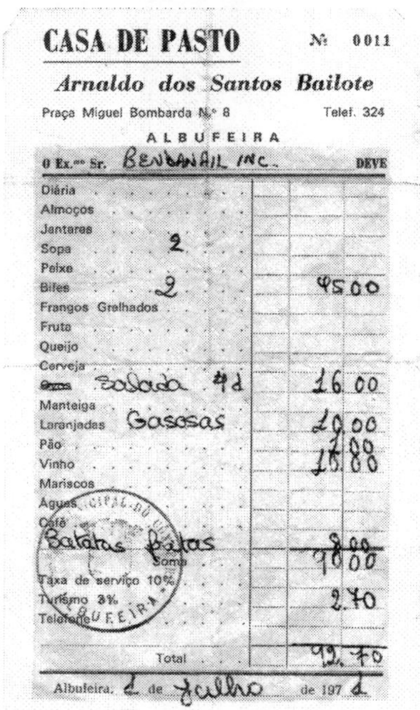

CASA DE PASTO Nº 0011

Arnaldo dos Santos Bailote

Praça Miguel Bombarda N.º 8 Telef. 324

ALBUFEIRA

O Ex.mo Sr. BENDANAIL INC. DEVE

Diária		
Almoços		
Jantares		
Sopa	2	
Peixe		
Bifes	2	45 00
Frangos Grelhados		
Fruta		
Queijo		
Cerveja		
~~Ovos~~ Salada	4d	16 00
Manteiga		
Laranjadas	Gasosas	20 00
Pão		2 00
Vinho		15 00
Mariscos		
Aguas		
Café		
Batatas fritas		8 00
Soma		90 00
Taxa de serviço 10%		
Turismo 3%		2.70
Telefone		
Total		92.70

Albufeira, 2 de Julho de 1972

8

For All Intents and Purposes

I THINK the mobile tent story got around, because the next day I was asked to visit the Marine Police in a little office on the cliff-top overlooking the fishermen's beach. I could still hardly speak a word of Portuguese, but somehow explained to them that I was camping on the hill "over there", pointing across the sea. I had to fill in a form saying how long I'd been there and what I was doing etc. I thought they may charge me with loitering with intent. Despite their harsh exterior they were very pleasant and said that there wasn't a problem, but that every visitor must have a document stating where they were staying and for how long. They typed out the form for me to sign and I noticed it said that my place of residence was called Scorpion Hill! I asked them why it had that name and they laughed at me and said, "Why do you think it's called Scorpion Hill?!!"

That night when I got back to my tent, I went out with my torch on scorpion patrol. All that time I'd been there I'd never seen one, but of course I hadn't really been looking for them. There were snakes, that's for sure, I hadn't seen any of them either, but I'd seen the dog chasing an invisible fast-moving target through the grass in zig-zagging movements. I had to fend off a few air strikes by huge armour-plated flying beetles, but they turned out to be harmless. Once, I got bitten in the night on my cheek and the whole side of my face was swollen for days. The experts said it was probably a spider – and to this day I can still feel a small lump under my skin where whatever it was bit me.

Camping in the wild with no facilities meant having to be at one with nature as it were. Most of the time I used the toilets in the cafes and had showers on the beach, or just went for a swim. On one memorable occasion I was lying in my tent at night and felt an urgent need to go for a number two. These fortunately rare events are a pain in the arse in more ways than one and have a certain unpredictability about them. Normally I would have had time to get myself organised, get the torch so I could see where I was going, if you know what I mean, a spade to dig a hole in the sandy soil that was about to be soiled, and of course a toilet roll to wipe my nose or whatever else you can think of. I would have usually gone up and over the top of the hill and hid in the bushes – not that there was ever anyone around, especially at night. This took time and time in this case wasn't on my side. I could feel the tell-tale rumblings of an imminent explosion. I heard myself saying, "Get out of the tent, get out of the tent." I flew out of the tent into the darkness, simultaneously pulling my shorts down, as I could tell there were only seconds to spare before blast-off, fell over the dog, rolled over, banged my head on a pine tree, then somehow managed to adopt the official crouching position before it came pouring out whoosh! Shitsville Tennessee!

I obviously hadn't had time to find any of the previously mentioned equipment, so to clean myself as best as I could, under the circumstances, I continued in the crouching position step by step back to the tent doing my version of a thin sumo wrestler. Fortunately, in the moonlight I spotted the toilet paper. After using a month's supply of bog roll I felt reasonably satisfied that I was presentable, found the torch and the spade and went over to the bomb site to attempt to hide the mess. I shovelled piles of sand all over the infected area. Bender joined in, doing his cat covering poo impersonation, I wondered what he had made of the evening's events? When I was convinced that it was safe to go back to sleep, I had a quick check with the torch that the area had been properly sanitised – and there in the middle of the disaster zone was a black scorpion! Any other time I would probably have shit myself, but I'd already done that, so I just stood there terrified staring at it. It lifted its tail, threatening me by pointing its sting at me. I don't know what came over me, but I ran up the hill shouting: "Fuck! Scorpion!" I had gone into panic mode and it took me a while before I plucked up the courage to go back. Even the dog had run off. I think he had felt the danger signals that I was transmitting. I'd heard that if you were stung by a scorpion you should go to hospital immediately. Then I wondered, 'What if a dog got stung? It might be lethal.'

It was really hot that night, so being a natural-born coward I went down to the beach and slept there. In the morning I went over to John's van for some moral support.

He came out and asked, "What's happened to your head?" I hadn't noticed, but I'd obviously cut my head open when I head-butted the pine tree.

As we climbed up the hill, I told him all about the previous night's encounter with the scorpion and my little accident. "Haven't you heard of the expression, 'Don't shit on your own doorstep?'" he asked.

He suggested that for hygiene reasons I move to a different spot a few metres away, which I thought was a good idea – but then he said maybe not to bother, as he and June had been talking things over and thought it was a good time to pack up for this year and move on and go somewhere else for the winter.

I was really shaken by this news. All good things come to an end sooner or later, but why now all of a sudden? He explained that it was October, they hadn't been selling well for the last few days, and felt it was a good time to leave. It would probably start raining soon and get colder at night and there weren't many tourists around anymore, so for them it was all over. My first reaction was to stay, but as the thought of being on my own began to sink in I realised how much I depended on them; things just wouldn't be the same without them. "We're thinking about driving across Spain and getting the ferry to Ibiza," said John.

"You can come with us if you want to."

"What about the dog?"

"We'll have to leave him here. He's not our dog for a start. This is his home and he can't go to Spain – anyway we've already talked about this." I could tell by John's voice that he was getting annoyed with me, but at the same time I knew he was just as upset as I was at the thought of leaving Bender behind.

9
My Albufeira

DURING those last few months, not consciously realising it at the time, I'd stumbled on by chance whatever it was that I was searching for.

Everything fitted into place. It was as if I was meant to be there. The fishing village, as it was then, was an idyllic spot. The now famous view from the Pau da Bandeira on the sandstone cliff top to the east overlooking the fisherman's beach is stunning, with the colourful fishing boats lying on the sand, the white houses all mingled together on top of each other on the opposite promontory. If you look a bit further to the west across the bay, you can see the pine trees and my ex-campsite! In those days you could walk around the village in five or ten minutes. You could go up and over through the narrow cobbled streets, or round from the fisherman's beach, via what is now known as the bar street, into the garden in the centre, then up to the left following the road where it gets very narrow between some houses, then left to the tunnel, and right, before the tunnel entrance, leading west out of town. You can also walk along the beach from the fishermen's beach onto the main beach (unless there's a high tide or rough sea) and go up the steps to the hotel Sol e Mar esplanade and through the tunnel that goes under the hotel. There were only a few cafes and restaurants in those days – and of course the famous Sir Harry's bar.

There were only two roads in and out of the village, one-way in the part near the tunnel area heading west because it was so narrow. I had to admire the skill of the coach drivers and how they navigated their way through the bends and up past the tunnel – some of them without even stopping.

A lot of drivers in a car couldn't even manage that feat. It was a nightmare for pedestrians. On many occasions I witnessed people nearly being crushed or run over. When there was an accident or an incident the whole place soon ground to a halt, especially around the central garden area, which brought on the inevitable cacophony of horn-blowing shortly followed by a lot of frustrated arm-waving and shouting until the GNR police arrived on foot, blowing their whistles at everybody and trying to locate the source of the hold-up. This was quite a regular occurrence, which sometimes at night was combined with a power cut and then the water being cut off. It happened so often that we had invested in camping gas lamps (more stuff to carry) but as was often the case it worked out well for us, as the tourists were going nowhere and, like moths, were attracted to the light.

Road rage apart, the local people were very mild mannered, especially compared to other Latin countries that I had visited. I'd found a lot of hostility towards foreigners in Spain, Italy and Greece – almost bordering on xenophobia. Here they were polite, helpful and friendly. If you asked where something was, they would soon realise that it was pointless trying to explain, drop whatever they were doing and, as long as it was nearby, they would take you there. They were honest and there was little or no crime. Someone told me that you could leave your belongings on the beach in total safety, as nobody would touch them. All the time I was up on that hill nothing ever went missing, yet the poverty level must have been way below normal European standards.

They appeared to be content with what little they had and accepted their lot. As foreigners it was as though we were from another world, but they didn't appear to be openly resentful, just curious. When we sold at night, we always had a crowd of the locals, mainly young men, just staring at us, watching in amazement at the amount of money changing hands. We probably made one month of their wages in one night. At the end of the evening's trading they would gradually make their way home having enjoyed the entertainment. The following night all the same faces were back again, quietly waiting for the show to begin. Hardly a word was ever spoken. After a while we got on nodding terms with some of them. Occasionally one of them offered a helping hand with something, but that's all it ever was. We never really made friends with any of them – which was strange, as we were open to friendship. It was as though there was an invisible barrier, as well as the language hurdle to overcome, before we would be able to connect with them.

It might have been down to the Salazar fascist regime and the fear of the PIDE secret agents that apparently were around in plain clothes keeping an eye on things. The GNR police in their Nazi-style uniforms, jackboots-and-all looked very unsavoury characters. Fortunately, they never bothered us because John had made a deal with the head of the 'Gestapo' (as I called them) by offering the mayor a painting in return for a verbal permit to sell in the tunnel.

The local people were not allowed to do almost anything: definitely not grow their hair long (the men of course) or camp outside the village (Gipsies excepted), let alone sell in the street. We had been warned about our wild behaviour on a few occasions, but John always managed to smooth things over with some kind of backhander. John often reminded me that it was him that had the permission and that I was unofficially in the same team as it were and as long as we behaved ourselves there wouldn't be a problem. No one else was going to be granted any favours and, as had already happened a couple of times, other foreign travelling artists and street sellers had set up in our place and it was John who had to politely move them on, explaining that otherwise we would soon be a hippy market and that we would all be chucked out.

One evening, the police chief himself had started shouting abuse at me. There was a lot of finger-wagging, backed up by a couple of his henchmen nodding away behind him. I didn't understand a word of what he was saying or what the problem was, I just kept saying "desculpe" (sorry). I got the distinct feeling that he didn't have much time for me or the dog. I was going to offer him a bracelet, a big chunky one that would complement his hairy wrist but thought better of it. He had strange pointed upside-down v-shaped eyebrows. I presume he'd had some sort of accident and had surgery that left him looking permanently surprised, as if he'd just heard that the local bank had been robbed and he'd got frozen in time. I always struggled to keep a straight face when he spoke to me. I wondered to myself what he would look like if he was really surprised. Maybe his eyebrows would disappear under his helmet.

I wasn't doing very well with learning Portuguese, as John always did all the ordering in the cafes and restaurants, but I did gradually pick up a bit. My first impression on hearing Portuguese was that it was a Russian version of Spanish. I could never work out where one word ended, and the next word started. When I was alone, I'd usually manage to get the message across one way or another. Very few people seemed to speak English.

There was a restaurant in the garden where I would sometimes have lunch, where the waiters were very friendly, and Bender was a regular. The only problem there was that, after ordering the meal and getting the obligatory bottle of wine on the table, it could take up to two hours before the food was on the table-during which time I'd usually drunk so much on an empty stomach that by the time the meal arrived, I and whoever I was with and most of the other clients were completely pissed.

If I was alone, mainly out of sheer boredom, I would pass the time – with the help of the waiters (who also wanted to learn the words in English) – trying to learn all the names of the objects in the restaurant, which started off as a harmless learning exercise but, as the minutes dragged on and the wine took hold, things often got out of control. Plate is prato, spoon is colher, fork is garfo, table is mesa etc.etc. The trouble began with knife which is faca which is pronounced more like fucca. I made the mistake of informing the waiter Martinho (who had a stammer) that faca sounded similar to a swear word in English. Before long he was going round the tables: "fffucker, fffucker", holding up a knife. When Portuguese customers sat down, after taking their order, he would point towards me holding up a knife "Que isto?"(what's this?) "Fucker" I'd shout across the room. He'd obviously told them what it meant. After a few "faca" shouts the whole place was in uproar and I had been turned into a performing seal.

Many, many, years later I went into a restaurant near Guia. To my surprise the owner was the same Martinho and we looked at each other and said "FACA!" in unison, followed by the usual hugging and shaking of hands.

There were many other words that confused me: puxe, pronounced "push", means pull. Hence the number of times I've banged my head on doors or nearly pulled my arm out of its socket. I once sneezed and was asked if I was constipated: "Estas constipado?" – which is actually, "Have you got a cold?" Hot is quente, pronounced Kent, which is where I was born; Cão, pronouced "cow", is dog; good morning (bom dia) sounds like "bombed here"; Peru means Turkey, which could upset your travel plans; A bifana (pronounced beefarna) is a pork meat sandwich. The most amazing coincidence in international swear words came to light one night when I was watching a football match on TV, and when there was a corner, they all shouted cant! which sounded to me like a cockney using the C word. The Portuguese equivalent for the C word sounds almost identical to corner.

10

Leaving Albufeira

HEAVY rain had been forecast. It had only rained once or twice in the four months that I'd been there. We decided that we would pack up and leave the next day, which I was quite excited about, but dreading the moment we had to escape from Bender. I say escape, because I could tell he knew that we were going to leave. A lot of animals have a sixth sense or some uncanny ability to understand your feelings. Bender was a canine psychic. It almost came to the ridiculous point where we couldn't talk in front of him. I'd hoped that we might just go without saying goodbye to him, which would have been unbearable but not as upsetting as actually seeing him watch us drive away. We had tried to put him in the back of the van once to take him out for a trip, but he refused to get in. John reckoned that he might have been caught by the council dog catcher. If they weren't claimed after a few days they were put down, so we heard. If that was true, maybe the little girl rescued him or, more likely, he got out on his own.

The next day we packed up all our gear and as soon as the tent came down, he knew what was coming. He looked so sad, nearly as bad as me. John and June gave him a big hug and got in the van, then I gave him a last big cuddle, trying to fight back the tears, I could see in his eyes he was saying, "Don't go, don't leave me." I jumped in the front of the van and off we went as fast as we could.

As we accelerated down the road John looked in the mirror.

"Shit! He's right behind us!"

"Go faster!" I screamed.

"I'm doing over thirty mph!"

"He's still coming, he'll get run over in a minute!"

"Or have a heart attack."

Finally, he slowed down and gave up. We were all crying our eyes out, to the point where we had to stop the van because John couldn't see properly through the tears. We had a group hug and got going, in case Bender had got a second wind and started chasing again – which wouldn't have surprised me.

We drove across Spain to Valencia, then took the ferry to Majorca. After a brief visit we went to Minorca then finally on to Ibiza. I know this book is about me and Portugal, but I've decided that I'm allowed to go off-piste occasionally. The sight that greeted us in Ibiza's main town in the west, San Antonio, was something I'll never forget. In the main square, instead of the normal Spanish people sitting around in the cafes, the whole place had been taken over by Californian 'Flower Power' Hippies. Wealthy Hippies. Businessmen who had 'dropped out' with their chicks. I thought I had long hair until I saw them – I felt like Yul Brynner. They were all drinking the local beer and firewater, zonked out on LSD, Mescaline and, of course, Marijuana; not that I was a drug behavioural expert. I found out all about this later. They were semi-naked, covered in beads and peace-and-love regalia. The ones who were still mobile were doing wheelies on their powerful Bultaco track bikes.

Peter Klopp

John led a genuine bohemian life-style out of choice, but detested anything or anybody associated with drugs, or what he would call 'Plastic Hippies'. We drove back out of town, ourselves almost hallucinating and still in shock. Somewhere en route we had made friends with a reasonably normal American, Peter Klopp. He was a New York Jew, he had friends in a beautiful, relatively undiscovered place called San Carlos. We spent a few days there, after which John and June decided to leave for the Canary Islands. We promised to keep in touch and meet up again next year in Albufeira.

I quite liked San Carlos, and with my new acquaintance Peter we rented a little house in the hills with a beautiful sea view. The house was very basic: no running water or electricity, not even a toilet, but we managed to get by. One day I was walking past the neighbouring property, which was surrounded by high walls, when I heard someone shout, "Morning!" in an upper-class English accent. I looked around but couldn't work out where the voice had come from. Then again, "Hello old chap." I listened carefully, I heard some kind of squeaking sounds coming from inside the walls and then I couldn't believe my eyes!

It was Terry Thomas the famous actor with the moustache and the big grin and the gap between his front teeth bouncing up and down on his trampoline! I could see his head only briefly, in intervals of a few seconds, so trying to have a conversion with a bouncing head – albeit a famous one – was impossible. I thought he might stop and lean over the wall for a chat, but he carried on, so I left him to it. I would like to have said that, as his new neighbours, he invited us round for drinks. But he never did.

A few days later I ventured a little further along the dirt track. I came across another quite luxurious villa. There was a couple sitting outside. They waved and invited me to come in. They were English and after sun-downers they insisted that I stay for dinner. How could I refuse! Over dinner we swapped stories and it turned out that they were guests of Diana Rigg, the actress of *The Avengers* fame. The house belonged to her and they were house-sitting while she was away. The couple were Delia and Brian who worked for the BBC. Delia had written the theme tune for Doctor Who. They were electronic music specialists working on an album called *White Noise*.

When dinner was over, I thanked them for a wonderful evening, said my farewells, but they refused to let me go until I had a quick tour of the house. The highlight was Diana's bedroom. The centrepiece was an enormous revolving round bed covered in cushions and pillows. They then decided that I had to stay the night, as it was far too late for me to walk back in the dark. We all sat huddled together on the sofa. A bottle of wine was opened, which soon disappeared, followed by another. We were laughing and joking when out of the blue Brian asked me if I'd like to sleep in Diana's bed . . . with him!

Up to that moment I had presumed that they were a slightly eccentric couple, but artists usually are. Maybe they were a couple, they'd been plying me with alcohol for hours, ménage-a- trois here we come! I'd been feeling a bit light-headed before Brian had made his intentions known. Now I was totally embarrassed, confused, shocked, and then I wondered if they had drugged me. All sorts of unpleasant thoughts were going through my head when, just as I was beginning to fear the worst, Delia came to the rescue.

"Look Brian, he isn't queer so let me have him."

She grabbed my arm and dragged me into her bedroom: "Just ignore him. He tries it on with all the young men once he's had a few!"

She was a tall, strong woman, almost manly, not my type at all, but I was so relieved to have escaped his clutches that once I was in bed with her all was soon forgotten.

The next morning the three of us had breakfast together with our hangovers. Brian asked me to forgive him – which I did. We shook hands. I kissed Delia goodbye and made my way back home. Peter and I spent quite a few evenings with them over the next couple of weeks, as they loved entertaining and it was sad to see them go.

Peter then bought a car, an old orange Citroen Deux Chevaux. A few days later he walked into a wall and broke his nose. He simply didn't trust the local island hospital, so he flew to England to get it fixed. I couldn't drive, but I needed to get around – so with a bit of trial and error I taught myself to drive on the dirt roads. I soon got the hang of things and within days I was rally-driving all over the island. One day, when I was out in the car, I picked up one of the American hippies. He asked me what I was doing, so I told him that I was learning to drive.

“Hey man, I love your British sense of humour!

Peter eventually returned with his nose patched-up. It was December, it was cold, so I left Ibiza and went home to my ever-suffering parents back in Bedford, England, as the Yanks called it.

1971

11

Back to Albufeira

MY second year in Albufeira started where I'd left off, almost exactly the same as the year before. I arrived in June with my friend Graham. We camped in the same spot. John and June were at the bottom of the hill in their van; next door was a military-style tent where John's dad Jasper was staying. I had an emotional reunion with Bender who, according to one of the locals, had sat in the tunnel for a few hours nearly every day during the winter, presumably hoping that one day we would turn up again.

John had been in Albufeira for a couple of months. It was still very quiet business-wise and they had been told by the police to move to the garden in the centre of town. The tunnel was a much better location for selling, as people were constantly strolling by. The garden was somewhere to sit and relax with no passing trade. However, despite the police's attempt at ruining our trade things worked out well for us and, as the summer progressed, we became a tourist attraction – much to the chagrin of the authorities.

Jasper Coy was 65, he had lived in forty different countries working in oil exploration. He had a white beard, white hair, weather-beaten complexion and shuffled along rather than walked. He looked to me like he'd been shipwrecked for a few years and just been rescued. He had a twinkle in his eye, was always laughing and joking, telling stories of his times in the Brazilian jungle or the Gobi Desert. He was also an artist, so he would sit in the garden during the day, selling his and John's paintings. Graham would spend hours with him in the garden, fascinated by his tales.

I don't know why, but my undying memory of him is seeing him moving a bit faster than usual across the road in the centre of town holding a toilet roll. He was heading towards the public conveniences. I was sitting in a cafe nearby – he spotted me and waved the toilet paper in the air, laughing. He shouted, "Guess where I'm going!" He didn't give a shit.

Over the next few weeks we had almost reached celebrity status with the tourists. We were invited to lots of dinners and parties at some pretty fancy places. In those days, before mass tourism, the majority of people on holiday in Albufeira were quite well-to-do as it was expensive to travel by air and accommodation was hard to find. There were a lot of famous faces around from the world of music, BBC personalities and film stars. The only ones I actually met were Lulu and Maurice Gibb.

After a party in a villa in the middle of nowhere Graham and I had to stay the night. We were put in a children's upstairs room in single beds next to each other. When I woke up, with the customary hangover, I could see Graham's feet with his white socks hanging out of the bed and I could hear voices downstairs, so I thought it would be polite to get up. Graham wasn't moving so I decided to wait for him to wake up. During the next hour I looked up every now and then to see if he had moved, but no sounds, no signs of life. The noise downstairs was getting more animated, I was sure that I could hear Graham's voice in the background. I couldn't lie there any longer. As I pulled myself up, Graham's feet strangely disappeared from view. I then remembered I'd borrowed his socks the night before, so I had spent the last couple of hours staring at my own feet in a mirror at the end of the bed.

Graham was a couple of years younger than me. He had been the barman in our local pub the King's Arms. As I spent a lot of time in there over the winter months, we became good friends. He was tall with long black hair, a bit of a "pretty boy" so he was very attractive to both men and women. He was a black belt in Judo, or so he said. A lot of what he came out with was difficult to believe, but that aside he was good fun to be around.

His looks and bullshit were ideal for holiday romances. With our suntans, local knowledge and being in the limelight every night we had our fair share of the young ladies. One girl stood out from the rest for me: her name was Carla, conveniently Graham got off with her friend. We had a great time together as two couples. Carla was a well-known fashion designer in London, I think we both felt at the time that there was something special between us. After she had gone back, we started writing to each other, which was a first for me.

One of the local girls took a fancy to Graham, although there was no chance of anything ever developing on that front. There was a very strict Catholic code of conduct in those days. Only men were out at night, except on special occasions such as a religious festival. The girl in question worked in the local Pensão, a type of small guest house. He soon had her doing our washing and letting us in for free showers when the boss was out. He'd probably promised to marry her to keep her interested. He'd say anything as long as our laundry service continued.

My brother David had been threatening to come over for a visit and after a couple of false alarms arrived in Albufeira with Irish Mick, the same young man that I travelled with the year before. They also had the technology to do a bit of nail bending but they had plans to try Cascais up near Lisbon. We had a few days partying together. One day we were having an impromptu afternoon beer session in the centre of town. There were a ridiculous number of bottles on the table, because the waiters didn't take them away so that they could count them at the end to work out the bill. My brother had mentioned that our local vicar, Reverend David Fricker, was in the Algarve with his family. He couldn't have picked a more opportune moment when, without warning, he was standing by our beer-cluttered table, family in tow.

"Fuck it's Fricker the Vicar!" I shouted.

"Sorry. It was the shock. God knows why I said that. I meant 'goodness knows' – sorry again!"

"I can see you're having a good time. Your parents asked us to look you up if we were in the vicinity, so I can now report back that all is well."

12

Things Go West

ALBUFEIRA had been very lucky for me until then, but things were about to go horribly wrong. It was the beginning of August and the height of the season was upon us when John was told by the police that we couldn't sell in Albufeira anymore. He said it was because we had become a "problem", following a string of complaints, and as far as they were concerned there were too many crazy drunken late nights. We had been warned before and had taken no notice. I had to agree that compared to the rest of the locals we were a bit boisterous, but we hadn't caused any trouble that I was aware of.

Sadly, Graham and I had to leave, John was annoyed with us for ruining his business. He had cut out some of the late nights because of Jasper, but he was still partially guilty for our expulsion. Graham and I decided to try our luck down the coast in Lagos. I had to say goodbye to Bender, as I couldn't take him with me on public transport, but John would look after him and I was sure I'd be back before the summer was over.

We arrived in Lagos, stayed at the campsite and started selling at the famous beach of Praia Dona Ana. We were the only ones there selling things, so business was good. Life on the campsite was a pleasant change as we now had washing facilities and hot showers. We would stroll into town at night, where there were a few bars and restaurants. It wasn't Albufeira, but a good second best.

I received a letter from another girl that I had met earlier in the summer saying that she would be back in Albufeira the next day and asking if we could we meet up. This was an opportunity that I could not miss out on. Her name was Kim, she was blond, gorgeous figure, posh and horny. She had approached me on the beach in her tiny bikini (those were the days) and it wasn't long before we were at it up the hill in my tent. We hadn't met each other an hour before and suddenly I was having the best sex I'd ever had. We met at the beach for sex every afternoon for the next two days – but then her dad caught us coming down the hill hand in hand with ridiculous grins on our faces. He dragged her away shouting, "How many more times?" I didn't see her again, but we had swapped addresses. I hadn't asked her age, but I got the impression she was about 17, a nymphomaniac and a serial maneater.

I caught the train from Lagos to Albufeira, – change at the strangely named station of Tunes, the ticket collector kept reminding me. Like some of the other train stations on the Algarve line the station is nowhere near the name of the place where you think you're going. Albufeira station is called Ferreiras, a few kilometres away inland. I thought that there might have been a connecting bus service, but of course there wasn't. A taxi arrived, which I shared with some other train passengers, which took us to Albufeira.

I went straight to the gardens to meet Kim but I couldn't find her; instead I was shocked, to say the least, to find John, June and Jasper sitting there with Bender, selling their paintings. John apparently had got permission to sell until the end of the summer, as long as they only sold paintings and that nobody else sold anything – meaning us basically. I was happy for them, but at the same time angry that it wasn't still me sitting there in my favourite spot and with my dog. We had a drink together and a good chat about it. There was palpable tension. I never thought anything would ever come between John and me. I felt Graham and I had been the sacrificial lambs. I think we both realised things would never be the same again between us. We had shared many memorable experiences, but that was in the past. We had to move on.

Kim finally showed up. I said my sad farewells to John, June and Jasper and then Bender, I promised him that I would come back next year. The only thing to do now was to drink to forget. After a few beers I took Kim to the beach where we soon made up for lost time. She had to be back early in the evening for dinner with her parents, and was leaving the next day, so I had another heart-rending goodbye to endure. I found a taxi and arrived at the station in time for the last train back to Lagos. I'd told Graham that I'd be back the same day.

I had time to spare at the station, so I sat in the bar and had a brandy to drown my sorrows. I'd had an eventful day even by my standards and there was still more to come. By the time I got on the train I'd already downed another brandy. I was drained mentally and physically and was looking forward to getting back to Lagos and my sleeping bag. The next thing I knew I was staring with bleary eyes, trying to focus on the face of a man in uniform who was shouting and poking me for some reason, at the same time holding a ticket and pointing at it as if I was an imbecile. I found a rectangular bit of cardboard in my pocket and showed it to him. He shook his head and no wonder: it was Kim's telephone number on a bit of beermat. At this point I realised I was slightly drunk and slurring my words – not that it made any difference in Portuguese. In fact, it probably improved matters.

"Bilhete, bilhete," he kept shouting at me. He was now joined by some of my fellow passengers who also joined in with the "BILHETE!" chant. After turning out all my pockets I found my ticket, much to the disappointment of the assembled crowd who were maybe hoping that I was a foreigner trying to avoid payment. But their hopes were raised again as the train person was about to punch a hole in my ticket held it up for all to see. "LAGOS!" he bellowed for the benefit of the whole train.

"So what?" I said in my best English.

"Lisboa" replied the ticket man making a kind of directional gesture towards the front of the train. I was quite accomplished in the gesture department and very quickly reached the conclusion that I was somehow on the wrong train.

"Tunes," he said, using his hands quite expertly to demonstrate changing from one train to another. It probably happened all the time. I had completely misjudged the mood of the other passengers and I could tell they were concerned for me by their worried expressions. I was on my way to Lisbon, so now what? After some time, the train stopped at a station where I was told to get off, everyone was shaking my hand and wishing me good luck. All I was thinking was, "Where the fuck am I?" The ticket collector had a word with a colleague on the platform, shook my hand with a big smile on his face, and jumped back on his train.

I was somewhere in the Alentejo that I did know – but exactly where I don't remember to this day. I've travelled on that line many times, but the stations all look very similar. They all have names in large letters but none of them sound familiar. All I could hear was the sound of cicadas. It was hot and very dark and there was no one around. I was trying to sober up and assess the situation when a group of people appeared and came over to greet me. They all shook my hand and I followed them to a café, where they gave me something to eat free of charge. I was then taken to what I presumed was a private house and shown to a bedroom with a toilet next door. They said good night and pointed at their watches at some- time early in the morning.

The next morning, they woke me up with some coffee and cakes. I got dressed and went outside to be met by a huge gathering of the local people. I offered to pay for the accommodation, but they politely refused. I could tell the train from Lisbon back to the Algarve was due in a few minutes, as they were pointing frantically at their watches. I took the short walk to the station, followed by what appeared to be the whole population of wherever I was. I bought my ticket and spent the next few minutes shaking hands and kissing everybody until the train arrived. As the platform disappeared, I could see them still waving. On the journey back I sat there mulling over the last 12 hours. It really had been like one of those incredible nonsensical dreams. I couldn't believe the hospitality I had received: it was as if they had never seen a foreigner before. Maybe they hadn't, but the outpouring of affection was overwhelming.

I remembered to change at Tunes. Graham was sitting by his tent when I arrived back at the campsite. He greeted me with, "Where the fuck have you been? There's a letter for you." The letter was from my parents with the news that my Dad had been promoted to be the Head Postmaster of Hertfordshire. They were leaving Bedford after many years and moving to Stevenage. Which was good news and bad news. The good news was that my parents would be better off financially. The bad news was that I had nowhere to live when I got back to Bedford.

We carried on selling until the end of September and then decided we'd had enough for one year. Instead of going back to Bedford I went to London and moved in with Carla and her three flatmates in Bayswater. We fell in love over the winter months, I couldn't bear the thought of leaving her to return to Portugal, so she did the only sensible thing she could do . . . she handed in her notice from an extremely well-paid job in the fashion industry, jeopardising her future career, which meant that we could go back together. And so, we did.

13
Driving Test

BEFORE setting off for Portugal, Mick (my friend from school) and I bought an old ambulance for the trip. We put some L- Plates on it. With Mick by my side I quickly grasped the basics of driving it. It was soon time for our departure, so I applied to take my driving test and got selected early due to a cancellation. I knew I probably had no chance, but you never know I might be lucky. I turned up in the ambulance as the rules stated that learner drivers could take the test in any vehicle as long as it was roadworthy. One of the examiners was notorious for failing almost everybody unless you looked smart and took the test in a British School of Motoring vehicle. His name was Fowler, he was a silly little man with a Hitler moustache and of course it was he who came out of the office. He looked me up and down and after writing something on the official form on his clipboard he ushered me outside.

"I would like you to read to me the number plate on that ambulance that is badly parked over there."

"JGY 678" (or whatever it was) I replied.

"Have you got bionic vision? You're not even looking at the nominated vehicle!"

"I know the number plate sir because that vehicle belongs to me."

"The next thing you're going to tell me is that you intend to take the test in an ambulance."

"The rules clearly . . . "

"Never mind the rules," he rudely interrupted. "If you think I'm getting in that heap with a long-haired hippy you can think again. How many driving lessons have you had at the BSM? Let me guess: Is it a round number by any chance?"

I was trying to speak but there was no point.

"Mr Marsh I'm obliged to inform you that you have failed your driving test."

"But I haven't driven anywhere yet," I protested.

He was looking very red in the face by now.

"Young man, you have been extracting the urine since your arrival, your vehicle doesn't look fit for purpose and, to be frank, neither do you. However, as you have paid your fee you are still entitled to take the test if you still wish to, but the decision is irreversible."

We went for a little drive round. Not a word was spoken. I was quietly waiting for the emergency breaking part when he told me he would shout 'STOP!' He was obviously a mind-reader as he was clinging on for dear life, so unfortunately, I didn't get my chance to injure him. I scared him quite badly when I pulled out into the path of a double decker bus; little did he know that I had lived in that area and that the Number 108 bus always turned left up Gladstone Street.

Later that week one of my best friends John took his driving test with Failure Fowler. John had been educated at a naval school on a ship docked on the River Thames. He was slightly out of touch with things on dry land. After he had taken the driving part of the test, he had to face a few questions on the Highway Code. One of the questions was, "When you are driving around in the countryside give me an example of one of the road signs you would expect to see?"

After giving the matter some thought he came out with: "Eggs for Sale." He failed.

1972

14

Portimão

BY MID-JUNE 1972 Carla, Mick Barker and I were in the ambulance on our way to Portugal. In the back, with all our luggage and equipment, was Jasper Coy who we had to deliver to his son John in Albufeira. John had been in touch and asked if we could bring Jasper back to Albufeira. Despite our falling-out from the previous year, all was now forgotten.

After a few days on the road we arrived in Albufeira, delivered Jasper, had a night out with John and June and Bender, swapped stories, and the next day drove to Lagos campsite. Bender had become John's dog, so I reluctantly agreed to let him stay with him. Carla suggested that we found a house to rent, which was almost unheard of in those days. Within a week we had moved into furnished accommodation at Nº 53 Rua Vasco Pires in downtown Portimão.

We found ourselves in the heart of the local fishing industry: a terraced house in one of the narrow streets by the port at the end of the 'Ponte Velho', the 'old bridge'. The house was very basic. It had two bedrooms, a kitchen, a living room, a bathroom and a roof terrace. It had a cooker that used a bottle of gas that also provided hot water that didn't work most of the time. We could just about drive the ambulance through the street without damaging anything or getting tangled up on all the washing lines, but to avoid blocking the road we had to park it a few streets away.

There were two cafes at the bottom of the road, a couple of grocery shops nearby, the fishing port was just around the corner. Walking up our street in the evening you would see a pair of freshly scrubbed wellington boots outside on almost every doorstep – and that's where they stayed until the owners went off to work early in the morning. I presumed they did this to keep the powerful stench of sardines from entering the home. Mick mockingly suggested that maybe they had acquired the Japanese custom of removing footwear before entering and were, instead, merely preserving the life of their carpets.

Mick, Luis and a neighbour

We soon began getting to know all our neighbours by frequenting the local cafes and shops on a daily basis. We were introduced to the local tradesmen who delivered to the door. The mornings nearly always began with a siren that was so loud it sounded as though it was next door. This was to let everybody know that fishing boats had arrived, and their catch needed unloading. The noise of the siren sent all the local dogs into a howling frenzy. The next noise was the milkman, who blew a horn to let you know his knock on the door was imminent and, to conform with local milk etiquette, we had to buy a standard aluminium one litre milk container which he filled up every day, except Sundays, from his churns hanging from his bike's handlebars.

He was there on the dot every morning at ten, the milk had come straight from the cow. Then there was the postman, who was relatively quiet, the dustmen and the road sweeper closely followed by the fruit and veg lady. Every now and then we heard the pan pipes of the knife sharpener who had a specially adapted cutting-edge technology bicycle. We even had a visit from the wooden coat-hanger man, who was dressed head-to-foot in coat-hangers. There was also the soap man who was a man of the cloth and had a colourful range of tea towels. We had to leave the house most mornings just to get away from it all.

Some of the local kids started coming round begging for money or food.Our neighbours told us not to give them anything, otherwise we would never get rid of them. That was easier said than done, as some of them were in a terrible state. They were dressed slightly better than in rags, painfully thin and filthy. Carla was the first to crack and invited two of the most persistent in for breakfast of cornflakes and toast. One of them was called Luis. He had a lovely smile which unfortunately exposed the black hole in his front teeth. His mother, who lived down the road at N°21, had just had a baby. It was her sixth child and only the baby and Luis were still alive. I've no idea what the infant mortality rate was in the sixties and seventies, but, as we got to know more of the kids, we heard many similar stories. Luis had at least managed to reach eleven years of age. His friend Carlos was much smaller, but at the same age he was covered in bruises, as was his mother who was in rags. They lived in the street behind. Some nights you could hear screams coming from their house.It was the drunken father beating up the mother and poor little Carlos, in an effort to protect her, took a regular pasting.

The furthest of the two cafes down the road soon became our local. It was run by Miguel and his wife Maria, who were very welcoming. This was quite a rough area; the cafe was frequented by some disreputable looking characters who mostly tended to steer clear of us. One night one of them sat down with us and introduced himself by breathing cigarette smoke and alcohol fumes over us from an uncomfortably close range.

His name was José Linha. Miguel told him to leave us in peace, but our new acquaintance pushed him away. The owner gave us the "be careful" sign, pulling down the bottom eyelid with his index finger. We couldn't really understand much of what he was saying except: tomorrow, sardines, dinner and pointing at the hands on his watch to make sure we understood what time to meet him.

Sure-enough the next evening he arrived at the cafe on time with a metal bucket with a lid on to keep the flies away from the contents. He tugged at his ear lobe and winked which was the sign for top quality. He gave the sardines to Maria who charcoal grilled them, then served them up with salad and boiled potatoes. They have a very strong flavour, best eaten by hand being careful to steer clear of the guts and bones; delicious. We ordered red wine; José joined us at our table for what we thought would be a one-off dinner. We did our best to converse with him and by the end of the evening we were already planning tomorrow's dinner. The word depend is the same in Portuguese pronounced differently of course so when I asked what was on the menu tomorrow, he said "depend".

His appearance was similar to almost everybody else that worked with the sardine trawlers Weather-beaten faces that made them look much older than their real age. Wearing caps, checked shirts and dark trousers it was difficult to distinguish one from another. He owned a big blue rowing boat which he used to collect the sardines and unload at the dock. We watched him one day going round with his bucket picking up all the fish that had fallen out of the wicker baskets that they used to do the unloading. If the boats came in at low tide, there was a big difference in height between the deck of the trawler and the level of the quay.

It was fascinating to watch the fishermen scoop up the fish from the boat into their baskets then throw them up to the waiting port workers who would catch the basket as it hovered in mid-air, just at that moment before the basket was about to drop back onto the boat. Simultaneously, as the basket went up, the catcher dropped the previous now empty basket down to the fisherman. Like anything else when you've done it all your life, they made it look easy. Now and then a fish fell to the ground – and there was our José with his bucket at the ready. The fish were packed into boxes, then taken by lorry to the nearby canning factories where hundreds of women were ready to start filleting, washing, salting and then cooking them in steam ovens, adding olive oil before trimming and putting the fish into the cans by hand.

For the last hundred years or so, generations of families had dedicated their working lives to the sardine canning industry. At one point there were 15 factories in Portimão alone, but since the 1920s the industry had started to decline due to overfishing, competition and then the arrival of frozen fish.I was told that there were seven factories still running at that time. A few years later they were all closed.

So, basically, our dinner depended on what type of fish he literally picked up – which was mostly sardines but often we had sea bream, mackerel, sea bass and a lot of weird looking varieties that probably hadn't been given names. We did this free fish dinner almost every night. We paid Maria for doing the cooking and for everything else, but the bill was virtually nothing compared to what it would cost in a decent restaurant, not taking into account that ours had been scraped off the cobblestones with all the rest of the crap. But once it had been washed and cooked who would know the difference. We hardly ever had bad stomachs or food poisoning despite the total lack of hygiene.

You can have too much of a good thing. After a while we started to get a bit tired of fish so I asked José if he could get any meat for a change. The following night he was there with his bucket pulling his ear lobe, but Maria was shaking her head pointing at us waving her index finger back and forth: obviously we weren't going to like it. When he wasn't looking, I peered under the lid of the bucket to find a huge eyeball staring at me. It was a sheep's head. Mick asked him where the rest of it was. They cooked it and served it up for us, saying that it was a delicacy. José started by sticking his fork in the sheep's eye and swallowing it, saying it was the best part. We were forced to try some of the meat, but we were overcome with a sudden lack of appetite. The whole spectacle was far too gruesome and barbaric. We'd seen other customers sucking on fish-heads before, but this was beyond the pale (and the bucket).

15

A Trip up the Arade

SUNDAY was a day of rest. No fishing boats, no delivery people. Instead, we had a trip with José in his rowing boat to look forward to. The first time we went I thought we were going quite a long way inland, as he had pointed north and mentioned Lisbon. We had to wait for the water level to start rising so that we could travel inland on the tide. Portimão up-river looks great when the tide's in, but as the water flows out to sea it gradually uncovers a muddy stinky silt. José Linha had all the equipment required for the picnic lunch: the ubiquitous sardines, charcoal, a portable grill, a massive loaf of bread and the biggest wicker basket known to man. We brought the wine and paper cups and a few essentials.

When the time was right, we set off, with José rowing up-stream. He didn't have an outboard motor, but we were moving along quite fast. We were a few hundred metres, maybe a kilometre, up-river looking forward to the next few hours experiencing the river views, Portimão had disappeared into the distance, and we'd successfully navigated a couple of bends when he stopped rowing and steered us onto the river bank and tied up the boat "Já Chega", that's enough, he said and started unloading. We followed suit rather disappointed with the duration of the voyage. We sat under a cluster of almond and olive trees while he set about lighting the charcoal. We were soon quaffing the wine while lunching on sardines on bread. Once we'd finished, he climbed into his wicker basket.He mentioned something about the time and then fell asleep.

Wondering what to do with ourselves, we thought about taking the boat further up-river, but without his permission we decided that was too risky. Option two was to walk up-river, which we did. It wasn't a very exciting trip, so after about an hour we turned back. When we returned, José was out of his basket – and his mind – shouting: "Uma hora" (one hour). I think we were supposed to wake him up. Anyway, I said: "It's water under the bridge now". And that was the problem. The boat was sitting in mud, the river was now a stream. We had to get in the mud, we sank in over our knees while trying to push the boat into the stream that was getting shallower by the minute. He couldn't row because there was no water to put the oars in. We were still covered in mud on the bank while he went to the stern, I believe it's called, and waggled one of the oars over the side to get some propulsion. He told us to walk with all the equipment as he gradually slipped down-stream. Further along, the water was deeper and wider until it looked like a river again. He generously rowed over and picked us up and by the time we went under the road bridge and back at quayside he had a smile back on his face. We swore that we would never do that again. But we did quite a few times.

16

The Rover's Return

JOHN Coy had called the cafe and left a message for me to phone him at a certain time in the evening. Most cafes had a pay-phone with a meter that charged by the "impulse", so you would hear a beep which let you know how much you were spending, which was fine at local level but with an international call you had more beeps than conversation. I spoke to John. He said that they had been out somewhere, lost the dog and went back to Albufeira without him. The next morning down at the port I spotted a dog that looked like Bender. I walked over and sure enough it was him. I couldn't believe it.

Was it just a coincidence, extrasensory perception or did he know? I took him home. Carla knew him from the year before and Mick had heard all about him, they were quite happy to keep him until John wanted him back and I got in touch with John who suggested we keep him for a while.

He soon settled into his new home. I couldn't really take him to the cafe at night because the owners had a dog and the cafe opposite had a much bigger dog, so it was obvious that there would be trouble if I took him there. The first night we locked him inside the house. He was a bit of a Houdini, but all the windows and doors had shutters so there was no way out. We had been in the cafe maybe thirty minutes when a neighbour came in shouting and pointing in the air: "Cão" (dog). We rushed up the street. We lived at Nº53 and Bender was trapped on the roof of Nº41 doing an impersonation of the Hound of the Baskervilles. Somehow, he'd escaped, run along the rooftops and then got stuck. There was nobody at home at Nº41, so Mick climbed up a ladder that suddenly had appeared, along with most of the local residents, and with great difficulty managed to bring him safely down. Bender was allowed in the cafe as long as he sat under our table. Their dog basically surrendered, and the other one next door kept his distance.

From then on Bender always had to come with us wherever we went. When we were at home he sat outside on the doorstep. At first there was a dramatic decline in the amount of child visitors, but as they got familiar with him the numbers were soon back to pre-Bender levels. When we went out selling, he came with us in the ambulance if we all went, otherwise he would stay in with one of us. Mick and I had a lot of problems with the police in Praia da Rocha which is the beach area of Portimão. Carla had started making halter tops, caps and T-shirts with some fabrics she had brought with us. She had an electric sewing machine and turned them out in no time. She walked into the town centre, found a busy spot, laid out her wares on a cloth and for some reason the police never bothered her. Her halter tops and caps were selling so fast she couldn't keep up with the demand.

She had also taken to making or repairing clothes for, first, Luis and Carlos, and then of course their friends wanted the same treatment. Carla single-handedly changed the look of all the local kids, with stars and stripes, union jacks, bright colours. Our house had become a day centre Dr Barnado's home or youth club. We took them in gangs of up to ten or eleven to the cinema, the beach and even to watch the Portimonense football team. It was very cheap, and we could afford it; we had by chance started our own children's charity. One of the films we saw was "Carry on Again Doctor" and near the beginning of the film our actual ambulance appears a couple of times. We know it as a fact because when we bought it, they told us it came from a film studio and was used in that film.

We also took them to the travelling circus where we sat in the front seats. It was about 100 years past its sell-by date. The same girl who took the tickets was also the clown, the trapeze artist, bare-back (the horse) rider and contortionist. Each time as she passed us she gave Mick a wink and then did the splits rather provocatively directly in front of him. Mick had fancied his chances until the juggler, acrobat, muscle man appeared glaring at him. On one of the beach trips Mick lost one of the boys. He found him in a cafe's toilet washing his whole body at the sink. There were paper towels and water splashed all over the floor. It turns out that this was the first time he'd had the pleasure of seeing hot water come from a tap, so he thought he'd make the most of it.

17

A Visit to the Hospital

WE NEVER patronised the other cafe at the bottom of our street, partly to remain loyal to our usual haunt, but also to avoid confrontation because the dog that was in residence was almost a match for Bender. The two dogs had declared a cessation of hostilities after the first encounter had ended in a tie. The local champion had been knocked down a couple of times but had recovered to give the contender from Albufeira a nasty cut over his left eye. Bender came out on top in the re-match, winning after a few seconds by submission. Later that same day I walked alone past the café. The place was packed inside and out.

The dog came charging out into the street and, before I had time to react, he had bitten me in the back of my thigh, much to the amusement of the audience. I was wearing shorts, there was blood pouring down my leg, nobody came to help, so I set off towards the hospital which was over the other side of town somewhere. After lots of pointing, numerous left and right turns and some straight-ons, I limped into the hospital.

One of my greatest fears of living abroad was ending up in a foreign hospital; another was getting rabies. A nurse asked me what had happened, and all I could say was "Cão grande" (big dog). I did my best biting impression, and they got the picture. They put me on a stretcher and wheeled me through a number of corridors, put me on a treatment slab, cleaned up the wound and administered a penicillin injection (I was allergic to tetanus) then told me to wait for a doctor. On my way to the room the conditions that I witnessed inside had sadly lived up to all my expectations. The waiting room and the corridors were packed with accident victims and the seriously ill, waiting for medical attention. There was a lot of blood on view, and the sound of crying and painful murmuring. It was reminiscent of those scenes from old films of the medical units from the world wars. I have no religious beliefs, but I remember thinking, "God help me if I have a bad accident and finish up in here."

I had been lying face down for maybe an hour, my thigh was throbbing, the pain was getting worse, no sign of any more medical attention. One thing I had learned about living in the Algarve was that things in general moved very slowly. The word 'fast' applied only to some of the drivers, so I was trying to be a patient patient. I was just beginning to think that they had forgotten about me when I heard a lot of shouting and screaming. I could hear the sound of agitated voices, then footsteps coming towards the room. They had left the door ajar. The door flew open with a bang, I looked up and there was Bender, who had followed my scent or the smell of blood all that way through the town. Three men out of breath in white coats were next in the room who naturally assumed that this was the dog that had bitten me. When they saw him licking me, and me patting him affectionately on the head, they were slightly puzzled. One of them spoke English and asked if that was the dog that had bitten me. I explained what had happened, they told me that dogs weren't allowed in the building and that the nurses had locked themselves in the toilet. I was swiftly bandaged up, no stitches and shown the way out. I offered to pay, the doctor waved me away, obviously glad to see the back of me and the dog.

A few days later the same dog bit Mick, but it wasn't bad enough to warrant an injection. The dog from the cafe was locked up for most of the time after the biting incidents; when we did see him he had a muzzle on, which didn't deter him from head butting me in the groin a few times.It's amazing how a dog can sniff out the one person in a crowd of people who is the owner of their enemy. Or maybe I just needed to shower more often.

18

Rocket Man

ONE Sunday at the end of August, the small village across the river, Ferragudo, had a religious festival in honour of Our Lady of Conceição. It was the talk of the town, everyone was going. At that time of year there seemed to be one or two festivals each week. These were the most important days of the year for any town or village, so the whole population would be in attendance in their Sunday-best, plus coachloads of tourists. We took some of our gang with us as they knew some short-cuts, where to park and how to avoid the inevitable traffic jams.

There were more horses and donkeys pulling carts than motorised vehicles. Using their specialised local knowledge, we took a wrong turn up a very narrow street, full of people on both sides, which was decked out in bunting, streamers, coloured lights and religious artefacts. While trying to avoid knocking down an illuminated picture of Jesus we hit a metal TV aerial support that was jutting out of a house. We heard a cracking noise, the kids in the back were screaming at us to stop. The metal end had penetrated the fibreglass roof of the ambulance. We were stuck on a hill. We couldn't go forwards or backwards and we had a metal pole inside. Any movement in either direction just made things worse. By now the usual village experts had arrived on the scene arguing with each other on what was the best course of action to take. I looked down the street and there, moving slowly towards us, was a priest carrying a huge cross and waving an incense burner from side to side, chanting away, closely followed by a statue of Our Lady of Conceição being carried by worshippers.

The priest was about fifty metres away when he looked up. He must have thought to himself, "What's that ambulance doing stopped in the middle of the road?" Panic had by now set in and we'd given up trying to drive our way out. The hole in the roof had doubled in size. The crowd were waving us to get out of the way as the procession was nearly upon us. With the help of the kids and a lot of bystanders we bumped the vehicle sideways at the back and then went round to the front and did the same until we were free of the offending object. We drove off and parked well away from the festivities in case of reprisals from angry residents. We then decided it would be safe to go and join the party.

When the procession had ended, a man with a wooden ladder – who was either inebriated or crippled, possibly both – slowly climbed to the top rung. He was the official rocket man who had the honour to do this task every year, and it soon became apparent why he had so many injuries. He was to give the signal for the celebrations to begin. He lit the fuse and with one hand on the ladder to steady himself and gripping the projectile in the other pointed it towards the night sky. The recoil of the explosion knocked him and the ladder into the expectant crowd below him causing a malfunction in the manual release mechanism. The missile's trajectory had been seriously compromised. We ducked as it headed towards us in the crowd. When it shot past it was no more than six feet above street level, which was fortunate as most people were only five-feet-six or less. The rocket man was not only injured in the fall but had also set fire to himself and broken his ladder. A tall person in the crowd had been badly hurt, Bender had run off, while the kids were having hysterics. I had to hold Mick back. I think he had temporary shellshock when he heard the cry for an ambulance. We had seen enough for one night. We found Bender trembling by our vehicle. I'd never seen him showing any kind of fear before that moment.

Possibly thanks to our festival incident the word had spread. These are close-knit communities, so stories soon get around and widely exaggerated. A few days later Mick was selling at the beach when the police arrested him for having the word 'AMBULANCE' written on the sides of the vehicle. He was fined about £1 and told to come back the next day with the word removed. We painted over the letters, showed the vehicle to the police, made a stencil of BENDANAIL and repainted it.

19

Match of the Day

THAT night in the cafe we had a really good time with a large group of fishermen who were from a town just south of Lisbon called Sesimbra. They convinced Mick into going out to sea with them for a night of fishing. Mick's passion was photography: He had taken loads of pictures of Portimão and the local characters, so he relished the chance of some nautical scenes and an adventure. When he returned from the expedition, he had lost his tan overnight. It had been a rough voyage and he had been very sea-sick (not to be recommended). When the boat was crashing through the waves it had been bearable, but somewhere en route they stopped and tied up to another boat. After being thrown around in all directions for an hour it had all been too much for him.

That evening, having dinner with Mick's fishermen's friends, one of the crew announced that his son was a footballer who played for his local side Sesimbra, who were playing in the Algarve the following afternoon against Olhanense in the second division. He asked if it would be possible for us to take him and the rest of the crew to Olhão another fishing port just east of Faro. It was a journey of about 80 kilometres each way, which doesn't sound too far, but driving on the main road which runs from one end of the Algarve to the other, the notorious R.N. 125, in those days was, to put it mildly a bit hazardous.

After far too much alcohol we reluctantly agreed to take the fishermen. It was not a pleasant journey: traffic-wise, there weren't many cars in those days. There was no such thing as credit, there were no car showrooms that I can recall, it was cash or nothing. Most vehicles on the road were either a donkey and cart – or the faster, 1 bhp version, the horse and cart. The road surface conditions didn't help either, with potholes all over the place: molten tarmac due to the intense heat and, inevitably, piles of horseshit everywhere. Any kind of accident would bring everything to a standstill in both directions and often cause another incident on the other side of the road – rubbernecking at its best.

We stopped for something to eat en-route which turned into the usual drinking session. As breathalysers hadn't yet been invented, nobody worried about the possible consequences of drink-driving. The drivers weren't that great when they were sober, but with a bottle of wine inside them, and a brandy for good measure, they morphed into rally drivers – resulting in carnage. After lunchtime was one of the most dangerous times to be on the road. The traffic mixture of animals, motorbikes, cars and lorries, all using the same narrow stretch of highway, was a recipe for disaster. Luckily on this particular trip nothing serious happened along the way but that was unusual.

The drink had taken effect: there was a lot of singing coming from the back. There were eleven of them, five on each bench along the sides and the captain at the back door sitting in the middle on a collapsible beach chair, Bender was by his feet. There was a hatch between the front of the vehicle and the back which was closed most of the time. If we needed to communicate, we slid it open for further instructions. As we approached the Olhão stadium we left the tarmac, as the last few hundred metres were on a dusty dirt road that led to the car park. The singing in the back turned to excited chanting, shouting and banging which we presumed was pre-match tension; then total silence for the last hundred metres, maybe they were praying, we thought. I went to the back to let the fishermen out. As I pulled the handle down, a pile of sand and dust poured onto the ground. They were all sitting perfectly still, covered from head to foot in dust. All I could make out were some mouths and eyes. They looked like the Portuguese version of the Terracotta Army. Bender jumped out, shaking the dust off, knocking the captain over backwards – who I just managed to catch before he hit the ground. One by one the crew climbed out and brushed themselves down. They were not amused, but once they could breathe again the mood changed for the better. The hole in the roof had widened and in all the excitement Mick had put his foot down for a grand finale and sucked in what appeared to be most of the top layer of the track.

We watched the game. I don't remember the result. It might have been a draw. When the game was over, we were introduced to the famous son and some of the other players. On the way back Mick drove very slowly out of the stadium until we were back on the black stuff to avoid another dust-up. It had been a long day, so by the time we got back home we were shattered and ready for bed. The fishermen who had slept all the way on the return journey had other ideas.

They had organised a special dinner for us in our honour in the usual cafe that was normally closed on Sundays. No fish, for a change, but prawns, crabs and steaks and plenty of beer and wine to wash it down.

Over coffee and brandy the captain stood up and thanked us for taking them, made a few jokes about the dust, and as a reward for our kindness we were all invited for their next fishing trip, embarking that Monday evening. Carla was adamant that she wasn't going. I wasn't that keen either, and Mick had already sworn never to go to sea again.

20

The Fishing Expedition

THE NEXT evening, after dinner all three of us and Bender were on board the fishing boat heading out into the Atlantic. There wasn't much room on deck, they showed us where the best place to sit was to watch the action and keep out of harm's way. We headed due west past Sagres and the most south-western point of Europe, Cape Saint Vincent with its famous lighthouse. As we passed the cape, the waves started to increase in size, the wind picked up and it was getting colder by the minute. Jorge, the captain, could see Carla was – as predicted – not very comfortable and took her below deck where there was a bunk bed and, fortunately, the one thing she had been concerned about: a toilet. The boat had three or four metres of open decking at the front, an enclosed cabin in the middle, where the captain was behind the wheel, and a few more metres at the back. It was powered by a diesel engine, so there were no sails to worry about. The distant lights of the coastline faded across the water. We were alone with the moonlight and the stars in the ocean with eleven fishermen who we hardly knew. Carla, was a very brave young lady to be out at sea, not exactly risking her life, but it was a far cry from the comfort of her flat in Bayswater.

I said goodnight to my shipmates and squeezed into the bunk with Carla. The noise of the engine and the movement of the boat made sleeping almost impossible. During the night the men were hard at work putting out thick nylon lines with baited hooks at intervals tied to a buoy. As dawn broke, we were told to get up – not that we needed waking up. The boat had stopped. We were moving up and down and rolling side to side, waves spraying over us. It wasn't cold, more of a shock to the system. We had reached the first of the buoys that had been left to wait for the fish to take the bait. Some of the men started pulling in the nylon lines and judging by the amount of effort they were putting in there were plenty of fish coming up. The ones that were doing the hauling in had rubber guards on their fingers like long thimbles to protect and give a better grip.

The deck was soon covered in long silver scabbard fish desperately flapping about. As soon as they removed the hook, another of the team hit the fish on the head to finish them off. Carla was the first to throw up. One of the men threw a bucket of sea water over her head, and he assured us that it would make her feel better. They told her to sit by the hatch just as a wave hit the boat and the hatch door came loose and hit her over the head. She had had enough and went below deck to lie down. Mick was next to succumb and got the bucket of water treatment. I started to feel sick, I tried to join in to keep busy and had a go at pulling in one of the lines but wasn't strong enough. One of the men was cooking the fish on deck cut into steaks. He told me to eat some and said that I would feel better. On the verge of vomiting, that was the last thing I thought I needed, but I took his advice and, sure enough, the nausea was gone in an instant.

Bender had been very quiet on the trip. He spent most of the time curled up at the back, away from all the excitement. He wasn't cut out to be an old seadog. We watched and waved to a lot of other fishing boats going by that day and it wasn't unusual to see a dog on board. Thankfully we didn't have to tie up to any of them, as they sometimes did, or we might have had a nautical dogfight on our hands.

It was early afternoon when we finally arrived safely back at the dock. We were so relieved to be back on dry land. Personally, it was an experience never to forget, nor to be repeated, I was a landlubber to the core. I was full of admiration for the crew and the tough life they led that I had now experienced at first hand.

It turned out to be a record catch for them: 1,300 fish that were, on average, a metre long and maybe ten centimetres wide; each one weighed two or three kilos, so the total weight must have been three or four tons. They concluded that our presence on board was a lucky charm so it meant we would have to do this more often. Before they got too carried away, we told them emphatically, "nunca mais!" (never again). I watched the captain distribute their hard-earned cash. Each crew member was given one share and he had twenty shares. It was his boat and they were on expenses. That evening we had yet another dinner with them and ate some more of the fish "we" had caught. It was delicious and well worth the effort. They left for Sesimbra the next day and we were sad to see them go. They insisted that we should look them up on our way back home. I may have been wrong, but I had got the impression that they were somehow friendlier and more generous than the Algarvians in those days.

21

The Olympics
(And Other Games)

WE WATCHED the drama of the Munich massacre in black and white down at the cafe with no subtitles, so we didn't really understand what was happening. I saw a lot of the Fischer v Spassky world championship which was fine in black-and-white. I was in the school chess team when I was 13, which was the only achievement that I could be proud of. The only 'sport' that wasn't considered by the school to be a sport. This meant I was never permitted to wear the 'house colours', a special tie with two thin stripes instead of one broad one. Even some of the fat boys had been awarded their colours for outstanding feats of endurance, like completing the hundred metres. While I'm on the subject: at 16 I was also the oldest pupil in the school's history to be wearing a white button on my cap, which signified that I hadn't swum 'The Pass', which was two lengths of the pool. Most kids had achieved that feat by the age of eleven at the latest as it was considered an embarrassment not to do so. This was my way of cocking a snook at the establishment. I did it eventually, due to peer pressure, and almost drowned in the process. I seem to remember that, like most boys, Mick had 'won' his colours, probably for rugby.

In the private backroom of the cafe there were four sickly-looking characters, who were visible through the glass, and were playing cards every night. The door was always closed. I asked the owner what game they were playing as I love a game of cards. Very kindly he invited me in to have a look I recognised their faces and they knew me. The first thing that struck me after the cloud of smoke was the powerful stench of pure alcohol. It was a mixture of two local spirits: Aguardente de Bagaço, clear firewater made from the residue of grapes and Medronho, another high-octane concoction made from the berries of the Medronho tree. They had the equivalent of shot glasses and a couple of bottles open at the table. I could tell straight away they weren't playing with a full deck and I noticed that some of the cards were missing too.

They were playing in pairs. The game is called Sueca and is very popular in Portugal. They were all far beyond being drunk, slurring their words, shouting every time they laid a card. When it was an important card, like an ace, or the seven called the 'Manilha', it had to be slammed on the table, which involved leaving the chair to gain height to give more downforce to the delivery. Sometimes the tremors nearly knocked over their precious drinks! They didn't look at all well: coughing and spitting, runny noses wiped on their sleeves, not many teeth between them, scabs and open wounds – like four hardened meths drinkers. I remembered that joke about the lepers playing cards when one of them threw their hand in. They made me sit down and play a few rounds and poured some fire water for me which had to be knocked back in one go. I managed to escape while I was still able to function and before I caught bubonic plague from shaking hands with all of them. I managed to escape the Middle Ages and get back outside to the twentieth century.

22

Leaving Under a Cloud

Rua Vasco Pires, Portimão

IT WAS mid-September, and the weather had suddenly deteriorated. At the beach the sun loungers had been stored away for another year, the sea was rough and grey, and the rain started chucking it down. Our season was over, we had paid the £28 for another month's rent, the kids had gone back to school, but only for a few hours a day, so the house became a juvenile day centre. We had two bicycles that we never really used, so the bigger ones borrowed them regularly. They played draughts, Ludo, cards and hit Bender with the football! They somehow destroyed the dartboard on the first day we bought it, probably just as well before one of them was injured. We incurred a lot of extra expenses feeding them with sandwiches, ice creams and drinks.

Maybe because of the rain the milkman didn't appear at the usual time. When he finally did turn up, I said to him, "Better leite than never!" (leite, pronounced 'late' means milk) which I thought was hilarious, but, as he obviously didn't get the joke, he thought I was laughing at him. I apologised and paid him the five cents. Luis was there and said that everyone else paid four cents a litre. I asked the milkman why we were charged extra and he explained that the custom was that when people could afford it, he took an extra cent for a tip. Bearing in mind that there were something in the region of 200 escudos to the pound and 100 centavos to the escudo it was irrelevant but at least he could have told us. I would have gladly given him ten cents, but it was a matter of principle.

Beggars were a common sight, but they do not normally make house calls. We heard a man, right outside our door, making all sorts of weird noises, lying on his back waving his arms and legs and having what looked like a seizure. Luis had almost taken up residence at this point; he told us that the man was putting it on and that there was nothing wrong with him. The next day he re-appeared so we gave him some money just to get rid of him and lo and behold, he made a miraculous recovery, stopped shaking, got up and walked off.

Boredom was setting in. There is a lot of truth in the old saying, 'The devil makes work for idle hands". Because of our perceived wealth and constant generosity, the locals had taken advantage of us on a few occasions, but we hadn't ever really been ripped off or had anything stolen from us. On Sunday's regular boat trip José had given permission for Mick to take another boat back down river and moor it next to his. The next day José demanded £7 to pay for the oars which allegedly had been stolen. This story didn't make any sense and some of the locals said he wasn't to be trusted. We refused to pay him so, as a result, he never spoke to us again.

Things soon took a turn for the worse: all our friends and neighbours were turning against us. Mick had collected photographs of all the local kids. He found a Time magazine centrefold picture of a group of Hell's Angels. To amuse himself he cut out all the faces and replaced them with some of his photos of our young friends. He stuck the finished article in our front window for all to enjoy. We were woken the next morning by loud banging on our door. There was an angry group of neighbours protesting that the images were disgusting and insisting that we remove them immediately. We tried to calm them down but one of the men pushed his way into our house and ripped it off the window and then into pieces. Some of the girls in the picture were wearing short skirts, others had bikini tops on. The mob were saying that we had made their daughters "prostitutes" and that we should be ashamed of ourselves.

That night in the cafe nobody spoke to us. Then the final blow was delivered when the owner came over with the bill and said that we hadn't paid from the previous evening. We always paid our bill; we even told him how much it was and when it was settled. But he wasn't having it. We gave him the money for the meal we had just eaten but declined to pay any more. We walked out and sadly that was the last time we set foot in the place. I could never have imagined that after three months of becoming part of their lives that one or two minor incidents would turn them against us. This was an unforgiving close-knit community joining together and slamming the door in our faces.

Fortunately for Bender he had run off with a bitch on heat the same day that the dog catchers, six old men with nets, arrived. It was a horrible sight to watch as they caught a few of the dogs that we had got used to seeing every day. After a struggle they threw them into a van and most of them, if they weren't claimed by the next day, were put down. Bender had a habit of disappearing, then turning up days later starving. We gave him a tin of sausages for a treat. He swallowed them all in seconds then went outside and vomited the whole contents in the street. We put him inside the house just as another dog walked by who then ate all the sausages. Bender had returned with a hole in his back, presumably from the fangs of another dog, just below his neck. It was so deep that flies disappeared down it out of view. We poured Betadine disinfectant down the hole until it was full, then beat a hasty retreat before he shook it all over us.

The cafe incident was the final straw. We had no choice but to pack our bags and drive back to England. Luis had begged us to take him with us but, although we had talked about it. It was never going to happen. We said goodbye to a few people who had remained loyal. We had a farewell drink with the kids that were still allowed to speak to us. We gave Luis and Carlos some money and a bicycle each and tearfully said our goodbyes. We'd had a great time while it lasted, it was such a pity that things had ended in such unfortunate circumstances.

That afternoon we drove over to Albufeira: a repeat process of the previous year where we handed over Bender to John and June. As usual it broke my heart having to leave him but at least he was with friends and back to his old familiar hunting ground. The next day, after the customary catch-up dinner at Arnaldo's, we left the Algarve heading for home via Sesimbra. We had promised the fishermen that we would visit them – it wasn't that far out of the way so why not?

We hadn't a clue where to find them when we finally got there. Sesimbra is yet another small fishing town so we soon found the port where all the boats were moored. As we strolled around looking for one of them or their boat everyone was staring at us. Foreigners stuck out like sore thumbs. We were on the verge of giving up our search when a familiar face came running out of one of the cafes. It was one of the crew, I couldn't remember his name. He was overjoyed to see us and greeted us like long-lost family. We sat waiting in the cafe until one by one the whole crew and then Jorge the captain joined us.

They insisted we stay the night and that we would all have dinner together. Jorge took Carla and myself to his house, where they had a bedroom prepared for us on the off chance that we would turn up as we had promised. The room was immaculate, with the dark brown wooden furniture that all the houses that I had visited seemed to have. The walls were covered in religious pictures and crosses. Mick was a guest of one of the others and the room he described sounded exactly the same as ours.

For some reason the three of us weren't feeling that hungry, possibly travel sickness. We went to a local restaurant where everything was already laid on for us as though we were royalty. We spent most of the evening apologising for turning away plate after plate of mouth-watering dishes. We weren't even able to drink as much as was expected of us. It was a very noisy affair that got even worse when the whole football team arrived. We must have shaken hands with half the town before we were finally allowed to go to bed. Poor Carla had to kiss them all twice: first when we met them and then again before we left.

In the morning Jorge's wife had prepared a huge breakfast of cheese, sausage, ham, eggs, bacon, bread, toast and coffee. Mick soon joined us but still none of us were that hungry. We didn't want to appear ungrateful but there was no point in forcing down food just because we were feeling uncomfortable. We left them with the impression that English people didn't eat very much. That's probably now part of Sesimbra folklore. They wrapped up most of our breakfast to take for our journey. After another round of kissing and handshaking they waved us off and wished us luck for the rest of our journey. That visit restored my faith in human nature after the Portimão debacle. Thinking back, maybe we had out-stayed our welcome in the Algarve – or had it all been an elaborate charade? I don't think so somehow.

The long trip back to England went well until we were about twenty miles out of Calais, when the engine started to overheat after climbing a hill. We had water on board, but we had learned that the engine had to be allowed to cool down before pouring cold water into the radiator. Half an hour later we got it running again.The road was one steep hill after another. Steam was gushing out from under the bonnet, we were coasting downhill and willing it to get up the next incline. We could see the sea in the distance, but we were forced to stop once again. There were plenty of ferries, so we weren't panicking. So near yet so far.

We filled up with water again but this time we couldn't get it to start. It was too heavy to push, there was nobody around to help so we tried bump starting it in reverse which miraculously worked. We coasted into the ferry terminal in Calais. We were unceremoniously pushed onto the ferry by some kind volunteers. The ambulance was cheered and clapped on board by our fellow passengers. When we reached Dover, we couldn't get it started so a tractor unit towed us out and deposited us on the seafront. The driver took a quick look at the engine and informed us that in all probability we had blown a head gasket and that it would need a new engine that would cost more than the ambulance was worth.

We hired a van, transferred all our belongings into our new shiny vehicle, said goodbye to the broken-down vehicle, imagining all the tales it could tell, and hit the road. Six months later Mick received a fine and a warning that if our vehicle wasn't removed in seven days it would be towed away to be scrapped as it was considered an eyesore. We paid the fine and let Dover Council carry out the death sentence.

(Three Years Later . . .)

1975

Revolução!

23

Tunnel Vision

I ONLY returned to the Algarve in September 1975. I drove down for a holiday with my new girlfriend Jenny in a green Volkswagen camper van. While I had been away there had been a virtually bloodless communist-led revolution on April 25, 1974. As a result, the army had overthrown the regime. The former fascist organisations like the secret police no longer existed. The workers had taken over businesses and farms, most of the rich had fled the country in fear of their lives, mainly to Brazil. I had no idea what to expect, I'd heard that the country was virtually in a state of anarchy. Foreigners were advised to be cautious if travelling in Portugal.

My first port of call was Albufeira. We'd been driving all day, and it was early evening by the time we arrived. I went straight to the tunnel in the faint hope that Bender would still be there after three years. I asked some of the local people whose faces I vaguely remembered, but there was no word of him. What I did notice was that lots of the young lads who used to watch us bending the nails were now selling their own things, mainly jewellery, in the tunnel, in the garden, in fact almost everywhere. A lot of them had grown their hair long and looked more fashionable than before and there were even some young women around.

We went up to see if Arnaldo's still existed and sure enough the three of them were sitting there just as before,Arnaldo,-Josélia and Bernadina.They were all wearing black and looking very despondent. They always looked tired at the best of times, but I sensed that something awful had happened. By working all hours day and night, and by economising where possible, their dream of wealth and a better life had come to fruition.

They had bought their son Armândio a three-litre Ford Capri, which was a very powerful expensive car. He already had a reputation for his crazy driving and had had more than his fair share of accidents over the years. He loved to brag about how fast he could get to Portimão and back.

I delicately asked them how Armândio was; they slowly shook their heads, looked down at the floor and pointed to the heavens.

"I think he's dead," I said to Jenny.

"Why don't you ask them?" she replied.

"Ele está morto?" (is he dead) I asked.

They all looked at me a bit shocked from what I'd just said.

"Não, ele está lá em cima no quarto dele!" (No – he's upstairs in his bedroom!)

There's me jumping to the wrong conclusions as usual and putting my foot in it. I spent the next hour apologising to them over dinner. They eventually saw the funny side of my gaffe. They were looking extra miserable because they weren't happy about how the revolution had affected a lot of the young people who had turned to drugs and crime and were understandably worried about their own personal and business future.

Pedro, an old acquaintance, came through the door. He had news of John and June. They were house-sitting for some people who had left the country until they considered it was safe to return. The house was in São Brás de Alportel, a small town north of Faro. Fortunately, he knew exactly where the house was and drew us a map. I was tired from our journey and didn't really fancy trying to find the house at night – but when he mentioned they had Bender with them I couldn't get back on the road quick enough.

We drove to Faro then up to São Brás. It took at least two hours. There were other routes across country, but I would probably have got lost. We eventually found the house and had yet another emotional reunion with John and June – but no sign of the dog. When the excitement of our arrival had died down John began to explain what had happened.

They too had kept away from Portugal and had been living in Spain, just over the border in Isla Cristina. The owners of the house where we were now had contacted them and offered it to them rent-free until they returned, if ever. John had been to Albufeira, found Bender and brought him back to the house. He loved that dog as much as I did, plus most thieves would think at least twice if they saw him barking at the gate. He'd settled in, happy to be back with his old friends again, until two days before when he suddenly started to behave in a very strange manner. He had gone very quiet and kept looking into the distance across the valley towards the sea. He wouldn't eat anything and ignored them when they called him. He then started howling and climbed on top of a wall. They thought he was going crazy or trying to tell them something. The next day he was gone, which was the day before. They hadn't seen him since.

We sat talking for a while, wondering what to do. It wasn't unusual for Bender to disappear for a day or two, especially if he caught the scent of a bitch. John had asked the neighbours if they had seen the dog, but nobody had. John suddenly jumped up out of his seat and said: "I bet he knew you were coming, and he's gone to find you in the tunnel in Albufeira! It's too much of a coincidence. You know that dog has psychic powers."

"He may be clever but how could he possibly find his way there? It's forty or fifty kilometres away," June exclaimed.

"I'm going in the van to find him now," John declared.

"It's midnight, you're mad, leave it until tomorrow," June protested.

Once he'd made his mind up there was no stopping him, and so off he went alone on a wild dog chase. Jenny and I were absolutely shattered, so we went to bed and were asleep in seconds. In the middle of the night I was awoken in the dark with something heavy on top of me licking my face. Jenny was very slim and had never done anything like that before. John switched on the light and there he was, my Bender, on the bed. I was so happy to see him I don't mind admitting that I burst into tears. How could he have known, how could he run all that way knowing which direction to go, and that after three years I would be there. And then, when he gets there, he can't find me – so he just sat there in the tunnel, waiting patiently. His intuition told him that one of us would be arriving shortly, as it was obvious to him that all our minds were synchronised, on the same wavelength.

Sure enough, John had found him curled up in the tunnel at two in the morning. As John remarked, you hear about these incredible stories in the newspapers about animals with supernatural powers and often wonder whether they are really true, or even possible, but here we were with living proof sitting at our feet.

We spent some time together reflecting on the previous few years: our ups and downs and how this amazing dog kept bringing us back to Portugal. Jenny and I were on a short visit so after about a week we had to pack our bags and leave. Poor old Bender. He must have been so confused as to what caused all the coming and going. As usual, I promised him and myself to come back and find him again as soon as possible. John and June were going to stay where they were until the owners returned, so Bender had a home – at least for now.

1976

24

Tragedy

THE FOLLOWING year I drove down to the Algarve in my trusty VW, this time alone. On arrival in Albufeira, I made all the usual enquiries – and of course found John, June and Bender, this time in a different house, somewhere up in the hills. I could tell something was wrong straight away. Bender was first out of the house, barking with glee and frantically wagging his stump of a tail. I presume he was expecting me.

June greeted me in tears. She was trying to talk, but sobbing at the same time; all I could make out was, "John, John!" When I asked her where he was, she pointed at a window upstairs. But I couldn't see him.

"What's happened?" I shouted, starting to panic.

For what seemed like ages she didn't speak, as though she didn't know how to say what was coming next. Then she looked me straight in the eyes and still crying, "He's gone mad. He's had a mental breakdown. He just sits there depressed, staring out of the window, not talking, I'm at my wits' end. I don't know what to do."

"When did all this start? Can I go and see him?" I asked.

"Yes. Go and try and talk to him of course, but I doubt if you'll get much sense out of him. Best not to ask him any questions for now. When you come down, I'll tell you the whole story – but you're not going to like it."

I went upstairs, wondering who I was going to find and what could have caused someone who I virtually idolised to apparently crack-up. Depressed! John Coy the most alive person I'd ever met, wit, raconteur, bon vivant, the man who taught us the brilliant Archibald Ascending joke (later . . .). As far as I was concerned this could not be happening.

Sure enough he was sitting staring out of the window. He didn't even acknowledge my presence at first. For a moment I didn't know what to say, then I blurted out: "What's up John?" Then I remembered, no questions! "Great to see you again John!" He looked away from the window and glanced at me briefly, then started to speak.

"I can't stay here for much longer, I've got to go back to England, the sooner the better or else I might ..."

He was almost whispering; he didn't shake my hand or appear to want to make any kind of contact with me. He seemed smaller, the big smile wasn't there, him, his normal self wasn't there, he looked drained of energy.

"Talk to June, I'll be here for a while."

As I went back downstairs, I was dreading to hear what June had to tell me. We sat down together, and she told me the whole story.

They had gone back to Isla Cristina for the winter, rented a small house in town and settled back in with the local community. One afternoon, they went for a walk in a nearby forest. They hadn't been there long when they heard the cries of what sounded like a wounded animal. They found a dog lying in the undergrowth, covered in blood, with a small hole in its head. It was starving and barely alive.

John carried the dog back to the van. They took it straight to the vets, where they presumed it would have to be put down. The dog had been shot and the bullet was lodged in its head. But somehow it had survived, and other than the small matter of having a bullet in his head he seemed to be fine. The vet asked them what they wanted to do, have it put down or keep the dog. They decided they would give the poor thing a chance. So they took him home, in the hope that they could nurse him back to health.

Over the next few weeks, his health gradually improved. He started to run around, and the wound healed up. He looked like new again, as though nothing had happened. They called him Bullet. He had a shiny black coat, was medium size and looked a bit like a labrador – four or five years old, the vet had reckoned. He followed them everywhere, even slept on their bed at night. They bought him a collar and put him on a lead if they went into the busier end of town.

One morning, they went to the local market with Bullet and sat down in one of the local cafes. They were just finishing their coffee when a policeman, who was walking past their table, suddenly turned towards them and pointed at the dog. He came over to them while taking a closer look at Bullet.

"I know this dog!" the policeman shouted at them in Spanish. "He killed some of my neighbour's chickens and bit her when she tried to stop him. Where did you find him?"

John jumped up and explained that the dog belonged to him and that he was just a harmless stray that they had adopted.

The policeman noticed the scar on the dog's head.

"This is the dog that I took to the forest and I shot him in the head because he's dangerous and shouldn't be alive!"

By this time a crowd had gathered round, and more police had arrived. The Spanish attitude to animal welfare, especially in those days, was appalling. From Bullfighting, maltreated donkeys and chained-up starving dogs – animals were animals, not pets, and being in Andalucia made things even worse.

The policeman in question was evidently the head of the local police, as the other police saluted him and were quick to follow orders. Three of the officers arrested John and handcuffed him before he had time to react. They ignored June, as women were considered inferior and, in many instances, treated almost as badly as their animals. The head policeman grabbed the dog, took him across the road, and in full view of everybody involved shot the dog in the head. This time, making sure that he was dead.

June, screaming hysterically, ran over to the policeman, knocked him over, punching and kicking him whilst trying to grab the gun out of his hand. Some of the spectators pulled her off the policeman, who got to his feet and punched her hard in the face. Swearing in Spanish he pointed his gun at her head, as the crowd held her down on the ground. Blood was pouring from her nose. John, despite the handcuffs, charged like a raging bull at the angry mob – smashing glasses and plates, tables and chairs flying everywhere before he was also subdued.

More police arrived in a Jeep, the dreaded Guardia Civil, their black shiny hats with the brim turned up at the back giving them the matador look. John and June were unceremoniously thrown into the waiting vehicle and driven to the local police station.

In a few horrific minutes their whole world had come crashing down.

They were pushed into separate cells, where they spent the night and were offered the luxury of a glass of water – but no food. Their first thoughts were of the tragedy of what had unfolded in front of them back at the cafe, their ill-fated trip to the market, and the barbaric murder of Bullet.

John and June could see each other in opposite cells, but weren't permitted to speak, June couldn't stop crying. Her face was swollen but nothing appeared to be broken. John was already planning revenge but was more concerned about what was going to happen to the pair of them. June was probably going to be charged with assaulting a police officer, and possibly attempted homicide, which would almost certainly mean many years in a Spanish jail. John was facing similar charges for assault and being in possession of a dangerous animal. Up to this point there had been no mention of any legal assistance.

When they awoke the next morning, they could hear a commotion outside. It sounded like objects were being thrown at the building. Their immediate thoughts were that there was a lynch mob baying for blood – theirs of course. There was a continual chant that was gradually getting louder:

"LIBERTAD! LIBERTAD!"

"FREEDOM! FREEDOM!"

It turned out that a large part of the local community, including friends and neighbours, were demonstrating against the police, condemning the brutal manner in which the whole matter had been dealt with, and were demanding the release of the foreigners.

One of the policemen was frantically screeching down the phone, asking for back-up, or for instructions on how to handle the situation. Nothing ever really happened in Isla Cristina and this was turning into not only an ugly situation, possibly an international incident. If the English tabloids got hold of the story, imagine the headlines: 'English Couple Beaten-up and Gaoled in Barbaric Spanish Town ... *while being forced to witness their pet dog's execution*.'

The Guardia Civil eventually arrived. In numbers. Armed to the teeth. They instructed the crowd to move back, most of them reluctantly obeyed, for fear of more violence. The National Guard were military police and had a reputation for taking matters into their own hands; dishing out punishment as and when they saw fit. Nobody in their right mind was going to stand in their way. The local police inside the police station opened the door and welcomed them with open arms, but were not greeted accordingly, as they walked straight past them and ordered the cells to be opened. John and June were handcuffed again, taken outside and bundled into the Jeep.

John had the temerity to ask where they were going, before bluntly being told to shut-up. John whispered to June that they were probably being taken to the nearest city – Huelva or maybe Seville? They had only been in the Jeep for a few minutes when they stopped and were told to get out. They found themselves outside the house where they were living. Totally confused they wondered what was coming next. Were they being let off and freed? Were the police going to search the property before taking them elsewhere? Were they to collect some clothes before going to prison?

They were ushered politely into the house by a sergeant who appeared to be in charge. The first thing June saw was Bullet's water bowl and broke down in tears once again. John put his arm around her and started to fall apart himself. The sergeant told them that they had thirty minutes to collect all their belongings, put everything in their van and were going to be escorted to the Portuguese border where they would be put on the ferry and be officially deported and were never to return to Spain. They put everything they owned in the van, said goodbye to a couple of their neighbours and drove the few kilometres to the border with the police Jeep following behind.

When they arrived at the ferry, the police handed them over to the border control customs officials, who then made sure that they drove onto one of the small ferries that crossed the river Guadiana. Ayamonte is the border town in Spain on the other side a few hundred metres down-river is Vila Real de Santo António, welcoming you to Portugal. In the summer months there was nearly always a long queue of vehicles on both sides of the river, as there weren't many of the small ferry boats and each one had room for only a few cars, crammed onto the open deck, often so close to each other that the vehicles were almost touching each other, just so that they could squeeze on an extra one. If you were stuck in the queue behind a lorry or, heaven forbid, a car towing a caravan, you could add a few hours to your expected arrival time.

This was early March and there was a long queue. The next ferry arrived and emptied its cargo of the foot passengers first and then one by one the various forms of transport rumbling noisily over the wooden planks. John, although he was at the back of the line, drove past the queue and was escorted up the ramp onto the boat by the customs officials. The people waiting in the row of cars started blowing their horns in protest that foreigners were getting special treatment. The ferry crew were, as usual, trying to find an extra few metres to make room for a Mini that they had spotted near the back of the long line of waiting cars. They waved the Mini forward to the front, the driver managed to manoeuvre into the tight space that was still available but knocked off the passenger's wing mirror in the process. This wasn't an unusual occurrence.

The frustrated passengers on deck, and those left on the quayside, began complaining, blowing their car horns and arguing with the crew.

John had hardly said a word since they had been evicted from their former home.

John turned to June, held her hand tightly and whispered, "I'm going back, don't try to stop me, I've got some unfinished business to attend to."

"I'll meet you tomorrow around sunset about a kilometre upriver. Don't worry, I'll be OK, I love you."

With that, he jumped out of the van and quietly shut the door. June looked on as John strolled casually over to the crowd of passengers who were arguing with the crew. When order was finally restored, thanks to a timely intervention by the police, John and all the other people who weren't supposed to be on deck walked over the boards back to their cars. In all the confusion he had slipped away unnoticed.

The ferry finally departed. The crossing took about fifteen minutes. June waited nervously in the van, waiting for her turn to go through customs. She was physically shaking, trying to control herself. She was an emotional wreck. The last 24 hours had been enough of an ordeal already. Now John, all she had left in the world, had suddenly abandoned her to risk everything on some senseless act of revenge.

June nearly jumped out of her skin as the Portuguese customs officer banged on her window demanding, "documentos por favor!" She showed him her passport and he waved her through without any fuss. He had probably noticed how distressed she was and decided not to add to her misery by searching the vehicle, or bothering with the polite greeting, "Bem-vindo a Portugal" (Welcome to Portugal). She drove to a nearby car park and tried to compose herself. She began by reliving the previous day's nightmare. The only positive thing that she could think of was that despite the living hell that they had endured, at least they were both free and still alive.

The next day, June drove the van down every dirt track she could find near the river area, looking for a good place to wait for John's arrival. She picked out what she thought would be the perfect spot to have a good view up and down the river, and where the van would be visible from the Spanish side. The Guadiana near the estuary is a few hundred metres wide, with a strong current, tidal and often teeming with jellyfish. She presumed that John would find some way of getting across by boat.

She waited and waited, staring across the river until she could hardly keep her eyes open.It was starting to get dark and chilly. There was no sign of any kind of movement on the river except the ferries going to and fro. She realised that in all probability something was wrong, and she might never see him again. She dreaded to think what he may have done, so she tried to keep it out of her thoughts.

She was peering through the semi-darkness at the opposite bank. Further up-river she saw what looked like a car's headlights illuminating the water, then flashing blue lights. She thought she heard what sounded like sirens in the distance, then barking dogs and gunshots. There were more flashing lights leaving Ayamonte, heading in that direction. She saw something moving in the water, maybe a hundred metres away. She could make out what looked like a plastic bucket propelling itself towards the riverbank. She ran along beside the river and there was John panting with exhaustion lying by the water's edge completely naked. He'd put his clothes in a washing bowl and somehow swum across from the other side.

"They're trying to shoot me; we've got to hurry!"

"What's happened, what have you done?"

"Something bad, I can't tell you, get me a towel. I'm freezing!"

John dried himself, got dressed and climbed into the driver's seat and off they went.

They headed towards Faro, then up into the hills where they stopped for the night. They had driven most of the way in total silence. June had been pestering John for answers but other than mentioning the obvious fact that the police were after him, and that they could never go back to Spain, he kept quiet.

John got out of the van, sat down and started to talk.

"Look, I walked back to Isla Cristina, waited until it was dark. I was angry and did something I shouldn't have done. I'm sorry but I'll never tell you what it was and I don't want you to try and find out. I wasn't going to let someone murder that dog in cold blood and get away with it. So you can think whatever you want to, but I don't want you – or anybody else for that matter – to know the truth. All I do know is that the Spanish police are looking for me, they probably know it was me that jumped in the river, so they know I've either drowned or that I'm in Portugal. The two countries are not exactly the best of friends so hopefully I, or should I say we, will be safe if we stay here."

June looked up at me. She had almost finished her story.

She called John to come down and join us, which surprisingly he did straight away. He asked me, "Did you hear about the dog?"

"Yes of course, do you want to talk about it?" I asked.

June looked at me and shook her head, whispering "No questions."

John looked at Bender and, holding back the tears, said, "I used to wonder whether if Bullet had come back with us, if he and Bender would have got on together."

I replied, "Bender doesn't make friends with male dogs. He might have made an exception as Bullet was your dog, but it would have been difficult."

"Well, for some reason, it was never meant to happen, so there's no point in us going on about it, is there. What's done is done, got to get over it." John was talking to himself, basically.

We had dinner together at the house, reminisced about the old days, and John even smiled a few times, which June said he hadn't done in ages. He said goodnight and went off to bed. June told me that she was frightened of what John was going to do next. He hadn't mentioned the word, but she thought he might be suicidal. He'd been in this state for three months or so. He'd stopped painting, they were low on cash and all he talked about was driving back to England, which would mean risking everything. They had to leave the house soon, as the owners were coming back. John had packed the van some weeks back and was ready to go at a moment's notice in case the authorities started making enquiries.

I stayed the night. I didn't know what to think or what to do. I kept wondering what he could have done. If it had been anything really serious, I'm sure we would have heard about it in the news. As he obviously wasn't behaving normally, he might have done nothing at all – but if so, why did he continue the charade and swim across a dangerous river? The policeman who shot the dog was the only target for revenge and he was armed. Maybe John knew where to find him, attacked him and beat him up. There were a few scenarios that I came up with, but all were pure speculation of course. Over the following years I kept planning to go to Isla Cristina and try to discover what exactly did happen. But I never did.

In the morning, I decided that there wasn't much point in hanging around any longer. I wished them both luck and to call my parents with any news. They said goodbye to Bender for what was looking to be the last time and after a few hugs etc. I drove off back towards Albufeira wondering what would happen to them and what could they possibly do. John would be crazy to risk driving through Spain, but all through his life he had often taken the hazardous path rather than the safe route, which was what made him the great human being that he was.

On the one hand, I was so happy to be back together with Bender and at the beginning of a new season; on the other hand, obviously upset about their dilemma and being unable to help. I was so lost in thought that I didn't really know, or care for that matter, where I was heading.

25

In Flagrante

That summer I spent most of my time camping in my VW van by a beach named Praia do Vau, which is the next big beach going west from Praia da Rocha. I'd spend most of my days swimming and sunbathing, enjoying the beach, while Bender sat nearby in the shade under the small cliffs. Despite the heat he would never go in the water, in fact he would do almost anything to avoid it.

One afternoon, I met a gorgeous blonde Australian girl on the beach. We went for a long walk by the sea and over some cliffs to the west towards Alvor. When we finished canoodling etc. and began our way back, we hadn't noticed how late it was, and that the tide had come in and cut off our beach route. Luckily the sea wasn't too rough – most days there were hardly any waves at all – but as usual the Atlantic water was cold. We swam the small distance round the cliffs, stepped onto the sand and ran over to our towels to get warm and dry.

I heard a familiar bark and looked up to see Bender looking down from the edge of the cliff. After meeting Sheila, or whatever her name was, I had understandably, bearing in mind the unusual circumstances, completely forgotten all about him. He was about 4 or 5 metres above the sea, there was no way for him to climb down. I assumed that as usual he would find a solution and so he did. He disappeared from view for a second, then took a flying leap and crashed into the sea.

There were a few people left on the beach, although the sun had gone behind the rocks, I suppose they were determined to get their money's worth. I heard a loud, American, male voice (it might have been a Canadian, I could never tell, but I didn't see the ubiquitous maple leaf anywhere on his clothing) shouting: "Martha did you see that?"

"No,Chuck,what was it?"

"My God I just saw a flying dawg. It dove off the cliff top into the sea!"

Bender paddled his way through the waves back onto the sand and then, looking a bit bedraggled, came over and began shaking himself all over us. Why do dogs always have to do it over somebody?

The Americans came over to say hello as they do. "Is that a Portuguese Water Dawg?" I resisted my natural urge to give a sarcastic reply as I was still trying to impress Miss Queensland.

"No, they are normally black, much smaller and have long curly hair. He's more like a Portuguese man-of-war!"

"Ain't that a poisonous jelly fish?" Chuck asked, trying to impress me with his expertise in wildlife.

Another dog strolled by at the very moment and, just as I was thinking of a way to extricate myself from getting involved in a longer conversation with Chuck and Martha, Bender went into attack mode and chased the other dog off the beach.

"See what I mean! Sorry, I've got to stop him before he does any damage!"

That night I was in the van having sex with Sheila when a loud bang on the van door brought an immediate halt to carnal proceedings – coitus interruptus at its finest.

"It's me Jenny!"

Before we had time to get dressed Jenny opened the door, quickly assessed the situation and went back outside again.

"Get her out of there!"

Sheila grabbed her things, gave me a quick kiss and a shrug of the shoulders as she turned to make her exit. Not a word was spoken as the two young women looked each other up and down, Jenny with her arms folded over her chest waiting impatiently for her rival's ignominious departure.

I couldn't help myself calling, "Next!" from inside the van, which exacerbated what was already a messy situation, in more ways than one. I prepared myself for the inevitable verbal stream of abuse, but only succeeded in making matters worse.

"I thought I'd come out here and surprise you."

"Well you certainly managed that!"

"Well who is she anyway?"

"Someone I bumped into on the beach this afternoon that's all."

"Didn't you read my letter? I said I'd be coming out soon."

"What letter?" I lied. "I'm sorry, I've been alone for a while, she seduced me, it was hard..."

"I bet it was!"

"...to resist her."

"Oh, you poor thing having to endure being violated by a gorgeous blonde. It must have been a dreadful experience."

"Well no actually..."

"Stop! I don't want to hear any more."

Then the crying started. I apologised, we had a kiss and a cuddle and soon after we were in bed, and all was forgiven. This was the first time that I had ever been involved sexually in a menage-a-trois, although the fact that one of the participants had fled the scene midway through would probably mean disqualification on technical grounds, so I didn't quite menage it.

Jenny, Bender and I spent the remainder of that summer in Lagos campsite. Most nights we would drive the short distance into town, park up with Bender locked in the van, and walk to our favourite restaurant. It would normally take Bender about ten minutes to find us. The owner of the restaurant had told us that no dogs were permitted inside the establishment, but after the third or fourth time he relented. One night, out of curiosity, we left the van where we could watch from a distance and looked on as Bender slid the front window open with his teeth on the metal catch then somehow squeezed himself through the tiny gap and slid down the side of the van scratching most of the paint off the door in the process.

To prevent any more damage to the vehicle we tried walking into town instead, which involved passing a few houses on the way. Outside one of the houses was a ferocious guard dog, behind a railing fence with a gate in the middle, that fortunately was always closed. Every night, as Bender went by the fence, the dog shot out of its kennel, ran up to the fence and the two of them began barking and growling at each other through the small gaps.

One night, the gate had been left open, the two dogs squared up to each other with no fence between them to prevent a bloodbath, but instead of attacking each other they moved along from the gate and returned to their normal positions, cocked their legs up a few times then when both contestants were ready started snarling, barking and gnashing teeth at each other through the safety of the iron bars. I quickly closed the gate just in case one of them had a change of heart.

26

A Few Anchors

In September, Jenny went back to the UK. The summer season was almost over, I was at a bit of a loose end, so I thought I'd take Bender on a trip to the Eastern Algarve and explore some of the towns and beaches. I was also searching for alternative places to sell my wares, which by chance took me to a Club Med resort called Pedras d'El Rei, which is situated just west of the town of Tavira. The resort itself consists of villas and chalets all painted white and surrounded by acres of grass. I'm not exaggerating when I say that there in the middle of all these luxurious surroundings were at least fifty dogs of all shapes and sizes, lying around relaxing in the shade almost as if it was them that were on holiday. I didn't fancy Bender's chances if the pack decided to turn on him, but after a couple of arguments they left him in peace.

To get to the beach we had to get a lift on a rowing boat to cross the narrow sea inlet that lies between the land and the beach. Once over the water there's still a long way to walk through the mud flats and sand dunes before you actually reach the sea. The beach itself is soft white sand that seems to stretch for miles into the distance in both directions. Along the sand to the east is the anchor cemetery, a relic of the bluefin tuna fishing days. There are the remains of an old fishing village and a miniature train, that I had presumed was built to save the tourists having to take the long walk in the heat but which was in fact used by the fishing community to get their supplies and transport the tuna back to land. There are about one hundred rusty anchors lying partly buried in the sand. They were used to secure the tuna nets not the boats. I learnt a lot about the history of the place because I spent my first evening dining with an English freelance journalist that I had met at the bar. We couldn't help notice each other as everyone else was speaking in French.

His name was Christopher Reed, and he was visiting the Algarve with his Japanese wife. He had come to Portugal to cover the revolution for The Guardian newspaper and in March the year before, while covering a riot in Setubal, was badly beaten up by left wing thugs who had turned on the press accusing them of being CIA. One of the more vicious members of the gang attacked him, opened his bag, tore the film from his camera and threatened to smash it over his head, before he ran to the safety of a local cafe. As he reported at the time, one dead 26 injured – make that 27! The police had driven off in their armoured vehicles and left the press to fend for themselves. The next day a battered and bruised Christopher's picture and story was headline news on TV and in the British press.

"I didn't think so at the time, but it was the best thing that could have happened to me," he told me.

His name became synonymous with the revolution making him probably the best-known foreign correspondent in Portugal at the time. Being a freelance he was now contemplating moving on to a new country and a different challenge. Before coming to Portugal, he had spent some years in Japan, where he had met his wife.

That evening the three of us had dinner together at a nearby restaurant. The place was full of Portuguese families, so there were noisy children running around out of control. I could sense that Chris was gradually losing his patience having to tolerate the slow service and the unruly behaviour. He told me that foreign journalists had a bad reputation for heavy drinking and that he was no exception. By the time we had finally finished eating we were slightly pissed, to put it mildly, and found ourselves having to almost shout to be able to understand each other. Chris had a booming voice. He was very eloquent and reminded me of Richard Burton.

A small child accidentally knocked into him just as he was pouring some more wine down his throat. When he had finished choking, he stood up and bellowed across the room in English: "This is supposed to be a restaurant not a fucking kindergarten!"

There was an eerie silence for maybe a minute. Some of the women were crossing themselves, a few asked for their bills, but soon the noise level was back to normal. I was ready to leave at that stage, before he got beaten up again. His wife bowed and made her way back to their apartment. I suspected that she knew that it was a good time to depart. Chris ordered an expresso and a Sol y Sombra, a Spanish concoction, consisting of half brandy, half anis that was served up in a huge brandy glass in over-generous proportions by our friendly waiter, who had become noticeably shakier since Chris's outburst. Chris insisted that I had an after-dinner drink with him (not that I needed a great deal of convincing).He gave me a long intellectual explanation of all manner of subjects, most of which went way over the top of the head of the ignoramus drunk person who was sitting in front of him.

We asked for the bill – he was on his third Solar system by then, I was lagging behind on my second brandy Macieira. The waiter seemed more relaxed by now, apologised for the slow-motion food delivery etc. and offered us a drink on the house which obviously we couldn't refuse. By the time we staggered out of the restaurant I was in such a state that I was actually instructing my feet to go forward in the correct order: "Left foot, your turn, now right – whoops . . . right straight ahead." I'd nearly gone ten metres in what seemed like twenty minutes when the waiter came running out shouting something about a dog. I'd forgotten all about Bender being asleep under the table. He'd probably passed out inhaling the alcoholic vapour. He ran out and licked my face as one of my feet had disobeyed orders and tripped me up, so I was lying flat out on the grass. Chris looked down at me and suggested that we went back to the bar in the resort for a nightcap. I couldn't stand up, so he basically abandoned me.

I woke up on the grass hours later. I was outside the restaurant, it was dark, it took me ages to find where I'd parked the van. I was desperate to take a slash, but I was still having co-ordination difficulties. I was so bad that I was going through a mental data analysis: put the following phrases in the correct order, A: unzip jeans,

B: take out penis, C: urinate. I must have chosen CAB judging by the wet patch I found in the morning; I use the word patch loosely. I remember my Latin teacher telling us the conjugation of a verb Po,Piss,Pit,Penis,Pistis,Pants.

Late morning, we met for a hangover breakfast, and amused ourselves by going over what we could recall of the events of the previous evening. He invited me to come and visit him in Lisbon. I agreed there and then.

CHRISTOPHER REED, the Guardian's correspondent in Portugal, in hospital in Lisbon yesterday after being beaten up in the Setubal riots. Reed, who is 36, had concussion. Below is his report from hospital.

Portuguese punch-up —diary of a victim

From CHRISTOPHER REED, Lisbon, March 9

If the personal experiences of myself and my press colleagues of the weekend's political terrorism in Setubal are any guide to events in the next few weeks, then Portugal's promised election on April 12 must be at grave risk.

I became the last addition to the statistics of 24 hours of violence in the industrial city south of the River Tagus, near Lisbon. It started on Friday evening and by yesterday afternoon the tally was one dead and 26 injured. By 9 o'clock last night there were 27 injured — the last one myself after I had been beaten up three times by a crowd of political thugs.

The violence began as the latest in a series of acts of intimidation against moderate and conservative political parties. The Popular Democratic Party had their meeting in Setubal wrecked by a mob of extreme left-wing elements. Later in the evening the violence increased and half the town's police force, including the Chief Constable, was besieged in its two-storey headquarters in a main street.

Although yesterday the Chief Constable, Major Joao Pascoa, said that in the confusion nobody knew who opened fire first, his men were certainly shot at. But eyewitnesses claimed that police fired from a first-floor window across the street at people coming out of a cinema. It was one of three who died later in a Lisbon hospital.

By yesterday evening a crowd of 300 stood behind the

Reactionaries blamed ... 3
Leader 10

pavement barrier outside the headquarters, which was guarded by troops and under the command of a paratroop colonel.

Just before eight o'clock the colonel announced through a loud hailer that the police were being taken away (catcalls from the crowd) but that the armed forces were "with the people" (cheers from the crowd).

At 8 o'clock, 21 hours after the siege began, uniformed police officers scrambled into two armoured cars and a military truck and roared off. It seemed curious that if this could be done so simply then it had not been done earlier when, the Chief Constable said, the crowd numbered only about 30.

This odd attitude of the forces was to cost myself, and five other foreign journalists, including three women, a terrifying hour. The crowd, noticing my camera bag and the presence of the British photographer Peter Cullis, had chanted: "Death to the CIA."

As the crowd broke up and we moved off I was suddenly surrounded by about 50 men and accosted by a man with a black beard who seemed a cut above the rather scruffy "local lads" who seemed to be on a Saturday night "aggro."

He accused me of being CIA, ripped open the bag, took the camera, tore out the film, and threatened to smash the camera on my head, demanding to know where Cullis was.

I said I did not know and he replied with a knee in my groin. I was punched and buffeted, but the crowd moved on to look for Cullis and I retired to a café nearby to recover. I could see no soldiers.

In a few minutes Cullis, a

Turn to back page, col. 2

27

Lisbon

I'D BEEN to Lisbon once before with John Coy, on our way to Ibiza. It's where I witnessed John at his streetwise best. A gypsy approached him in Rossio, a famous square in the centre of the city. The man showed John a fake Rolex wristwatch. He made him try it on, John wasn't interested and put the Rolex back in the fancy presentation case that the man was holding, put his own watch back on his wrist, said no thanks and we walked away. We hadn't gone far when the gypsy came running after us waving John's watch in his hand. John was wearing the Rolex, acting very nonchalantly as though nothing unusual had occurred. The gypsy, instead of being angry, was impressed by John's sleight of hand and, after they swapped the watches back, he congratulated John, shook his hand, checking to make sure he hadn't switched them again and said something like, "You're worse than me!" Which was quite a compliment.

In those days there was no such thing as a motorway in Portugal. The A roads were more like B roads and so on through the first letters of the alphabet. Crossing the hilly part between the Algarve and the Alentejo was about two hours of bends at 30/40 kph most of the way unless you were stuck behind a lorry; then it was even slower as it was almost impossible to overtake safely, which didn't seem to bother many of the Portuguese drivers as they had this uncanny ability to see round corners.

When you finally reach the flat plains of the Alentejo, the straight road begins, and all those drivers that were queueing up behind, that hadn't been brave enough to have risked their lives beforehand, made up for lost time by over-taking en masse – sometimes three abreast, covering both sides of the road, often with traffic hurtling towards them doing more or less the same. There wasn't a great deal of traffic between the capital and the Algarve then, but even so there was plenty of roadside debris, evidence that there were frequent accidents. When there was a pile-up it meant everybody had to stop and get out of their vehicles. Their ghoulish curiosity could not be resisted, which often resulted in another crash on the other side of the road.

It took me at least five hours on this occasion, before I reached the 25th April huge red suspension bridge with the stunning view of the old city of Lisbon and the river Tagus. After such a long drive, through somewhat monotonous countryside, it really is a fantastic sight.

Chris had a rented apartment in the heart of Lisbon. I'd researched the location before I'd set off, so I had a rough idea of how to get there. The main route into the city led me down to the Marquês de Pombal roundabout which consisted of at least three, maybe four, lanes of traffic and was basically mayhem on wheels. The only good thing I spotted was that at least all the traffic was going around the old architect's statue in the same direction. It took me three laps before finally taking the turning I wanted – and I still had an argument with a taxi.

Chris's place was surprisingly easy to find. Before going into the block of apartments I took Bender to a park to let him do his business. Thankfully, after running off to relieve himself, he came back to me. I had a piece of rope in the van, so I tied it round his collar. I shouldn't have brought him really. I began to wonder what I would do if I lost him in a city of this size.

Chris and his wife lived on the third floor of a large building that overlooked one of the main avenues. After dinner we sat on the balcony with our brandies, watching the madness of the traffic below. One of the new political parties, I think it was the right wing CDS, had somehow painted their circular logo in the middle of a busy junction, so some of the drivers treated it as a roundabout – or through respect didn't want to drive over it – whereas the majority of the vehicles drove straight across. I'd never heard so much horn blowing and screeching of brakes. And this was at 10 O'clock at night.

After a long evening, Chris told me that he had been asked by The Guardian to travel up north to a religious pilgrimage site called Fatima. The newspaper wanted an independent viewpoint from him as an atheist. He asked me if I would drive him there, stay for a couple of nights and help him in his research. Being a non-believer myself, I agreed and so the next morning off we went.

We had to take the main road to Porto for the first 100 kms. The road was bumper to bumper lorries, vans and diesel fumes. There were hardly any safe places to overtake for the faster cars, so yet another quite scary and dangerous trip. Luckily, we made it to the turn-off and headed into the hills where we eventually found our holy destination hidden away in the middle of nowhere.

Fatima is where three young children were herding their sheep and "saw" over a period of six months, between May 13th and October 13th, 1917, various apparitions of the Virgin Mary. The Catholic church conveniently considered their tale as "worthy of belief" and constructed a sanctuary facing a concourse twice the size of St. Peter's in Rome, in honour of the miracle of Fatima.

On arrival, Chris found himself a room for the night while I decided to stay in the van because I wanted to keep an eye on Bender. That evening we found a restaurant; Bender ran off with a bitch who was probably on heat. We got pissed, had an argument with a table of Americans who were from the Blue Army that was going to, as they put it, "defeat the commie bastards of the Red Army".

The next day I was assigned the task of counting the gift shops, taking note of what was on offer and checking the prices of the candles that were in the shape of body-parts.The theory was that if you had a withered hand for example you would purchase a hand shaped candle and light it and your hand would miraculously repair itself.The candles weren't cheap either,infact larger parts of the body cost an arm and a leg.The sheer size of the place was overwhelming and what's more very exhausting. This was the Portuguese answer to Lourdes. It was early October, the big day of the year was the 13th and pilgrims were already arriving – most of them on their knees, shuffling down the concourse, after some of them had apparently been walking for days. We had seen hundreds of them by the roadside, making their way on foot.

I'd gone there with an open mind and I must admit you do tend to get caught up in the religious vibe. It's hard not to feel a certain creepiness about the place. When I had finished my part of the investigation, I re-joined Chris, who was interviewing more members of the Blue Army. I could tell by the look he gave me that he'd already heard enough religious claptrap.

After lunch we did the tourist bit and saw where the children met Mary. Chris was convinced that the whole thing was fabricated by the church and the Government of the day, and the sooner we left the better. Bender had disappeared, it was too late to drive back to Lisbon, so we spent another drunken evening arguing with members of the Church.

The next morning, we had planned to leave reasonably early, but there was still no sign of Bender. Chris needed to find a phone that functioned properly to call in his story to The Guardian in London, which entailed a visit to the post office. I arranged a time to meet him and began my search for the missing dog. I began by walking around the centre shouting "BENDER!" at the top of my voice, which raised a few eyebrows amongst the burgeoning crowd of worshippers. Maybe they thought it was a new chant that hadn't reached the Iberian Peninsula. I was hoping that they might join in with me, thousands of worshippers wailing 'BENDER'. I didn't care, I was starting to panic, I even considered buying a candle in the shape of a dog, lighting it and placing it with all the arms and legs and other parts of human anatomy that needed invisible mending.

In desperation I went back to the van, hoping that by now his sixth sense would have kicked in. And, sure enough, there he was, looking very sorry for himself and almost as tired as I was. I gave him a jumbo size tin of dog food, which he wolfed down in two or three gulps, got him in the van and drove back to the post office. We were late, and Chris was nowhere to be seen. I peered through the windows of the post office and could see him in one of the telephone booths waving his arms in the air. Things didn't appear to be going smoothly.

I waited patiently outside contemplating the thrills to come on the return journey, while at the same time feeling so relieved to have found the missing animal. Chris had been in there for over an hour when he finally came storming out of the building followed by a group of nuns waving their wooden crosses at him. He stopped to confront them and shouted for all to hear: "I'll tell you what the miracle of Fatima is, it's an uninterrupted fucking phone call to London!" With that he turned his back on the nuns who were crossing themselves in disgust, jumped into the van and slammed the door. "Drive, get me out of here before I'm arrested by the Papal Guard."

When he'd calmed down, I said, "I found him."

"Who? God?"

"No. Dog!"

"Oh, thank God for that."

"Who?"

"Just drive the bloody van."

How a Blue Army aims to lower the Red Flag

From CHRISTOPHER REED: Fatima (Portugal), October 13

One of the largest manifestations of Portugal's poor in 2½ years of political turmoil took place today in what was once a tiny village 70 miles north-east of Lisbon. Now, among hotels, boarding houses, souvenir shops and a basilica facing a concourse twice the size of St Peter's in Rome, the Catholic Church honours the "miracle" of Fatima—and quietly continues a thinly disguised anti-Soviet campaign.

Fatima still holds a mystical attraction for the 100,000 poor Portuguese workers who flocked to this year's main event with a devotion the Portuguese Communist Party might envy.

Many arrived in pouring rain and blustery winds shuffling painfully on their knees in penance. Others trudged barefoot for miles and still others arrived in the backs of open and drenched lorries. The better off packed hundreds of coaches. Only a small proportion arrived in cars and a tiny fraction flew from abroad.

Even the poorest still found money to buy trashy "artigos religiosos" at hundreds of shops, even supermarkets, among the 40 religious institutions at Fatima. They were offered plaster virgins, hardboard crucifixes, plastic rosary beads, nickel medallions, 6ft. candles and an appalling collection of kitsch junk souvenirs. This commercialisation is all the sadder because Portugal is usually noted for restraint in tourist exploitation.

All this may be regrettably familiar to visitors to other famous Catholic shrines but the Fatima legend is perhaps the most curious.

In uncanny concurrence with events in Russia in 1917, three poor, illiterate shepherd children, saw visions of the Virgin Mary in or near Fatima. In October the final apparition appeared above an oak tree to Lucia, one of the children, but not to 70,000 people watching. Suddenly, it is said, the heavens parted and the sun whirled in growing intensity for ten minutes.

Two of the children died in two years from the great flu epidemic and the third, Lucia, who was then 10, is in a convent in Coimbra. An anti-Soviet militant Catholic organisation called the Blue Army of Our Lady of Fatima with 30 million members in 37, 80, or 100 countries (depending on which member or which brochure one consults) is based on the vision's message and has its international headquarters at Fatima.

The Fatima message seems at first to be a simple rallying cry by the Church — hard pressed in Portugal in 1917 by the anti-clerical Republic. But there is a startling anti-Soviet message. In the words of this year's official Fatima brochure, Our Lady warned that "if people do not do these things Russia will spread her terrors throughout the world, causing wars and persecutions against the Church. Many will be martyred. Several nations will be annihilated." The explicit words of Mary apparently, recalled by Lucia were: "In the end my Immaculate Heart will triumph. Russia will be converted, and an era of peace will be granted to humanity."

The sceptical view is put succinctly by Antonio de Figueiredo in his book "Portugal: Fifty years of Dictatorship." He writes: "That Portugal should have been elected to receive such an important message by a Portuguese speaking celestial visitor from the top of an oak tree as a suitable place for a shrine and sanctuary capable of accommodating hundreds of thousands of pilgrims and vying with Lourdes, is one of those natural mysteries that a good Catholic nationalist Portuguese is expected to accept without question."

Last year at the height of Portugal's revolution the Fatima theme was "reconciliation" — a slogan promptly adopted by the conservative CDS party whose huge hoarding looms from a hill over the main road to the shrine. This year with the Communists regrouping after a setback the political message was muted.

In a chapel at Blue Army HQ in Fatima is what they claim to be the priceless Kazan icon from the basilica in Red Square, destroyed during the revolution. At Fatima they say they will return the icon "when the site is reconsecrated as a cathedral of the Red Square basilica rebuilt."

The devotions at Fatima, which verge on the hysterical, are a matter of belief and taste. But it is difficult to reconcile the call for peace and brotherhood at today's service with the crude anti-Russian sentiments.

28
The Marginal

WHEN WE got back to Lisbon, I dropped Chris off at home, we said our goodbyes and promised to keep in touch. A year later I received a postcard from him from California, which was the last time I heard from him.

As I was in Lisbon, I decided to go to Cascais for no particular reason, before returning to the Algarve. I'd heard it was one of the most scenic coast roads in Europe. I'd also been told that it was one of the most dangerous roads in the civilised world.

Going back to my driving test days, I'd taken the examiner's advice and had a lesson in a BSM car which I then took the test in with the same examiner, and this time I passed. In order to make up for lost driving time, I threw myself in at the deep end by blagging my way into a driving job. I became a "trade plater" which meant delivering brand new vehicles to their destination and getting back usually by train. The way to earn extra cash was instead of taking the train you hitch-hiked back and legitimately collected the money for the train fare. I was an experienced hitcher and, as an added bonus, I was armed with a set of personal red number plates. These plates virtually guaranteed success, a kind of 'Get Out of Jail Free' card.

Lorry and van drivers knew that you were working and that you were part of the driving community, so it was relatively easy to get picked up. As I was a rookie, the boss – who had a very close resemblance to Hitler – gave me all the jobs that nobody else wanted or trips to London, which was impossible to hitch back from. The Fuhrer had only government contracts so I often had to take half-built tractor units (the front part of an articulated lorry), where I had to climb up a ladder just to be able to get in the cab, army lorries with no windscreen, GPO vans that had speed limiters, sometimes as far as Scotland.

And then the return trip, trying to get back home to Bedford from remote locations, often in the freezing cold or torrential rain. If that wasn't hard enough, I had to suffer hour after boring hour with all kinds of nutters. Most lorry drivers were glad of the company and loved to chat, unfortunately I was usually shattered and half frozen and almost always fell asleep after about five minutes. Most of the cab interiors were erotically decorated with Playboy and Penthouse centrefolds; you could hardly see out of the windows for tits and bums.

One particularly unpleasant driver in London had a hole in the crotch of his filthy stained trousers which exposed his manhood. He said it was for pissing into a bottle so that he didn't have to stop so often. After allowing a reasonably attractive member of the opposite sex to walk over a zebra crossing, he commented, "I bet her shit doesn't smell", grabbing hold of his crotch, followed by, "I'd shag that."

I mumbled under my breath, "I bet it does, and no you won't, you big fat ugly twat," before politely agreeing with him and asking him to drop me off at the nearest station.

I got the sack shortly after that. I'd broken down just north of London, so I had to phone Adolf for assistance. When he asked me for my exact location I said, "Potters Bar" (a town in Hertfordshire). I was already on a yellow card for a previous incident involving a London Routemaster bus. "You can't hit them, they're big red things!" he'd screamed at me.

"Potters Bar? I told you no drinking on duty – leave the vehicle there with the keys in it and come back here. You're fired," he announced, and slammed the phone down before I had a chance to explain. I then graduated to taxi driving, where I quickly developed my driving skills, and so I presumed I would be well prepared for a short trip along The Marginal.

As it turned out, I don't think any amount of training would have been sufficient. It certainly lived up to its dangerous reputation. I hardly had any time to take in the view. The road itself runs between Lisbon and Cascais along the Tagus estuary, passing through a number of towns. With the sea on one side, sometimes with the waves crashing over the sea-walls onto the actual road, and built up urbanisation on the other, it was a dual carriageway with no central reservation, junctions that crossed both sides, pedestrians crossing, a lot of them in swimming costumes coming from the beaches, meaning one small bikini and the honking began from the horny drivers who obviously kept only one eye on the road at best.

I first tried the inside lane at a sensible speed, but there was too much traffic muscling its way in. The outside lane was seriously fast, with the boy racers flashing their headlights behind, telling you to get of their way, who would then out of frustration undertake on the inside lane giving the middle finger sign as they shot past. I felt as though I'd been dropped into the middle of the Monaco Grand prix.

When I went past the chequered flag, I found a place to stop, let Bender out, sat down on some grass and tried to relax. I was shaking with nerves. I remember punching the air with a loud self-congratulatory, "Woohoo, I've done it!" I had a stroll around the town and it certainly had charm and signs of wealth, I quite liked it, somewhere for the future maybe. The neighbouring town of Estoril, famous for its casino and sophisticated lifestyle, wasn't for me and Estoril wouldn't have wanted me either. Apparently, Salazar lived there, and it took him so long to get home from Lisbon he ordered the construction of the 'Avenida Marginal'. It was also an international spy centre during the second world war. Portugal was neutral, despite their fascism, as they were also Britain's oldest ally – so I suppose everybody was welcome. Fascinating times. I can imagine the Monte Carlo of Iberia, maybe.

Like those terrifying rides on the fairground that you're scared to go on but then love it once you've done it and conquered your fears, I couldn't wait to have another go on the Marginal. It didn't disappoint, really exciting and I even saw the aftermath of a head-on collision; well worth the effort. Just imagine having to do that journey every day. I wondered what the life expectancy was among commuters. There was a perfectly good train service which ran along beside the road, obviously the safer option.

I had just crossed the bridge on my way back to the Algarve and was going flat out downhill when one of those small pick-up trucks that farmers and builders use pulled out in front of me, giving me virtually no chance to avoid it. I slammed on the brakes. Bender, who was lying in the front seat, smashed into the windscreen. I swerved full lock in an attempt to miss them, went up on two wheels, somehow just scraped the front of the truck, went off the road as the van righted itself back onto four wheels, and stopped on the verge facing the opposite direction. Bender had hit the split windscreen with an almighty bang but hadn't broken it. He was lying on the floor. I thought this was the moment I'd been dreading. I ran to the other side and opened the door and he jumped out, I grabbed hold of him before he ran off. He had a swelling over his left eye but seemed to be OK. I hadn't even worried about my own safety or the damage to the van. I put Bender back in the van and ran over to the truck. They hadn't even got out or come over to help, they wouldn't open their windows until I started banging on them and shouting in my best Portuguese, "Idiotas, estúpidos, meu cão está ferido!" (Stupid idiots my dog's injured). They started to apologise, they asked if I was alright and said that they hadn't seen me – by which time the rubberneckers had arrived and all the traffic had stopped. I was shaking like the proverbial leaf, people were offering me water, and to be fair they were very kind and helpful.

An argument broke out, so I left them to it. The van wasn't really any worse than it already was, Bender appeared to be alright. I cuddled him and stroked his head and for no particular reason burst into uncontrollable sobbing. I suppose I was in shock, hardly a surprise under the circumstances. I loved that dog so much, we'd been through so many adventures together that just the thought of him dying one day broke my heart, so I put it out of mind and pulled myself together.

The van started, nothing seemed to be wrong with it, so I left the scene of the near accident, drove until the first cafe, sat down and ordered a large brandy. I sat there for a long time going over what had just happened and counting my blessings. We could have easily have both been killed or seriously injured. How the van didn't turn over I'll never know. How ironic, after dicing with death on The Marginal.

I spent the night in Setubal, a city south of Lisbon that lies on the Sado river. I was feeling a bit 'sado' myself, because I knew when I arrived in Albufeira it would soon be time to leave Bender behind again. In the morning I caught the ferry across the river estuary over to Troia, even saw some dolphins, which was nice. On the other side I very slowly made my way back to Lagos and then on to Albufeira. Bender didn't seem to be suffering from any after effects, so I started building up the courage to leave him.

I found an old friend who knew the dog well, he held on to him while I made my getaway in the VW. I hadn't said farewell to Bender this time, I thought I'd just go, just leave him, he'll work it out by himself. I couldn't face going through all those emotions again. As I left, I promised myself that whatever happens, that if I find him again next year. I'll never leave him again.

29

Stratford-upon-Avon

AS SOON as I arrived back in Bedford I got in touch with June. She told me that John had been in some kind of mental institution but had recently been released and that they were living in Stratford on a canal barge moored on the river near the city centre. A few days later I drove up to see them. John seemed to be back to his old self, we spent the afternoon together by the river, everything appeared to be perfectly normal. I heard all about their drive through Spain – they had only stopped at remote service stations, paranoid that the police were searching the country for them.

John stood up and left June and me alone for a few minutes, giving us an opportunity to talk to each other in private.

He'd been behind bars, locked up in a type of secure mental hospital as a precaution. June had been to see him almost every day. On her last visit he had handed her a large kitchen knife through the bars of the cell, saying, "I don't think I'll need this anymore." How the knife ever got in there in the first place was a complete mystery – John up to his tricks again.

When John returned to join in with the conversation, he knew that we had been talking about him in his absence. He looked at me closely in the eyes and without averting his gaze he said, "Does he know?" June nodded her head and almost in tears just said, "Yes." I didn't know what to say or where to look. We sat there in silence for a while. I was starting to feel uncomfortable when John held my hand across the table. "I'll be OK, and thanks for coming, I'm going for a nap, keep in touch," and off he went.

When he'd gone, June told me that she thought he was gradually getting better but had her reservations about whether he would ever make a full recovery. Would he get back to being his old self and maybe start painting again? I'll never know, because that was our final moment together. Despite both of us promising to phone or write, neither of us ever did. So that was my final confused memory of two remarkable characters who had had a profound impact on my life.

As a tribute to John, here is his favourite anecdote that is best recounted after a lot of practice and make sure plenty of alcohol has been consumed by your audience before you start.

A new boy has arrived at school and the teacher introduces him to the rest of the class. She then asks John Smith to stand up and spell his name out loud using the special technique that they had developed. (You say the letters one at a time then how it sounds phonetically, e.g. C-A-T there's your CAT. The faster the better.)

J-O there's your JOE,

H-N there's your HN, there's your JOHN,

S-M there's your SM, there's your HNSM there's your JOHNSM,

I-T-H there's your ITH,there's your SMITH,there's your HNSMITH, there's your JOHN SMITH.

"Thank you, John, that was very good. Now Archibald as the new boy it's your turn to spell your name out loud to the class."

He stands up and off he goes:

A-R there's your AR,

C-H-I there's your CHI, there's your ARCHI,

B-A-L-D there's your BALD, there's your CHIBALD, there's your ARCHIBALD,

A-S-S there's your ARSE. There's your BALDASS, there's your CHIBALDASS, there's your ARCHIBALDASS,

E-N-D there's your END, there's your ASSEND, there's your BALDASSEND, there's your CHIBALDASSEND, there's your ARCHIBALDASSEND,

I-N-G there's your ING, your ENDING, there's your ASSENDING, there's your BALDASSENDING, there's your CHIBALDASSENDING, there's your ARCHIBALD ASSENDING.

John was a master at telling it and because of the raucous laughter that usually started about halfway through, he very rarely got to the finishing line.

1977

30

Big Dick

THAT winter I resumed my career on the taxis with a company called Blue Circle. Most of the drivers were hardened professionals who had no time for the likes of me. I had to prove myself capable before being taken seriously. When we weren't busy, we sat around in the rest room drinking tea and coffee waiting for the phones to ring. One week each month we were obliged to work the night shift.

On one of my first night shifts a call came through about 2am one morning to pick up a customer called Dick West. He was a notorious hard man and womaniser, a well-known face around town. Luckily it wasn't my turn – but all the other drivers in front of me in the queue refused to go for one reason or another. The night controller came in the room and asked whose turn it was. All of them were pointing at me.

"Well get your skates on. You're already late. He'll be on the blower again in a minute – and don't ring the bell!"

I raced through town up to the then new part called Brickhill, found the address but no sign of my reputedly problematic fare. I sat outside the house for a while and called in on the radio to check I was in the right spot. The sound of my radio had awoken some of the neighbourhood, as upstairs lights had started coming on, probably expecting to see a police car. The passenger door flew open, nearly coming off its hinges, then slammed angrily.

"Where the fuck have you been? You couldn't have made more noise if you'd tried. Look at them nosy bastards, they'll all be gossiping about me shagging Mandy while her husband's on nights. Muswell Road!"

By the time we arrived at his terraced house we'd got acquainted. We'd seen each other around in the pubs, so we kind of knew of each other's existence. As he got out of the car he gave me £1.35.

"Well they told me it's £1.65," I muttered nervously.

"Tell them to stick their fare up their arse I always pay £1.35."

"Waiting time?"

"It was me that was fucking waiting, why didn't you ring the bell?"

"They told me not to."

"Oh yeah, true. Come inside and have a beer, you cheeky little twat."

I weighed up the situation very carefully before finding the courage to venture indoors. Two beers later I knew I shouldn't have gone in. I was supposed to be working and I could hear them calling me on the radio – but I was enjoying myself being in Dick's company, so I thought: why not? Our chat came to an end when his wife shouted for him to come upstairs.

"You'd better fuck off, I've got to give her one now, know what I mean." He winked.

"I'll be off then. See you around Dick."

"Yeah, I'm usually in the Clarence. You owe me a pint!"

When I got back to Blue Circle HQ the drivers said, "Where the fuck have you been?"

"That's the second time I've heard that tonight," I laughed.

"Smells like you've been drinking, what happened to you?"

"Well, as you had all anticipated, he was nothing but trouble, so I decided that it was high time that someone taught him some manners," I lied.

"Huh! You and whose army? Bet he never even paid you, the tight bastard!"

"Did he pay you?" the controller asked.

"Yes, some of it in cash, the rest in refreshments."

"What? You've been inside his house with him? Are you mad?"

"Actually, he seemed like a good bloke. I don't understand what all the fuss is about."

"Wait until you get on the wrong side of him. You'll finish up in hospital like the rest of them," warned one of the drivers.

Over the winter months, Dick and I became good mates. We'd hang around the popular pubs where the opposite sex was more readily available. We had separate groups of friends and Dick was three or four years older than me. He had his own roof tiling business and employed a lot of the town's trouble-makers, the kind of muscle-bound bullies that were always looking for a fight.

One of them picked me up by the scruff of the neck with one hand one night after I'd commented on his ridiculous tattoos. The ceiling in the centuries-old pub was very low, and he was in the process of pushing my head through the plaster when I heard: "Put him down or I'll have you. He's alright."

"Sorry Dick, I didn't know he was your mate, he was taking the piss."

"Yeah, he does that when he's had a few."

Dick told me to buy my attacker a drink and then we would all be friends again.

Going out with Dick was like having Clint Eastwood by your side. He had a lot of respect amongst the more aggressive and undesirable members of Bedford's nightlife. After a while I noticed that most of the troublemakers left me in peace. Some of them even went as far as giving me a friendly nod, whereas before I would get a threatening: "Who are you looking at?"

Dick was six-foot-three, with curly, mousy hair, good looking, usually with a big grin on his face. He was wiry not stocky, all arms and legs and huge hands and apparently lightning fast and vicious. He told me that if he started throwing punches to get well out of the way, not that I needed any advice in the running away department. My brother David was standing in the queue for late night fish and chips in the town centre when three burly lads pushed in at the front. Dick was canoodling at the back of the line with that evening's conquest when somebody pointed out to him what was going on. According to my brother it was only a matter of seconds before all three of the queue jumpers were lying unconscious on the pavement.

He also had a reputation for the length of a certain part of his anatomy that hung between his legs. No wonder he was named Dick. He would stand in the pub and deliberately leave his foot in the way, often near the ladies loos where there was more female traffic. Now and then an unsuspecting young lady would trip over him, usually apologising with, "Oh, sorry, was that your foot?"

He always replied with, "No, it's only eleven-and-a half-inches – I don't use it as a rule!" Once when I went into a pub looking for him, his girlfriend was there sitting alone, so I asked,

"Where's Dick?"

She replied, "He's in there shaking hands with my best friend," giving me a knowing look, pointing towards the toilet. I thought to myself, what the hell is Lisa doing in the men's toilet. When he came out doing up his flies, with no sign of Lisa, the penny dropped. I wondered if any girl had ever said that about me. Little chance of that, I decided.

One night Dick was upstairs in one of the local discos having a good time with one of his Italian friends, Angie Russo, who owned a fleet of ice cream vans. Dick's younger brother Steve, who was also a bit of a handful, was trying to get in the club, but he wasn't wearing a tie, so the doormen weren't allowing him in. He tried to force his way in, got shoved down the stairs and the inevitable fight broke out. Almost single-handedly Dick put five bouncers in hospital and injured a couple of policemen. Apparently, Dick was covered in blood, none of it his own.

When the three of them came to trial, it was reported that Dick had smashed some of the doormen's faces repeatedly onto tables full of empty glasses, causing severe facial injuries. Steve and Angie got off reasonably lightly, but Dick was charged with GBH and was given a one-year prison sentence, suspended for one year as long as he didn't re-offend during that time.

Afterwards Dick told me that the bouncers were beating the crap out of his brother, so he had had no choice but to get stuck in and destroy everything in his path. He had a terrible temper and once the red mist came down, he just lost control. He wasn't proud of what happened, but his street cred had soared. He came to the conclusion that he would find it almost impossible to keep out of trouble for a year, as for sure there would be revenge attacks, so he would have to leave town, maybe the country.

"When are you going back to Portugal?" he asked.

"Next month, probably. Why? Don't tell me you want to come with me!"

"Yeah, why not? I've got plenty of money, we'll have a laugh."

"What about your wife and the rest of your harem?"

"There's plenty of fish in the sea, mate. I'll sort the missus out... anyway, I've had the VAT inspectors round, the business is up shit creek, so I might as well disappear for a few months."

I put my reasonably normal-sized hand out in acceptance. He was so grateful he gripped and hugged me enthusiastically, crushing my fingers and ribs simultaneously. Quite painfully!

31

John Greene

John at the wheel of his coach

AT SOME point during the course of the winter, through a mutual friend, I met John Greene, who also lived in Bedford. He'd travelled a lot and was planning a trip to Portugal with his very attractive blond girlfriend Lorraine. John's parents were Irish, he had two sisters and a younger brother. John was a very handsome young man, he had a black stubbly beard, and he reminded me of my idol George Best.

He didn't have a great regard for the law, he was involved in dodgy money-making schemes, credit card fraud, bent cars, etc. etc. He moved down to London where the pickings were easier. Despite his criminal tendencies he was the nicest bloke you could ever meet, and I don't say that lightly. He was like Robin Hood. If he'd made some money, he'd treat everyone to a slap-up meal. Easy come, easy go. He'd recently purchased a 44-seater coach that he was going to convert into a mobile home. He had the vehicle parked outside his rented flat in London and was getting three parking fines a day, as he was blocking three meters. By the time he left for Portugal he had accumulated a £900 debt to the local council and was up to his eyeballs in unpaid bills and other financial obligations. He said he wasn't ever coming back, so he didn't give a monkey's.

The previous year he'd copied a painting technique that he said would be the first step on his way to making a fortune. He'd stocked up with raw materials, so that when he arrived, he would start mass producing his artwork. Before they left, John ripped out all of the seats in the coach except the front two rows, and it was the middle of May when the two of them headed off for pastures new.

A week or so later, John phoned to say that they had arrived in the Algarve and had rented a house in Vale de Éguas, near Almancil, and that there were two spare rooms for us. A few weeks later Dick and I arrived in the VW van and moved in with them. The house was a typical old terraced building in a cul-de-sac. It had a small garden and patio, and was also reasonably quiet, but a bit out of the way. We soon made friends with the neighbours, except one of them, Fernando, a man probably in his thirties who was apparently a die-hard communist with a left-wing revolutionary beard to match. He wasn't very sociable and owned a dog, a large male German Shepherd. I thought, if we find Bender there's going to be fun.

John had started his painting mass production in the garage. He'd parked the coach, which he had now emptied, on some waste land nearby, and was drawing up plans for his mobile home conversion. While John and Lorraine had been driving through Spain they went through a lot of small towns and villages, obviously a few minutes ahead of the local bus because as they approached each place the waiting passengers ran out into the road to greet them carrying their suitcases, shopping bags, live chickens and ducks etc. waving frantically, screaming and shouting for them to stop.

After about the fifth village, John decided to start picking them up before someone was run over. Of course, apart from the front two rows there was nowhere for them to sit, which didn't seem to bother them, especially as it was a free ride. Once or twice John had to brake hard. With no seats in between the front and the rear all the passengers slid to the front of the bus almost knocking John and Lorraine out of their seats. Eventually, while John was in the process of dropping off and picking up more passengers, the real bus caught up with them. The driver got out, berated them for stealing his fares, but then calmed down when he realised that it wasn't a rival bus company. He saw the funny side of it, shook their hands and wished them a good trip.

32
Dognapped

ONCE we'd settled into our new home, Dick and I drove to Albufeira in search of Bender. My heart was thumping with anticipation when we arrived at the tunnel, but he wasn't there. I started asking around, but nobody had seen him for a long time. Albufeira had changed since I was last there. The centre was full of rough-looking undesirables: young Portuguese from Lisbon and Porto looking for the good life, camping wild in all kinds of places near the town, street-selling all kinds of junk. I began to wonder if any of this was my fault.

The garden in the centre was still the main official selling area. I was well-known amongst the now more established local traders. They weren't that pleased to see me back again and most of them gave me a wide berth. I don't know what they had against me. I had a feeling that this was now their patch and foreigners, even non-Algarvean Portuguese, were not welcome.

I also noticed a few black people were around. I'd hardly ever seen a black person in Portugal before. They were "Os retornados" (the returned ones) mainly from Angola and Mozambique, which along with some other countries were Portuguese colonies. After the revolution the two countries gained independence, so the Portuguese citizens started to come back en masse. At one stage 4,000 were arriving per day and the population increased by over a million in a very short time. The majority were white, a lot of them successful business people looking to start a new life. Over the next few years these people, many of whom were smart, hard-working entrepreneurs, began to change the dynamics of the Portuguese business world. The tourist trade was ideal for them, so numerous new cafes, restaurants and shops started to appear.

Before the revolution there were colonial wars in Angola and Mozambique that were ruining Portugal's economy. Most young Portuguese men were conscripted to fight in Africa. I'd heard a lot of horror stories about the wars in Africa from former soldiers whose only previous view of black people was through the sights of their guns. As one ex-commando told me, "One day they are trying to kill me, now I'm supposed to accept them as friends!" The talk in the bars and cafes was openly xenophobic.

Many of the new Portuguese hippies were ex-army or draft dodgers who had returned from Europe now that it was safe again. A lot of them had got into serious drug-taking and with that,of course,came the crime. With the police operating with at least one hand tied behind their backs, Albufeira in particular was becoming like the Wild West.

Dick and I were having a beer in Sir Harry's bar by the garden. I'd almost given up on Bender for the day, when one of the more amicable street vendors said that he thought he had seen Bender, on a chain, with a group of scruffy Lisboetas (people from Lisbon) who were camping just outside town. He warned us to be careful as they were drug dealers and not to be messed with.

Dick would have nothing to do with drugs, and worse still hated drug dealers. His younger brother Bubba was destroying his life injecting heroin, he was the runt of the litter, he made Keith Richards look healthy. Dick had spent a lot of his spare time in Bedford tracking down the dealers in a futile effort to save his brother's life. By banging a few heads together, he was hoping to stop Bubba getting his supplies. Unfortunately, he couldn't match their resourcefulness.

We took the short walk to where this drug gang were supposed to be hanging out. The first thing I saw was my poor Bender chained to a tree. Without thinking, I rushed over to him, he stood up and put his front paws on my shoulders and slobbered all over my face.

One of the druggy people shouted in English: "What the hell do you think you're doing man? Leave our dog alone and fuck off out of here!"

I laughed at them. "Can't you tell he's my dog? I'm taking him with me. You have no idea what this animal and I have been through together over the past few years."

Luckily for us and them (knowing that I had my own Wild West backing me up) they looked like they were 'high on their own supply'. Two or three of them were comatose, the other two shakily stood up to try and stop me taking the chain off. Dick hadn't said a word during the proceedings up to then.

"If you touch him (meaning me) I'll chain you up by your necks." I don't think they understood the significance of the threat, and they gave each other puzzled looks as if to say, "So what?"

I gingerly unclipped the chain. I walked past the two of them expecting some kind of reaction. I could see Dick was winding himself up getting ready to start, but the two of them just stood there as we walked away. They looked totally bewildered as to what had just happened. We were a safe distance away from them when one of them shouted out some Portuguese swear words. Dick was still annoyed, but kept control of himself, which is what I'd asked him to try and do in these situations, otherwise we'd be in big trouble sooner or later.

When we arrived back at our new home with our new housemate, I introduced him to John and Lorraine. They were a bit wary of him at first, but soon saw how soft he was with people. We went outside with him so he would get used to his new surroundings and meet the neighbours, which went well until our communist friend came out with Trotsky, or whatever his dog's name was. Although Bender was now showing signs of old age (he was about 14 or 15 years old by then) he hadn't lost his street-fighting skills. Within seconds the poor animal was knocked off its feet with Bender standing over him. I think Bender sensed that the other dog was young and not really a threat, so there was no damage done. It was just a warning to put the dog in its place. Our neighbour wasn't very happy seeing his supposedly tough dog being humiliated, so he angrily took a swing at Bender's head with his boot, which, fortunately for all concerned, missed the target. Dick growled at Fernando and poked him in the chest. I think he got the message. Territorial disputes all but solved in a few minutes, the day couldn't have gone much better really.

33
Mind the Jap

WE ALL started trying to sell in the centre of Albufeira, but it wasn't easy as there was far too much competition. We didn't have anything particularly original on offer, just a range of wholesale semi-precious jewellery that we had invested in back in the UK. John was doing reasonably well with his paintings but had trouble finding space to exhibit them all. The only person who had a novel idea was a Japanese guy who wrote your name in silver wire and put it on a chain as a necklace.

He had the best spot in the centre of the garden with his small table neatly laid out with some examples of common names. He was done up in full Japanese traditional dress: a white kimono with a red sash around his waist and a black bandana with Japanese writing on his forehead; a diminutive figure always bowing and smiling, a complete contrast to the majority of the unwashed hippy layabouts polluting the town.

He had some specialist pliers which he would use to skilfully bend one piece of wire into whatever name was written on the paper in front of him, with added flourishes at the beginning and end of each name that gave the finished article an artistic touch. He hardly said a word to anyone just the occasional "Arigato!" He made the names to look like they were written with the first letter as a capital, the rest in small letters with a loop at each end to connect to the chain which was cut to measure. It seemed that every young girl and boy around town was wearing them. The list of names on the note pad in front of him was never-ending, he was always struggling to keep up with demand. I estimated that he was making 100 names a day at 100 escudos each – about £40-a-day, which in those days was serious money.

I couldn't let an opportunity like this pass me by. If I could bend nails, I could soon learn how to bend wire, probably not up to his standard, but good enough to sell to the public in another town somewhere. I spent a day or two mulling over the idea. I didn't like copying other people's products, but the Japanese took my Dad as a prisoner of war for three-and-a-half years, so I reckoned they owed my family a favour. I was wondering how I could broach the subject with him, until one day fate took a hand.

I was sitting in Albufeira selling my wares when one of the local characters that I had known for years told me not to come to work the next day as there was going to be trouble. He told me to warn John Greene and the Japanese man. I took the threat very seriously as I could tell the local people weren't happy with what had become of their town. I walked over to the oriental name writer and tried to communicate in English and Portuguese, but without much success. He must have understood some of what I'd said but as I'd never spoken to him before he politely ignored me. So, I wrote down a message on his pad trying to explain the situation in English with some sketches of police with knives and guns attacking street sellers the next day. I pointed at myself and John and then him and tried to mimic us getting our throats slashed. I'd gone slightly over the top for maximum effect, but he still didn't say anything. As I was about to walk away frustrated with his lack of communication skills he said, "Tomollow no come... velly much danger... understand, arigato!"

The next day we did what we were told and kept away from Albufeira. The day after that we went back into town to see if anything had changed. The centre of town was completely deserted, and except for the Jap and one or two of the locals there was nobody else selling in the street. Apparently, fishermen, businessmen and able-bodied residents had ganged together and formed a kind of militia to rid the town of the drug and criminal elements – by the looks of things very successfully. There had been some violence but most of them had packed up and gone without putting up much of a fight. The local people of Albufeira had made a stand and taken the law into their own hands. People were smiling again, the status quo had been restored thankfully.

After that there were just a few us left selling in the garden and business was booming of course. The Jap, which is what we had always called him up until then, came over and introduced himself. His name was Nobu, he was from Kyoto and had been travelling through Europe and had decided to stay in Albufeira as he was doing so well. He thanked me for warning him and said, "My Engrish not good but now I can one day help you." He was living alone renting a room in town near the garden. He said he hadn't made many friends as he was shy and Japanese culture was so different that he was home sick but still enjoying his experience.

During the next few days we took him out with us a few times. It was hard work at first getting him to relax and let his hair down but once he had drunk one small beer he changed into a giggling wreck. I thought he'd be under the table after two or three, but he didn't seem to get any better or worse, which was just as well probably. He started to open up and became more confident, his English also improved dramatically. One night I asked him if he would teach me how to make the necklaces. He thought about it for a moment before agreeing to do it, but then asked me to respect two conditions before we went any further. One was that I promised that I wouldn't sell the necklaces in Albufeira while he was still there, which went without saying as far as I was concerned.The other was that if he taught me it was a Japanese custom that as he was the master and I was the pupil there would be an everlasting bond between us where I would maintain the quality of my work and that he would always look out for me. I of course agreed and even though he didn't like shaking hands and I didn't do bowing we understood each other.

Over the next few days I had a crash course in wire writing. I couldn't believe how difficult it was, especially judging the length of the wire to be cut. It was silver-plated copper wire that we managed to find plenty of in Faro along with the rolls of chain. This was like the good old days with the horseshoe nails, learning new skills. At the beginning I was probably wasting half the wire, as one mistake and the whole thing was ruined so I had to start again. I couldn't find the correct pliers, so I had to improvise and file down standard flat nose ones into special shapes.

After a while I got the hang of it and made my first public performance in Albufeira with Nobu looking on giving me some guidance. I was fine with *Ana* or *Joe* but completely fell apart when *Christopher* turned up as I ran out of wire by the time I got to the letter '*p*'. (I convinced him that *Chris* looked much better.) My efforts were pretty poor quality compared to the master but not bad, and good enough to sell that's for sure.

All I had to do now was to find a good location to sell. I remembered the Club Med near Tavira and wondered if they would allow me to sell there. It was a long way to drive but I quite liked it there and Dick could sell the jewellery nearby maybe. We drove down to Pedras D'el Rei and spoke to the boss, who was a very kind young Frenchman. He gave us permission to sell the necklaces, but nothing else was allowed. The first day I sat near the entrance with my pad ready for action and it was an instant success. What I hadn't taken into account was that half the population of France had at least nine letters in their names *Bernadette, Antoinette, Dominique* or, even worse, double names like *Jean Claude.* Doing a double '*t*' was one of the trickiest, so it was never easy, but it was good money. I never arrived there very early and often by the time I did turn up everyone had gone to the beach. So I would leave my order pad and pen overnight, on arrival I would have 50 or 60 names to do and had the best part of the day to make them.

The manager of the resort was so pleased with me he asked me if I could try their other resort Pedras da Rainha which was just a few kilometres away on the other side of Tavira. I gave it a try, it was equally as good and with more Portuguese clients so smaller names. I was struggling to keep up with demand, Dick wasn't selling much, so there was only one solution – I'd have to teach him how to do it, then we would be able to cover both places and try some other spots as well. I wasn't sure if I was allowed to pass on the old Japanese art to my partner without permission from my master, but the memory of Changi Jail lingered on . . . and needs must. I discussed the issue of betrayal of trust re our Japanese friend with Dick who very succinctly expressed his feelings with, "Fuck him we need the cash!"

Within a few days Dick had more or less got the hang of it, so two or three days a week we went off to the Club Meds with Bender who liked lying in the shade on the grass. After a hard day's bending, instead of going home, we drove into Tavira for dinner at a very exclusive French style restaurant upriver from the Roman bridge (it isn't Roman but apparently built on the remains of the original foundations, just in case you were interested). The restaurant was the Beira Rio and catered for the French clients from the Club Meds. This was fine dining at its best and reasonably cheap considering the quality. The waiters had all been trained by the Maître D, a local chap, who himself had been schooled in the culinary arts in Paris. The owner of the restaurant also owned a chain of cheap clothes shops called 'Pago Pouco' (literally pay little) where all the waiters worked during the day.

Downstairs in the restaurant was a different section where they had grilled chicken and so on, where you could eat as much as you wanted for a set price. With our new-found wealth we couldn't bring ourselves to mix with the hoi polloi. We wanted linen napkins, chandeliers and quails' eggs; they even let Bender sit under the table, hidden by the tablecloth, and allowed us to give him luxury scraps.

34
Queue Bridge

WHEN we weren't travelling to Tavira we all went into Albufeira for dinner in John's coach. There were two routes into town, one of which involved crossing a very narrow single lane and quite a long old bridge. For some reason John preferred this route rather than the longer trip on the EN 125 through Ferreiras and then turning left. By the time we reached the start of the bridge, John's face had come out in a red rash brought on by the stress of whether we would make it safely across to the other side. Part of the problem was that (as he had discovered in Spain) the front of the vehicle wasn't lined up with the back. Consequently, he had left a trail of devastation behind him, especially traffic bollards and the occasional cyclist. He would approach the bridge at maximum velocity assuming that nothing would be coming the other way. His theory was that the quicker we crossed the bridge the better and if you happened to be coming in the opposite direction and saw a coach hurtling towards you, your immediate reaction would be to wait for your turn. There were no traffic lights, no rules of engagement, you just hoped for the best.

More often than not there was already something on the bridge coming the other way which meant slamming on the brakes, often with no warning to us passengers, so we all finished up in the front as we had usually forgotten to hold on. The amount of arguments and near misses we had there, sometimes in the middle of the bridge face-to-face with a lorry, another bus and once even a horse and cart. Traffic backed up on both sides with everybody refusing to budge, total chaos. If that wasn't bad enough, we then had to get through the centre of Albufeira.

The road leading up to the tunnel was only a little wider than the coach, so pedestrians had to step into the recesses of doorways, or in some cases run for their lives, to avoid being squashed. I heard about an overweight butcher who was crushed to death by a bus in that very street. After that we had to navigate a very tight bend that set John's rash off again. I told John that I had seen the professional bus drivers do it in one go, but it usually took two or three attempts before we were on our way out of town and up to Catunas restaurant in Patio.

35

Catunas

THE ONLY place to eat for us and clearly a lot of other people was Catunas. It was so popular that there was nearly always a long queue outside. It was impossible to book a table; it was first come first served. Upstairs inside there were long wooden tables and benches so each group sat together, but you couldn't have your own table and you had to sit with complete strangers. I say inside but the whole place was really outdoors – luckily it hardly ever rained. This seating arrangement encouraged the clients to mingle and get to know each other, so there was a drunken party atmosphere every night. The food was always excellent, everything was cooked on a huge charcoal grill by the two brothers João and Fernando. Apart from the usual delicious and cheap chicken piri piri or sardines they also catered for the wealthier clients with king prawns, enormous steaks, pork chops and even bigger portions of sole that would hardly fit on the plate.

The waiters were great fun too, despite being rushed off their feet. Over the season we became well acquainted with most of them. When the eating was over, and the coffee and brandies were being served they would bring out an enormous china phallus with balls that contained the local firewater and pass it around to the ladies to take a sip from. Watching some of those high-class middle-aged women sucking a giant penis took some beating especially the night when one unsuspecting German lady screamed in disgust and dropped it on the floor smashing it to pieces.

One of the benefits of working there, apart from the regular large tips, was the number of females that the waiters attracted, so Dick and I often met up with them later to give them some assistance. We always finished up in Sir Harry's bar, which in those days, apart from Julio's Snoopy's bar and one or two others, was the place to go. I'd got to know the owner of Sir Harry's, Harry Warner. With his distinctive handlebar moustache, he looked like a retired RAF Wing Commander. Unlike most of the foreign business owners he had managed to maintain ownership of his bar throughout the time of the recent revolution. The place obviously wouldn't have been the same without him.

The first time I went in there with Bender he politely told me that no dogs were allowed on the premises. I laughed at him and said, "This isn't a dog, it's Bender."

He replied, without batting an eyelid, "Oh, that's alright then." One of the more bizarre conversations we had.

Dick had picked up a few important words in Portuguese to help in exactly that: picking up Portuguese women. Unfortunately, after asking what the word for 'well' was, he was told it was "poço" which is a well, as in a hole in the ground with water in it, whilst what he wanted to say was, "Well!", as in look at you gorgeous, standing there with his arms open wide with his six-foot wing span looking like a frustrated hairless orangutan ready to grab his next target. 'Poço' sounds exactly the same as 'posso?' which means, "May I?" And somehow, despite making a complete fool of himself, he often managed to pull it off.

He also upset a lot of people, especially the boyfriends or husbands of attractive ladies with his novel chat-up line. He of course didn't care about the men, what could they do? One or two of them had a go at him but he had also learnt to say "Desculpe" (sorry) which usually defused the situation, or failing that he would poke the irate male in the chest and give them a nasty look.

"I always give them a warning first, so usually nobody gets hurt."

After Sir Harry's we would try Silvia's disco. We were friends with the doorman João who usually let us come in. One or two of the regular local playboys made it quite clear that we weren't exactly welcome in the club – we were a threat to their sexual conquest success. One of them, Vitor Bacalhau, regularly picked on me by sticking his face in mine and pinching my skin on my chest and twisting it spitefully. It was quite painful, but I didn't rise to the bait. He also had a reputation as a tough guy and womaniser, so Dick had regular confrontations with him and one or two of his cronies – fortunately nothing ever kicked off.

Richard, a good friend of Dick's, came out from the UK for a quick visit. Dick warned him that if he met up with this Bacalhau to keep quiet and just shake his hand. He also made the mistake of telling him that Bacalhau translated was codfish. That night in the disco after slightly too many cervejas (beers) Dick introduced an inebriated Richard to Bacalhau. Richard, slurring his words, looked at him and said, "Alright Codface?" then slapped him on his back nearly knocking his whiskey out of his hand. Codface grabbed hold of Richard, shouting for him to come outside with him. Dick picked Bacalhau up with his left hand round his throat and his right fist in his face, then dumped him on a bar stool while threatening to kill him if he touched any of us again. We were then told to leave immediately by the management and never to come back. The following night we apologised to João saying it was all a misunderstanding. He wasn't bothered. He'd seen it all before.

36

Catastrophe

BACK at home, two of John's friends had arrived from England. They had driven down in a Mini that belonged to John and were going to spend some days with us before flying back. They were a couple also from Bedford, Scooby and Caroline, and we found room for them in the attic. John now had a car that he could use so he made the most of it and was always rushing here and there running errands.

One morning he flew out the door, jumped into the car, and shot off spinning the front wheels. As he accelerated past the front window, a black cat that had recently adopted us, had been asleep on top of one of the front wheels. Its squashed lifeless body did a few somersaults through the air before landing in a bloody heap in the neighbours' patio. Lorraine came running out having heard the cat's death-screams, closely followed by some of ours. She was hysterical when she saw the body of the flat cat, and the neighbours weren't too pleased either. Poor old John, who loved animals, was getting attacked from all sides: "Assassino!" from the Portuguese and "Murderer!" from the normally restrained Lorraine. It was an accident waiting to happen. Why the cat didn't react quicker when the engine started, we'll never know. Lorraine was furious with John, she even threatened to leave at one point.

A few days later John came home with a litter of five feral kittens that someone had given him to help him get over his loss. He had expressed earlier that he felt that he owed the cat world a favour and from now on would do his utmost to repay his debt to feline society. He hadn't really considered anybody else's opinions on the matter except cat-loving Lorraine who was over the moon, which meant that he was now forgiven. The one thing John hadn't taken into account was Bender. To be fair he couldn't really be bothered with cats as a rule, but five kittens running riot on his patch was never going to work. Countless times I heard John shout, "No Bender! Drop it! Open your mouth!" Miraculously, John managed to train Bender to leave them alone. I couldn't believe my eyes when all five kittens walked in through the front door inches from Bender's nose. He didn't move a muscle, just let out a disgruntled sigh as if to say, "The things I have to tolerate living with this lot!"

John continued his kitten love affair, which meant his whole body was covered in scratches, even his face didn't escape their claws. Over the next few weeks the kittens gradually started to disappear until we hardly saw them anymore – gone to live in the wild I suppose. The coach was rotting away in the field nearby, John's conversion plans never materialised, so he decided he would sell it. Brent the local English mechanic found a buyer for the engine and sold the rest for scrap. It was mid-September, the season was coming to an end, we had all done reasonably well financially, so we now had more time for leisure activities.

37
Film Night

WE USED to collect our post from the Almancil post office a couple of times a week, which meant queuing for ages, showing your passport and then watching the grumpy postmistress flick through the Poste Restante tray – usually to be told that there wasn't anything for us even when there was. She seemed to have a grudge against foreigners receiving mail. She was always dressed in black and consistently unhelpful. I often saw a letter addressed to me as she went through them, so I would demand that I could go through them myself and almost always found letters for me or one of us. I told her in no uncertain terms that my Dad was very high up in the Post Office and that an official complaint would soon be made at executive international level. Myopic old bag deliberately making our lives a misery.

Near the post office was the cinema, which occasionally had a half-decent film showing. As with the TV the Portuguese films weren't dubbed but were with sub-titles, so despite the lack of quality we were at least able to understand. One evening we decided to give it a try, the only problem being Bender, who still insisted on coming everywhere with us unless someone stayed with him at home. We put him in one of the rooms, locked the door, closed the windows, closed the shutters on the inside and the outside. We then drove the couple of kilometres to the cinema and sat down to watch the film. About thirty minutes into the film there was a bit of a kerfuffle at the back of the cinema that got louder and louder. The film stopped, the lights came on, the staff were panicking and there was Bender running down the aisle towards us.

We were,of course,booed out of the establishment and told never to return, nobody seemed to see the funny side of it as usual. Bender was covered in bits of glass, wood and blood. When we got home, we found that he'd managed to push up the inside shutters, smash the window, bite through the wooden outside shutters, jump down and run all the way to the cinema. He'd done things like this before, but this one took the biscuit. How did he know where we were? Could he follow our scent from there? He should have got a job with the police according to John. Once more the canine Houdini had amazed us all.

38
A Trip To The Vet

THE SEASON was almost over and we started thinking about the winter. Dick decided to fly home. He'd had a good time over the summer, but he had enough of the Algarve and was basically homesick. He'd made a few sexual conquests during his visit but as he kept reminding us, his success rate was nothing compared to what he was used to on home ground where he was a big dick in a small pond.

John and Lorraine had heard about a campsite in Gran Canaria, where a lot of other English who worked the season in Spain spent their winters having fun and soaking up the sun. I'd decided some time ago that I would never leave Bender again, so the Canaries sounded like the logical choice. Bender would need a dog passport which meant a trip to the vet for his rabies injection and a check-up.

Jorge, one of our friends from Sir Harry's,was a vet. He was a big man about thirty-five, he was very charming, the women loved him. He had already had a couple of run-ins with Dick when they were competing with each other for some young ladies' affection. He was a "frienda Bender" and was more than happy to treat him. Jorge's practice was in Faro, so I booked Bender in for his injection. I put him on a lead, which was a new experience, in the likely event that he caused any trouble.

There were a few other customers in the waiting room, small pedigree dogs and a couple of cats in boxes. All was quiet until an Englishman came through the door with a Rottweiler. The pair of them nonchalantly brushed past us in an attempt to reach the reception desk. Before I'd had time to react, Bender had the Rottweiler by the throat with me still attached. I was dragged to the floor, my face inches from the Rottweiler's fangs.

Everyone picked up their pets and ran out of the room screaming, barking and screeching. Hearing the commotion Jorge came into the room and laughed at me lying on the floor still trying to hold on to Bender. He suggested that I came back when the coast was clear. I apologised to the owner and offered to pay for any repairs to his dog.

"At least you're in the right place," I said, trying to defuse the situation.

There was nothing wrong with his dog, but the man still wasn't satisfied. He was a stocky ex-military type who had that "don't mess with me" look about him.

"Next time it will be me and you sunshine!" he warned me.

I was considering a reply of something on the lines of, "My mate eats people like you for breakfast" but managed to restrain myself.

Bender and I sat outside in the cafe over the road, which was handy. There's usually a cafe nearby wherever you are in Portugal. There's probably one cafe per 100 people and most of them are full of men drinking bicas (expresso coffee) in chavenas, the small cups that have maybe less than a mouthful of liquid in them, which you would expect would speed them up and spur them on to greater things, but no, except for their driving, life generally moved at the proverbial snail's pace.

It was getting late when Jorge called me from the other side of the road to let me know it was finally our turn. I apologised again for the earlier disturbance. He shrugged his shoulders and said, "These things happen, the dog was just shaken up. I don't like that man or his dog for that matter. He thinks he looks tough and likes to bully people, arrogant bastard!"

Together we lifted Bender onto a stainless-steel treatment table. He was a very good patient and didn't even flinch when he gave him the rabies injection. Jorge did some quick tests then pronounced him fit and well. He reckoned Bender was about 15 years old and in pretty good shape for a big dog of that age. But then he said (there's always a but isn't there):

"I'll have to remove these lumps or growths that he has on his stomach area as they might be malignant tumours."

"What does that involve?" I asked nervously.

"I'll cut them off then cauterise the wounds. It will be painful and unless he's unconscious he wouldn't let me do it. I'll have to put him to sleep for the duration of the operation."

"So when are you proposing to do that?"

"We might as well do it now, it won't take long."

"Are there any risks?"

"Unfortunately, with older animals there's a slight chance that he might not wake up again. This drug is used a lot on horses. I have to be careful to get the dosage correct. There's one injection that knocks out the patient and then another one that wakes them up."

I had a feeling something wasn't quite right and decided that it wasn't worth taking the risk, but Jorge convinced me that it was a simple routine surgical procedure and guaranteed that everything would go to plan.

To reassure me he told me a story about an English vet who was administering this same drug to a horse. At the moment he inserted the needle into the animal it kicked out and somehow the vet managed to inject himself instead of the horse. He collapsed and, as there was nobody else around at the time to give him the antidote, he tragically died.

Jorge calculated the dose based on Bender's weight and stuck the needle in. Bender was soon asleep and together we carried him into another part of the surgery and laid him on a different table. I didn't really want to watch or get in the way, so I left him to it. He closed the white plastic curtain behind me. I sat down terrified something was going to go wrong.

I smelled burning flesh, then began wondering if I'd made the right decision, all sorts of things were going around in my head. Was he a good vet? Had he told me the whole truth and nothing but the truth? I suppose it's called worrying.

After what seemed like hours Jorge backed through the curtain with Bender in his arms very much asleep.

Jorge looked distraught and said, "I'm sorry. I'm going to have to put him down."

"WHAT!" I screamed. "WHY?"

Jorge laughed. "Because he's too heavy! English humour, eh Paul!"

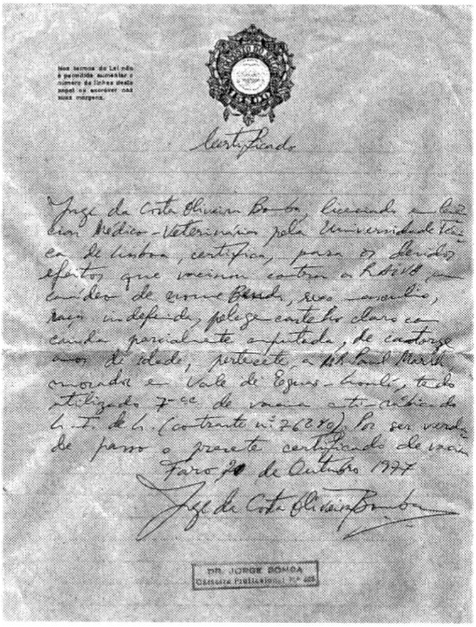

Certificado

Jorge da Costa Oliveira Bomba, licenciado em Ciência Médico-Veterinária pela Universidade Técnica de Lisboa, certifica, para os devidos efeitos que vacinou contra a RAIVA um canídeo de nome Bender, sexo masculino, raça indefinida, pelagem castanho claro com cauda parcialmente amputada, de catorze anos de idade, pertencente a [illegible] Paul Mart[illegible] morador em Vale de Éguas - Almancil, tendo utilizado 7 cc de vacina anti-rábica do [illegible] (contraste nº 26280). Por ser verdade se passa o presente certificado de vacina

Faro 20 de Outubro 1997

Jorge da Costa Oliveira Bomba

DR. JORGE BOMBA
Carteira Profissional Nº [illegible]

Rabies Certificate

"There's a time and a place for jokes (how many times have I had that phrase aimed at me?) and this isn't one of them," I shouted.

"I'm sorry, I couldn't resist giving you British some of your own medicine. Anyway, now I'll give him the antidote and he will wake up."

But he didn't wake up. Jorge's jovial mood suddenly changed. "He should be awake by now, his heart's beating but very slowly."

Out of sheer panic I screamed “BENDER!” and banged my fist on the metal table. I started to cry, screaming his name and banging the table. Jorge gave me a worried look. I was already thinking how I could inject him with his stupid drug. I shouted once more out of sheer desperation. Bender’s eyes opened for a second then he lifted his head before it dropped back onto the table, but he was breathing. Jorge calmly checked his heart rate (the dog’s, not his own) with his stethoscope and gave me the thumbs-up sign.

Jorge came over and hugged me. I could feel him shaking with emotion, we were both sobbing uncontrollably. Two grown men beside themselves over an old dog. It sounds ridiculous but that’s how the love for an animal can get to you.

His receptionist came in and looked slightly embarrassed when she saw the pair of us wrapped around each other.

She looked at Bender. “Is he dead?”

Jorge looked up at her. “No, thank God, but it was a close call,” he said, wiping away his tears.

She hadn’t finished. “I’ve never seen you like this before, is he a special dog?”

“Yes, that’s the word, that’s exactly what he is... special, you can go home now Teresa.”

“What about the bill?”

“No charge.”

We carried Bender in a blanket to my van then went over to the cafe for a couple of quick brandies to calm our nerves. We shook hands and I drove the patient home to Almancil.

John and Lorraine helped me carry him indoors and we made him a bed, which was a new experience for him. He woke up in the morning and I watched him as he struggled to stand up. To say he was thirsty would be putting it mildly as one bowl-full followed another and then another, until he went back to his new bed and slept there all day and night. It was a few days before he was anything like his normal self. He looked like a Bender who had been on a bender. I was convinced that Jorge had given him an overdose.

But Bender was now legal and fit to travel. He was back to his old self and we were all ready for the Canary Islands.

39
Gran Canaria

AT THE end of October, we bid farewell to Vale de Éguas and our neighbours. John "gave" a lot of his paintings to Fernando who promised to sell them in Lisbon at Christmas and would give John half of the proceeds on his return which seemed like a good plan at the time.

Bender had fully recovered from his ordeal and was back to his old self when he had another near-death experience at Praia de Castelo. He attacked a dog the size of a sheep, but this time had met his match. The other dog quietly sat on top of him, no biting involved – pure body weight was enough. Bender was crying out in agony. He couldn't move. It was like all-in wrestling. Big Daddy was sprawled across his victim waiting for the arm to rise in submission, but there was no referee to count to three.

By the time I arrived at the scene the owner had managed to drag his sheep off poor old Bender.

"Iz yor hunt crazy?" the owner laughed at me.

Bender sulked off, struggling to breathe after losing his unbeaten record of any fights that I had witnessed.

"What breed of dog is that?" I asked, ignoring his question about Bender's state of mind.

"He's a fat Belgian sheepdog and I'm Rolf ze big fat German owner."

I looked at the dog's name on his collar and I read it as *Dieter*, as in someone who was trying to lose weight.

"In English, dieter means someone who is on a diet, so he's basically an oxymoron."

"Vy you call my hunt a moron?"

"It's because he's fat and his name is dieter – a contradiction in terms."

"You say his name like Deeta!"

He looked angry and confused so I switched back to polite mode and asked, "Does he sit on a lot of dogs?"

"Not really, Zwei Dobermans until today. Most dogs aren't stupid like yours!"

"Well actually he's... never mind, no harm done, auf wiedersehen, Rolf."

Later that day, we loaded the VW van with all our belongings and drove to the border, crossed the Guadiana on the ferry into Spain and passed through the customs without problems. I kept hearing, "Perro peligroso" (dangerous dog), as we walked around Ayamonte. I was toying with the idea of stopping off in Isla Cristina to try and discover the truth about John Coy. I broached the subject with my two travelling companions, who pointed out that Englishmen and dogs didn't appear to be very welcome there especially ones that ask questions.

"That policeman might shoot Bender or you or all of us," Lorraine chipped in cheerfully.

"Don't be ridiculous. As if anyone's going to shoot at us or the dog. It's 1977, we're in Spain, not in a banana republic in the middle of a civil war," I shouted.

I liked Lorraine. She'd been sharing a house with three men all summer and it was a testament to our friendship that we had rarely fallen out with her. John and Lorraine stayed in a lot, they didn't drink very often in the bars, and on the rare occasions when John did come out, he would always try to pay for everything – then usually fall asleep in the bar. Dick and I used to wind him up that Lorraine was wearing him out at night, which he strenuously denied; narcolepsy was mentioned a few times.

We drove for two or three hours until we reached the ferry in Seville, which was a strange place to set sail from as it's nowhere near the sea. Fortunately, the river Guadalquivir flows from there into the Atlantic where, a few hundred years before, Magellan set off on his voyage to circle the globe – or as I heard an idiot explaining to a fellow passenger: "He was the first man to circumcise the world."

It was a two-day trip. We had cabins, but Bender had to go on the top deck with all the other cats and dogs. The cage was at head height and it took four of us to get him in. He wasn't at all happy. We were allowed to let him out twice a day for exercise etc. I've never mentioned this before, but I'd never seen Bender have a Number Two. He was almost human in the way that it was a private matter for him, and he always sloped off somewhere to avoid public embarrassment.

The first time we went up to release him, I threaded his lead through the bars of the cage and slowly opened the door. To say that he was eager to get out would be a slight understatement.

As soon as he saw his chance to escape, he knocked the metal gate open and leapt out, nearly taking John and myself over the side of the ship. He cocked his leg up everywhere he thought necessary, but that was all – unlike the rest of the animals on board, who seemed to have gone overboard (a nautical term) on the defecation front. There was dog shit everywhere; maybe that was the poop deck.

I had to fill up his water bowl on a regular basis as it was spilling everywhere with the movement of the ship. He wasn't eating much of his food and was probably feeling seasick as a dog. On one of my top deck visits some bastard blew the ship's foghorn at the very moment that I was walking past it. The blast can be heard for miles and it was just a few metres from my ear. My feet actually left the ground in shock and for the second time that day I nearly jumped over the railings. I swear that anyone of a nervous disposition could have died on the spot. It took me some time before my heart and hearing recovered.

After two days at sea we arrived at the bustling port of Las Palmas. It was the afternoon and very hot. We disembarked without any problems and were soon driving south on the coast road that took us past the sand dunes of Maspalomas, on to Puerto Rico and finally the camping site at Tauro.

40

A Shot in the Dark

WE REGISTERED at reception: one van, one tent, three people,and one Bender and were told to find a suitable spot in the centre, where the English community had taken control of the middle ground. The Germans had the area surrounded in their luxury motorhomes and caravans. There were white concrete huts to rent but they were fully booked by the regulars. The beach was a few hundred metres away, where the bar and restaurant were to be found.

Once we'd settled in, the three of us took a stroll down to the sea. The entrance to the beach area was secured by a couple of scruffy uniformed guards, who had two dogs pulling on their leads – German Shepherds of course, trying to get at Bender. We did our best to steer clear of them, but once the growling started, I couldn't hold him back, and the fight started when the guards let their dogs loose. It only took a few seconds for the guard dogs to give in and then run off whimpering, covered in blood. The guards went crazy and began shouting at us and pointed to the exit. Some people came over to see what all the noise was about – and then I saw one of the guards unbuckling his gun holster.

Some of the bystanders tried to intervene, but I didn't waste a second before I started to run back through the campsite with Bender on his lead and with the guards giving chase. It was getting dark by the time I found some trees and a stream. I was literally running for my life and I could hear them still following us. I looked back and saw torch lights and then a 'Bang!' I couldn't believe it: they were actually shooting at us. Then another bang and, I'm not kidding, a bullet literally whistled past my head. I let go of Bender and ran, as fast as I could, in blind panic through the woods until I reached a road. I sat down exhausted. Then I heard something coming through the bushes... it was Bender.

It wasn't long before the police came flying past with sirens wailing and the obligatory blue flashing lights. They saw me, screeched to a halt up the road and then reversed back, got out of their squad car, pointed their torches at me and started chattering on the two-way radios. A police van soon appeared which took me and Bender back to the campsite.

We were greeted by a volatile crowd of mainly young Englishmen arguing with the guards, the receptionist and the police. Even some of the Germans were getting involved. When things calmed down, I was told to leave the campsite and take my dog with me and never come back. I was escorted to my van and then to the gates. One member of the crowd came over and told me to drive down the road to a cafe and wait there until help arrived while they sorted things out.

I drove off, found the cafe, but sat in the van. I was still shaking uncontrollably, trying to come to terms with what had just happened. Talk about over-reaction by the guards. Was there no law and order around here? They just tried to kill me for doing virtually nothing for God's sake! I was trying to work out what attempted murder was in Spanish when a car pulled up beside me. John Greene jumped out with a couple of other blokes and, after a hug from John, one of the others said, "You've been re-instated at the campsite mate so you can come back. We'll see you're alright."

"No chance of that. I'm not getting shot at again by those crazy bastards, and nor is he," I said, pointing to Bender.

"You'll be safe with us mate; the police have given the guards a bollocking and confiscated their weapons. In all the years I've been coming here, nuffink like this has ever happened. Even some of the Krauts are threatening to leave in protest."

"More like cos they're shit-scared," his pal chipped in.

"Let's have a beer and get you calmed down. Brenda's a fucking hero mate, we all hate them Alsatians."

After a few beers they convinced me to go back with them and found me a good spot to park-up, surrounded by tents and other vans. I was of course the centre of attention, everybody wanted to hear my story.

Lorraine came over and smothered me and Bender in kisses and said she would be leaving as soon as she could and had to have a dig at me with, "What did you say the other day about getting shot at? Huh!"

That night, in bed in the van, I couldn't stop going over the day's events in my mind. I wouldn't go so far as to say I was lucky to be alive, but I'd certainly dodged a bullet.

The next morning, I was awoken by the vibrations of the van shaking – it was Bender, who was trembling with fear or rage. I peered through the curtains. The same guards were outside with their bandaged dogs. In front of them were a group of men with more dogs, three of the largest and nastiest specimens I'd ever seen. The men were gesturing for me to come outside and face them. They started making chicken noises. A crowd had gathered, an argument started and before long most of the campers were getting involved. The giant dogs were showing their teeth and straining on their leashes.

First, they try to shoot me and, having failed, now they were seeking revenge. One of the crowd was having a heated discussion in Spanish with the guards and their friends. A few of the English section of the crowd bravely stood around my van and told me to stay inside – not that I had considered any other option apart from driving off and leaving them to it.

After a lot of pushing and shoving, the guards and their friends walked away with their vicious animals. I finally plucked up the courage to step out of the van and face the public with Bender by my side. The young Englishman who had basically defused the situation explained that this had been a warning. The giant dogs were the local Canary mastiffs native to the islands: 'Perro de presa Canario' with their brindle coats. They were used for protecting cattle from wild dogs. Bender was basically a mastiff, but these dogs were at least 50kg and much larger than him.

Once again, I decided the only sensible thing to do was leave, as we clearly weren't welcome. I'd had more aggravation in the last 24 hours than I'd had in all the years I'd been in the Algarve. I spoke to John and Lorraine and told them how I felt and that I was leaving before someone got hurt. Lorraine was in total agreement and said she would come with me, which put John in an awkward position. We spent most of the day trying to come up with some ideas of where to go next, but nothing could be agreed on. There were plenty of other islands to choose from: Tenerife, Lanzarote, Fuerteventura etc. Ferries could take us almost anywhere in the archipelago.

Over dinner that night we were joined by a group of campsite winter regulars; some of them had been coming for years. They tried to convince us that this was by far the best place in Europe to spend the winter. It was warm, entertaining, cheap and certainly crazy. We'd been unfortunate and got off to a bad start. We really enjoyed ourselves that evening in the company of seasoned travellers, so we delayed our departure to the next day and then the next day... in the end we decided to give the place a chance. One of the best things I ever did.

The next few months were some of the most memorable and enjoyable of my life. The place was a magnet for the strange and the eccentric, young people looking for an alternative way of life before probably succumbing to the inevitability of normality.

There were all kinds of characters – some of them extremely intelligent, others nearer the lower end of the mental spectrum. Drunks. Junkies. Crooks. Out-and-out nutters. All living side-by-side, mainly in tents, on a small plot of land on foreign soil. Not including the Germans in their luxury mobile homes, there must have been two or three hundred happy campers;

predominantly Brits but most European countries had some form of representation, plus the usual Americans, Canadians and Australians. A crazy league of nations if ever you saw one.

There were a few gangs, or groups of friends to be more accurate, from Lloret de Mar, Jersey, and other seasonal workers from European hotspots. I was neighbours with two Swiss poofs, as everyone called them (they didn't seem to mind) who lived in a big van, and some Californian surf dudes who were into drinking seawater even when they weren't surfing (all those years ago they had already begun weird diets).

"Cleans out the shit that's been in your body for years man!"

Then there was Electric Annie with her dog named Pisser and her boyfriend/slave Paul, also van people. She used to have sex with other men, and bizarrely she was attracted to the ones that she didn't like. John and Lorraine were nearby in a tent and John had managed to convince a couple of lads to let him use their concrete hut as a studio. John soon had his painting production line up and running.

The tenants of his studio were called Jimmy and Tommy. Jimmy was a Liverpudlian and staunch Everton fan, Tommy was from Glasgow, or Glasgee as he pronounced it, and a Rangers fan. The pair of them had spent the autumn grape picking in France and were now selling John's paintings on commission in nearby Puerto Rico, which was still in its infancy as a resort but already had a busy tourist trade, and business was going well. So well that John invested in a transistor radio with a cassette player so that we could listen to music – but more importantly listen to the football commentary and results on the World Service on Saturday afternoons, which was probably the highlight of the week for most of the inmates – except maybe for the fancy-dress parties on sangria nights.

The local electricity company were installing overhead cables by the campsite and conveniently left a large wooden cable drum by the road. Between us we managed to roll it into the camp and laid it down flat it in the centre of 'our area'. It became the place to sit around and chat, eat meals, play cards and most of all to listen to music. Fleetwood Mac's 'Rumours' album is the one that brings all the memories back for me, and then there was Supertramp's song 'Dreamer' and Queen's 'We are the Champions', and so on and so on. A classic era for music.

Burky was another interesting character: a cockney, loud, tough, bushy moustache, earrings, tattoos, rings on all his fingers. Strangely enough, it turned out that he was a bouncer in a nightclub in Lloret, Spain. What else could he have been? Luckily, he was very amicable, and everybody loved him on the campsite. He was also very dry. He wasn't interested in the football but once he popped in and asked, "Ow's Queen ov the Sarf gettin' on?"

There was Noisy Billy who was built like a Marine and twice as fit. He would run up and down the beach at high speed with a few other training recruits, shouting at the top of his voice. He kept going for miles, as one-by-one the rest of them collapsed with exhaustion. He very kindly used to do a lot of our supermarket shopping. He would come around and collect our shopping lists and deliver the goods a bit later that day at very reasonable rates.

It was only after a few weeks that someone told us that he was a professional shoplifter. If he got caught, he would run away – and of course nobody could catch him. All part of the training I suppose.

I hung around a lot with a good-looking young man named Fred. He was one of Burky's mates, also a Londoner, a real Jack the Lad and what he hadn't done wasn't worth doing. He was in his twenties, but if everything he said was true about his life, he would have been at least 50. I called him Freddie Whicker, after Alan Whicker the travel TV presenter. Whatever you'd done, or wherever you'd been, he had a story to top it – but he was harmless and great fun to be around.

Burky, Fred and Me

41
Fancy Dress

THE FIRST fancy-dress party Fred organized; our group decided to get dressed up as Zulu warriors. I was put in charge of nose-rings, collecting canes for the spears and the grass skirts. There were at least 12 of us so there was a lot of work involved – not that we were exactly rushed off our feet. A couple of hours before the party started, we dressed each other and then added the final touch, which was the burnt cork to blacken all our visible skin. We even practised a couple of tribal dances.

The venue was the cafe on the beach. A few people had made a bit of an effort, blokes dressed as women and vice versa, doctors and nurses etc. But we were undoubtedly the stars of the show.

One of the Canary Island men had decided to join in the fun and was dressed as the arch baddy gunfighter from a western movie. He was wearing only black, including his Stetson, and instead of pistols he was waving a couple of knives about. It was at that point we realised he wasn't play-acting. He was one of the local nutters and was actually threatening to stab people. Burky went straight over to him, fearlessly grabbed the two knives and snapped them both in half, then literally picked him up and threw him out of the door. The weapons were only large penknives, but who knows what damage he might have done.

After we had shown off our tribal dance skills the disco got into full flow and I was lucky to get off with a Canadian girl, Michelle from Quebec. She was very pale and had only just recently arrived. She came back with me to the van and we spent the night together.

When I woke up the next morning, the previous evening's events were a bit fuzzy. I peered under the duvet and there was a naked black girl lying asleep right next to me. I quickly pulled the covers back over her. I couldn't remember any black girls being at the party. I had another quick look and she'd turned over: her back was very white, and she muttered something in French. I was in bed with a multi-coloured bi-lingual stranger. I got up and took a quick peek at the mirror. I had two black eyes, but nobody had hit me. The body in the bed moved and a head appeared with a "bonjour". It was a black-faced Michelle. Of course! How could I have forgotten that a few hours ago I had been a Zulu and some of my personality must have rubbed off on her.

A few parties later, just as we were running out of themes, we came up with the idea of going as Burky. This involved false moustaches, dark glasses, striped t-shirts, a lot of rings and tattoos. To be as authentic as possible I borrowed a t-shirt from the man himself. Then Jimmy and Tommy did the same. By the time the fourth person approached him for clothes he told them to "Piss off! I won't have anything left to wear at this rate!"

He was obviously getting suspicious, but completely baffled about what was going on.

He came over to me and reasonably politely asked, "What's your little firm up to? Summink funny is going on, ain't there, and what yer getting dressed up for, as this week no one's said nuffink to me about nuffink?"

Can't tell you mate, mum's the word, hush-hush, top-secret, get the picture?" I replied.

"What about me then – who am I going as?"

"Just come as you are," I laughed.

"Well I ain't got much fucking choice – I've got no fucking gear left thanks to you lot. Why can't you let me in on it like normal?"

"I just can't, you'd have to torture me first."

"I could do that. Dunnit before, like."

We made signet rings out of cut-up sardine cans and metal tubes, burnt cork again for moustaches, felt pens for the tattoos and even cockney rhyming slang lessons.

When we made our entrance at the party the bar was packed, and Burky was already there. After the cheering and laughter had died down, Burky started walking towards us with a puzzled look on his face. When we had first come up with the idea, none of us were quite sure how he would take it.

"Very funny lads, but who the fuck are you supposed be?"

After the laughter subsided, again Jimmy comes up with: "You, you twat!"

Burky thought about it for a while, then there was relief when he put his arm around me and said, "Brilliant! I knew you were up to no good. I'm really proud you chose me, it's an honour!"

After thinking a bit longer, he said to me, "That's why you couldn't tell me innit and that's why you needed the clothes. So, I am part of the gang after all. I thought you'd Ostrich-sized me."

A few weeks later Burky was up in front of the camp commandant for stealing large amounts of young ladies' underwear from the washing lines. He got off with a severe reprimand. He wasn't that bothered about it, it was more like a hobby to him.

"I got a bit of a fetish for panties, can't help it, and now I've been nicked for nicking knickers."

42
Breakdown

ONE MORNING I couldn't get my van started. We tried everything to get it going, but no luck. I had a book '*How To Keep Your Volkswagen Alive: A Manual Of Step-By-Step Procedures For The Compleat* (American Rubbish Spelling) *Idiot*' by John Muir. Over the past few months I'd learnt a lot about the engine in my vehicle thanks to Mr Muir and was actually able to fix most things myself – but not this time. My Swiss neighbours were mechanics and soon had the engine out in what seemed like hundreds of pieces.

The verdict was worn piston rings, which they could fix as long as we could find the parts. This meant a trip to Las Palmas. I got a lift with Alan who was, quite simply, a gangster. He'd been in hospital in England for a few months, recovering from being deliberately run over by a rival. He wasn't a member of the campsite community but had a few acquaintances amongst them.

He drove a big Mercedes – "Safest cars on the road, Paul" – and rented a big villa in the hills nearby, where he lived with Shirley, his blonde moll. Every now and then a few of us were invited to his house for dinners and get-togethers. I was warned not to ask any questions, but once he got to know you, he would open up about his past. He was a Londoner, about 40 years old, medium height and build and looked the part. Burky was very wary of him despite the fact that they were the best of mates.

Alan was his real name, but he had different surnames.

"Never change you first name," he confided in me. "When yer on the run you can easily get caught out if you let yer guard down."

He had seven passports, all with different names and nationalities, piles of cash in all sorts of currencies. On the way to Las Palmas he started to chat about the bloke who ran him over.

"I spent months in that hospital bed planning my revenge, that's what kept me alive basically. When you've been in pain like that, with so many broken bones, it focuses yer mind."

"So, what did you do when you finally recovered?" I asked.

"I did the same to him. I waited outside near his gaff one morning in a Transit van with the engine running, and as soon as he stepped onto the pavement I accelerated down the road and knocked the bastard over. They say he'll be in a wheelchair for the rest of his life poor sod, and they done me for attempted murder. An eye for an eye – know what I mean?"

I could tell he hadn't finished so I kept quiet.

"You gotta stand up to these people or else they'll walk all over you. If you've got a reputation for being a hard man you have to show people who's boss."

I was trying to think of something pertinent to say when we had to stop at Maspalomas to drop off our other passenger, 'Fatboy Frank'. He was overweight and still a boy really, a late developer maybe. He'd got himself a job selling hotdogs to the Germans on the nudist beach and had sold out on his first day. However, the naked Germans had complained that he shouldn't be allowed to wear clothes on a naturist beach. Frank was embarrassed about the size of his bratwurst but had managed to get around the problem by having a wooden tray hanging around his neck on a piece of string strategically positioned to cover his nether regions.

This was a sight not to be missed: an obese, unclothed, red blob impersonating one of those cinema usherettes that sold choc-ices in the interval. His original plan to hang a frankfurter between his legs hadn't gone well during trials, when a stray dog took a bite out of his dangling sausage and nearly castrated him in the process. Despite covering himself in sun cream he still got a burnt arse and for a couple of days he couldn't sit down.

His career was short-lived after one of his customers stuck his German dick in the bread roll, spread some ketchup on it and asked Frank if he would like to take a mouthful.

Alan dropped me off with Bender in Las Palmas. We had already driven past the airport, but he kindly offered to take me the extra few kilometres into the city before heading back to catch their flight. I didn't hear what happened to them until I arrived back at the campsite.

43
Las Palmas

WALKING around the city with Bender turned out to be a very big mistake. The place was teeming with people. As usual, he wasn't on a lead – which I admit was foolish, but he didn't like it and neither did I. Once, in Lisbon, I nearly had a dislocated shoulder as my arm was almost pulled out of its socket when he suddenly jerked the lead as he went for another dog. He always stayed right beside me when we were in crowds. I noticed that he kept bumping into people and panicking a bit when he lost me for a second or two.

I soon found the Volkswagen dealer and they had the parts that I needed. I'd planned to take the bus back, but when I arrived at the bus station, they told me that dogs weren't allowed on public transport unless I was blind, or if they were in a cage. For a few seconds I thought about buying a cane and painting it white, then dismissed the idea as quickly as it had come into my head: bad karma and all that stuff.

The other solution would be to hitch it back, but with Bender in tow I decided against it, even though this was the isle of dogs. I hadn't noticed that the Canary Island flag has what appear to be two lions guarding a shield, but on closer inspection are in fact rampant puppies and what's even more fascinating (that's if you're in the slightest bit interested) is that the Canary Islands are named after the Latin word for dog, '*canis*', and the native canary birds are named after the islands. I opted for plan C which was to stay the night somewhere and worry about getting back the next day. After hours of searching I found a pet-friendly hostel near the centre. I had planned to lock Bender in the second floor room, but after giving it some thought I realised that I probably wouln't be able to afford the repair bill, as in my absence he would have probably used all his escapology techniques – which usually included serious property damage.

I was becoming more and more concerned about him. All of a sudden, he seemed to have started losing his sense of smell, sight and maybe hearing. He was at home at the camp site, but the crowded noisy city was too much for him. I promised myself I wouldn't bring him again.

After going out for dinner, I went for an evening's stroll to see what Las Palmas had to offer at night. It's an interesting place, in that the port is on one side and, at its narrowest point, the beach is just a few streets away on the other side. It was somewhere around that area of the city that I stumbled upon, completely out of the blue (well actually green) an amazing product for the first time. In an instant I had a gut feeling that this would be another game-changer for me.

A young couple walked past me, and they were both wearing it – a green luminous necklace. Then I saw another one and another, then suddenly they were everywhere. There were some Spanish guys selling them for something like 100 Pesetas each. They were making a small fortune, and this was an opportunity not to be missed. I hung around for a while until they had sold the last one. Somehow, I had to get to know them and find out as much as I could, without making it too obvious that I was intent on copying their business.

I got chatting to them as they were packing up. I offered to buy them a beer, which usually helped in these situations. As it turned out, they were from Argentina and they sussed me out straight away. I'd bumped into a few South Americans in my travels, mainly men unfortunately, although I did have a sexual encounter with a stunning Chilean girl in a campsite in Florence, Italy.

I must have been about nineteen at the time. I think she'd spent too much time that day drooling over Michelangelo's statue of David. She was in the tent next to mine with her parents. I'd said hello but she had just smiled. I was going to pluck up the courage to speak to her, but she was so gorgeous I would have probably started dribbling before any words had come out of my mouth. That night she crept into my tent, pulled her t-shirt over her head, exposing her enormous breasts, and then put her hand inside my sleeping bag and grabbed my erect boyhood.

"Hey Gringo, let's make ze love," she whispered.

Unfortunately it was a case of *coitus notonitus*: as soon as she touched me I exploded all over her hand; overcome with pleasure I let loose a guttural cry of, "AAGH!" so loud that I woke up half the campsite; her parents were of course included in that fifty per cent. I heard a lot of shouting in Spanish, there were a lot of flashing torchlights outside. A frustrated Miss Chile had quickly crawled out of my love nest, probably into the welcoming arms of her father. I didn't have much luck at that camp site. The previous night I'd drunk some of the roughest wine known to man, staggered up the steep hill which was at least a 1-in-3 gradient overlooking the ancient city, got into my sleeping bag and passed out. The next morning, still in my sleeping bag, I woke up in a French family's tent. During the night I'd tossed and turned so much that I'd slid out of my tent and slipped about fifty metres downhill, before crashing into chez Claude et Monique. At least they offered me a croissant before showing me the open tent flap.

I'd found Argentinians were usually very savvy, street wise and not to be trusted. They certainly weren't giving any secrets away. I didn't blame them, at least they hadn't told me to piss off. I told them straight that I was on the look-out for new ideas in Portugal, hoping that they might give me a clue or something to go on. But no, they drank their beers and left me. They had given me one of the necklaces that they had been wearing. I noticed that the light was fading. It was a transparent plastic tube with a liquid in it, bunged up at each end and attached at the back with an empty piece of the same tubing. The only question was what the hell this magic liquid was and where I could get it.

I was completely wrapped-up in thoughts, my head was spinning: How do you get the liquid in the tube? Where do you buy such thin tube and what's it normally used for? I looked around – where's Bender? In all the excitement I'd forgotten all about him which normally wouldn't have been a problem, but this was different.

I called him, asked passers-by if they had seen a 'perro grande'. I tried everything. I presumed he'd gone off for some reason and couldn't find his way back. I went back to the hostel, but he wasn't there and hadn't been seen. I went back to where I'd last seen him but there was no sign of him. I tried to remain positive but was beginning to panic. I walked all over the place shouting his name. The beach, the port area, some of the narrow streets. It was hopeless. I was worn out, so I went back to my room at the hostel.

The next morning, I was sure he'd be sitting outside, or waiting for me where I'd lost him – but he wasn't. Up to that point I'd been strong, but I was on my own, I only had myself to blame. I sat down on a bench and had a little cry – surely it couldn't end like this after all these years. We'd done so much together; he was lost and so was I without him. I held my head in my hands, and my little cry turned into uncontrollable sobbing. I must have looked a sorry sight, but I didn't care, I had to let it out I suppose.

I was having one of those moments when everything gets on top of you, when you begin to question your lifestyle and start feeling sorry for yourself. I was wallowing in self-pity, lost the dog, the van's broken down, no girlfriend, no home, no future, no money, the world's against me – my alter ego had taken me to a low point. I'd been there before once or twice. Hitchhiking all day in foreign lands in the pouring rain and not getting anywhere – hungry, nowhere to sleep, all self-inflicted. I had learnt that you need to actually experience genuine utter hopelessness before you can appreciate how fortunate you really are to be having such a great life.

To put things into perspective, when my father Leonard was about the same age, he was also enjoying his youth. In 1939 he married his childhood sweetheart, my mother, Phyllis. A few months later, after enlisting as an officer in the Royal Artillery, he finds himself being beaten and starved in a Japanese Prisoner-of-War camp and forced into hard labour building a railway in a Burmese jungle. For three-and-a-half years my mother never knew, except for the occasional post card, whether he was dead or alive. A month or so after the Japanese surrendered, his troop ship arrived back in England and my mother, along with all the other wives and families, went to greet their loved ones. She described him as a living skeleton. He had lost half his body weight. A lot of his young comrades had died, and it took him years to fully recover.

Three of his brothers had died because of the war, and then my parents' first child was stillborn, probably due to rationing, lack of vitamins, minerals, proteins. My Dad never spoke about the war, he didn't want us children to hear about the atrocities that he had suffered. The only thing he mentioned was the heat in the jungle and the size of the hornets. National Service, or conscription, ended in 1960, so thankfully I just missed out on being called-up to join the armed forces.

I'm mentioning all this now because, when I was young, the last few generations had all lived through wars. All the talk was of guns, tanks, bombs, trenches, suffering and death. At that time, it seemed quite logical to me that sooner or later it would be my turn, so in my immature teenage brain I was determined that I would have as much fun as possible before it was too late. Very selfish and absolutely ridiculous reasoning – and anyway they would never have got me in any army. I would have run away and become a nun or something.

A kind lady asked me if I was OK, I nodded and tried to pull myself together.

"I've lost my dog," I whimpered.

"Well go to the police," she said in Spanish, then said something like, "You'll find him."

That sorted me out. I actually shouted at myself: "Grow up for God's sake, he's lost not dead!"

I went to the police and gave them a rough description. I called the camp site and left a message for John to call me at the hostel, which he did. Three hours later about twenty friends from the campsite had arrived in cars and vans. We split into groups and combed the city for hours. It was an almost impossible task, so once it was dark, I called off the search and we all took the long drive back to the camp site. I thanked them all for their help and support – I was really touched by the community coming together.

That evening a few of us sat at the round table and came up with a few ideas of how to trace Bender. We decided that 'lost dog' posters might work, and maybe try an advert on the local radio and the newspaper. All this meant another trip to Las Palmas, which I wanted to do anyway, as I had a feeling that if I hung around the city long enough, I might just find him.

The Swiss put the van engine back together and got it started but they said that the pistons and cylinders needed a proper overhaul. I could use it, but when I did there wasn't much power anymore and a lot of smoke was pouring out of the exhaust. But at least I was mobile again.

44

Accidents Will Happen

LATER that evening I heard the news about Alan and Shirley. On their way back to the airport a small hire car driven by another foreigner came hurtling round a bend on the wrong side of the road and hit Alan's Mercedes head on.

The impact of the collision broke Alan's foot, which had been firmly pressed on the brake pedal. Shirley was badly shaken up but unhurt. The driver of the hire car was killed instantly. Alan was taken to hospital, where they put a plaster cast on his foot and ankle half-way up to his knee. When I saw him at the bar a bit later, he was visibly drunk. The first thing he said to me was, "This is what you get from doing someone a favour!"

"Come on," I shouted, forgetting who I was talking to. "Surely you're not blaming me?"

"If I hadn't taken you, I wouldn't have a broken foot and I would have got on that plane."

I wondered what was coming next.

"Now I'll have the cops on me for manslaughter or dangerous driving or something and then they'll start nosing around – which is all I fucking need, you prick!"

I walked away from him as quick as possible before I did something nasty in my underpants.

The next day Alan was hobbling around the campsite. He saw me before I had a chance to avoid him. I felt the blood draining from my face as he approached me and was thinking to myself that this is definitely going to hurt.

"Sorry about last night mate. According to Shirl I was right out of order. I was off me face on the vodka."

"Apology accepted, no hard feelings. To be honest I thought you were going to beat the shit out of me," I laughed, with a huge sigh of relief. He shook my shaking hand and said: "I wouldn't hit you, you're one of us. I might run you over though," he laughed. "That's if I had a fucking motor of course."

The next day the police turned up with the news that as the accident wasn't Alan's fault, and that no Spanish nationals were involved, the matter was closed. The bad news was that the Mercedes was a write-off. So, Alan went out the next day and bought another one – another Mercedes.

45

Las Palmas Revisited

I DROVE back to Las Palmas, which took longer than ever. Jimmy and Tommy came with me to help and for moral support. We parked at the beach that night and visited my Argentinian friends again. They were a lot friendlier than last time and agreed to have dinner with us, as long as I paid. Over the meal they hinted that they would sell us some of the stuff I needed, but only when I could show them a ferry ticket to prove that I was leaving the island. This was exciting news for me, but I had no intention of leaving for a while. It was only December. I wasn't planning on going back for a while; I could wait.

The next day we put up '*Missing Bender*' posters that we had had printed. We placed an advert in the paper and got a free spot aired on the radio – the Spanish people were very sympathetic to our cause. Keeping busy kept my mind off things, but I realised that it was, in all probability, a complete waste of time and effort. We walked along the long beach in the hope that if the dog was free and alive, he would be looking for me there, rather than in the chaos of the all the traffic and pedestrians.

Every time we saw a dog, we were sure it was him. Your mind starts to play tricks on you when you're desperate. Most dogs hung around with other dogs, but unless there was a bitch on heat (which was one possibility) he would be alone for certain

We had tried to imagine what could have happened to him and then work on those theories. He could have gone off to die, but there weren't any signs that he was suffering or sick. He could have been taken by the dog catchers if they existed here, or, as someone suggested, maybe somebody gave him some food and took him in and kept him as a guard dog. If they had, he would have almost certainly have escaped and destroyed their house in the process – unless he was chained-up outside, hidden away somewhere. In the end it didn't really matter: He was gone, we'd done all we could.

While we were out at night, we saw another interesting product that was selling like the proverbial hot-cakes, and this one was very similar to what I was already doing. They were necklaces again, with names, but with silver-coloured individual moulded letters that had two rings above each one which enabled them to slide onto a chain. The salesman had the letters separated in plastic boxes. All he had to do was pick the letters and slide them on the chain. Easy to make, no skill involved, and they looked great.

In those days it was very difficult to source products other than by asking the seller outright. I used to get this all the time, and, completely out of character, I would usually give silly sarcastic replies. In this case we tried a bit of industrial espionage looking for addresses on the boxes under the sellers' table, while dropping a coin in the near vicinity – diversionary tactics, bribery, anything. After wasting time and achieving absolutely nothing an impatient Jimmy piped up with:

"Why don't you just fooking ask him?"

"As if he's going to tell a stranger where he gets the stuff – and I doubt if he speaks English," I mocked. "You have to be subtle in business. I should know, I've been doing it long enough."

After carefully listening to my advice, Tommy went over to him. "Where do you get the letters from mate?"

The young man looked up at Tommy and said, "Oh, you're from Scotland. I used to live in Brighton, England. You can get them in a wholesale shop in Barcelona or go to the factory in Murcia."

"Can you give me the addresses?"

"I've got them somewhere. I'll give them to you when I'm finished in about an hour, but don't come selling them round here though will you!"

I couldn't believe my ears – was this bloke for real?

Tommy was what he called 'made-up' with his successful introduction into the world of commerce. "There's no point in messing about with these people – either ask them nicely or else."

"Or else what?" I asked.

Jimmy stepped in: "We have ways, let's leave it at that."

We drove back to the campsite the next morning. I was hoping that there might be some good news after all our efforts, but no such luck. Three or four days had passed when I was called to the reception desk and, miraculously, there he was, a dishevelled-looking Bender. When the kissing and cuddling had died down, along with my heart rate, I asked where he'd appeared from. Apparently, a young couple had found him wandering around on the beach in Las Palmas. They had heard the advert on the radio, he fitted the description, so they had driven him to the campsite, and then left without leaving their names – so I was never able to thank them personally.

Bender was much thinner and was wearing a brand-new green leather collar, which made it obvious that someone had taken him in and had intended to keep him. I wondered if it had been that couple and that they hadn't realised that he belonged to somebody. With a guilty conscience there was only one thing to do, take him back to his owner. Maybe a neighbour spotted him and told them, or maybe they were telling the truth and didn't want to make a fuss. In the end it didn't matter. I couldn't believe that we were back together.

When the rest of the campsite heard the news, I was overwhelmed by the amount of people who came over to shake my hand; some of them were total strangers. I certainly bought a few drinks that night and fell asleep on the floor of the van with Bender in my arms.

The next two months were spent mainly at the camping ground. The van was on its last legs, so I kept trips down to a minimum. Bender was visibly getting older and slower. He'd been attacked quite badly by a nasty German with his giant Borzoi. He had a long, pointed nose and sharp teeth – and the dog was even worse. It looked like a greyhound wearing a white woollen pullover. It ran so fast that it was actually quite beautiful to watch it in full flight – that is until it homed in on its target.

Poor old Bender never knew what hit him: it was like an exocet missile with fangs. One minute Bender was strolling along the beach minding his own business, the next minute he was covered in blood and needed stitches in the wound. I had a furious row with his owner, then I remembered the old proverb, 'live by the sword, die by the sword', so I left it at that. After a series of complaints from various quarters he was told to keep the vicious bastard on a lead at all times, but he simply chose to ignore all warnings.

As the weeks went by, people started to leave for one reason or another. Alan eventually got rid of his plaster, and he was very tanned except for the lower half of his right leg. Fred was still regaling us with his ridiculous stories, Lorraine had flown back to England and it was late January when John chose to return to Portugal. I took him to Las Palmas to catch the ferry the next day. Despite all that had gone before, I had no choice but to take Bender with us. That night we slept at the same hostel. We walked around the bustling streets, but this time with the dog on the lead. I wasn't going to make that mistake again.

That evening, after we'd had dinner, we went back to the hostel for an early night, as John had some things to do in the morning before boarding the ferry. I reminded John to be careful not to let Bender out if he got up first. I gave Bender a goodnight stroke and a pat on the head. Sadly, that was the last time I ever saw him…

When I woke up the next morning John and the dog were both gone. When John finally appeared I could tell by the look on his face that something was wrong. He looked at me and started to explain:

"I could hear Bender scratching on the door. When I opened it, he followed me downstairs and into the street as he always does, but before I had time to put on his lead he was gone. I have been looking for him for over an hour. I hoped that he might have come back."

"Oh, no! I can't believe it, not all this again," I shouted in despair.

John had bought his ticket for the ferry and it was leaving shortly. We went to the quayside where we said our goodbyes. He was going back to the same house that we had rented the previous year, to get his painting production line started so that he would be ready for the beginning of the season.

I went back to the hostel, collected my belongings, got in the van and started cruising the beach area. I was quietly confident that I would find Bender, or that if I walked for a while that he might see me – but it wasn't to be.

I tried all the same methods as before, with the local radio station and all the rest, then drove back to Tauro campsite. I waited and waited for any news. As the weeks went by, I began to accept that this time it really was the end, and was resigned to the fact that I would have to leave the island of the dogs without him. I blamed John for what had happened, but at the time I'd kept it to myself. I knew he felt responsible and it must have preyed on his mind for a while. A few weeks ago, I'd done exactly the same thing. It could have been worse If I'd actually seen him die or had to have him put down. He was 16 years old, which was a good long life for a quite a large dog. I only hoped that he enjoyed the rest of his days and that he didn't suffer any cruelty.

It was time to return to Portugal and the Algarve. Jimmy and Tommy had asked if they could come along and see the place for themselves. We'd become the best of friends over the past few months, so I was happy for them to join me. On the day we left the campsite some local people came to the van with a present for me... a black and white male puppy!

They had obviously heard about my loss and they didn't want me to leave their island with sad memories. They explained that Bender had been sniffing around their bitch a few months ago, so there was a possibility that he could have been the father. I decided to accept their kind offer, and called him Benson, having bought into the theory that Bender was indeed the daddy. He was about a month old, had floppy ears and big feet, a sign that he was going to grow into a big dog.

Our last night in Las Palmas was spent with the Argies. I first had to show them my ferry ticket, as agreed, before having a quick lesson on Lumie-making. They sold me a few rolls of tubing and gave me the name of the magical product which was a safety light used mainly in the nautical trade and sold by ship chandlers. It was a 'Cyalume lightstick' and it was that which contained the special liquid. This would have to be found somewhere when I got back, as they didn't have any for sale – or so they said. They explained the manufacturing process and reminded us that the finished article must always be frozen, the colder the better. I had a feeling we were being ripped off somehow, but I couldn't imagine how, as I hadn't paid much for the tube. Maybe I was wrong. They were very similar to gypsies: you know you've been outsmarted, and they pretend to be your friends, but it's never genuine.

On a clear day on the beach at our old campsite you could see a white triangle sticking up on the western horizon: this was the tip of a volcano. Out of curiosity I wanted to get closer and see it, as I might not get another opportunity in the near future. So, instead of catching the ferry directly back to Spain, the three of us plus new dog went to Tenerife.

Mount Teide is the highest point in all of Spain and a few years before, they had constructed a cable car that almost reaches the top. As soon as we landed, we made our way to the cable car station. When we had reached the top there was still a short walk to the summit. We were young and reasonably fit, but to reach the peak took us ages because of the rarified atmosphere. At over 12,000ft every step was an effort. Some of the older tourists gave up after an hour or so with breathing problems. The clouds of stinking sulphur pouring out of cracks in the ground didn't help either. When we finally reached the top of '*Pico Viejo*', as it's called, the amazing views had made it all worthwhile.

The next day we were back on the ferry, and two days later we were back at the same house in Vale de Éguas. John was there to greet us. He had already prepared everything for us and was covered in paint from his production line. The neighbour with the German Shepherd had sold all of John's paintings but had moved away and kept all the money.

Gran Canaria had taken my incredible dog, but in exchange had given me an experience never to forget, some new friends and two potential money-making ideas.

1978

46

Paint it Black

IT WAS the beginning of March and Easter would soon be upon us. Jimmy, Tommy and I, as we had planned, decided that we could all work together. We got in contact with the factory in Spain that manufactured the letters that we had seen in Las Palmas. The only way we could buy them, other than driving a few hundred kilometres across Spain, was to have them sent to the nearest Spanish post office where we would pay the invoice at the counter and then they would give us the merchandise.

We couldn't have them delivered to Portugal, as the goods would go through customs and we would then have to pay exorbitant amounts of import tax and other duties. This would have made the product so expensive, probably double the price, that it wouldn't have been economically viable. The other worry was that in those days the Portuguese postal system wasn't very reliable, so our only realistic option was to go over the border and bring the stuff in and hope that we didn't get stopped at the customs.

We phoned through our first order to our supplier and were informed that on a certain date, only a few days later, our package would be at the post office in Ayamonte on the other side of the river Guadiana. We drove to Vila Real, took the quick ferry trip as foot passengers, changed our escudos into pesetas then waited in the queue at the post office. I was convinced that something was bound to go wrong -- but the goods were there as promised.

The only problem now was to get back into Portugal without being checked at the customs. There was a thriving trade between the border towns as certain products were cheaper or unavailable in Portugal, so it was better to buy in Spain and to a certain extent vice-versa. There were probably all sorts of dodgy dealings going on, so we weren't that concerned about being caught. Even if we were, we could have probably talked or paid our way out of it, but it was still quite nerve-wracking.

We were dressed like all the young tourists, complete with our back packs – except that ours were filled with silver coloured letters instead of clothes. We'd tied on sleeping bags to look the part and nonchalantly strolled through the customs shed without any bother. We'd heard about further customs checks on the road out of town, so we weren't out of the woods yet, but after a few minutes we stopped off in Monte Gordo to celebrate the success of our first run.

We then began getting organised as to where we would sell and if we could get away with it without licences etc. It was still very early in the year, so to begin with we took it in turns to sit in the garden in Albufeira. It was strange to be back there without Bender. Some old friends came by and asked after him, so I told them the story and introduced them to Benson who was growing bigger and crazier by the day.

The van was still mobile, but I knew it was only a matter of time before we were going to need a new vehicle. John was in the same position. His Mini had reached the end of its days, so one morning he suddenly announced that he was going back to England there and then. He had a minivan at his parents' house back in Bedford which he would drive back and would pick up Lorraine at the same time. He had invested most of his cash in materials, so he opted to hitch back. If he struggled for lifts he was going to take public transport, as he was in a hurry to get there and back as soon as he could, so as not to miss the Easter holiday when business always picked up.

One afternoon three or four days after he'd left, I was sitting in the Albufeira garden when a young Portuguese chap came over and spoke to me in English:

"I'm sorry to hear about your friend being killed in France."

"What are you talking about, what friend?" I screamed.

"John with the beard, the painter . . . it was on the news."

"NO, NO, it's impossible . . . it can't be him!"

I ran straight to the public phone box to call my mother. I was in such a state that at first, I couldn't remember the number, a number that I had called a thousand times. I calmed myself down and eventually it came back to me and I got through to her. She hadn't heard anything, so she said she would call John's mother and call me back.

I stood by the phone, my whole body trembling, praying that there had been a dreadful mistake.

The phone rang . . . as soon as I heard my mother's sobbing, I knew that John was dead. Mrs Greene told her that John had arrived two nights before, about ready to collapse after his long trip, slept the night on the sofa, got up the next morning, had some breakfast with the family and then set off in his minivan for London to collect Lorraine. They caught the evening ferry to France and on arrival, instead of having a rest, drove through the night.

Lorraine was asleep in the back. At dawn, as the sun rose, they were travelling along one of those tree-lined routes. The sun rays were flashing through the trees, which can have a hypnotic effect on drivers, especially when you're tired. John had obviously nodded off at the wheel as, according to the French police, there were no brake marks and he hit the tree with such force that it split the car into two halves.

John was killed instantly. He never had a chance. Lorraine survived the crash and was taken to a nearby hospital with multiple injuries including severe spinal damage. We were told that she probably wouldn't survive but if she did, she would be paralysed.

I drove back home trying to see the road through the constant wiping away of my tears. I broke the news to Jimmy and Tommy, and we all cracked up together. We had just spent nearly every day of the last few months together with John, and to some extent Lorraine, and now he was gone for ever. Only 23 years old. He was probably my best friend at the time. We never argued. I was only annoyed with him the one time when he lost Bender – and now I'd lost him too.

About a week later I flew back for the funeral. John had a younger brother and twin sisters. His Mum and Dad were in a terrible state and because I had introduced him to his life in Portugal, they told me that all this wouldn't have happened if it wasn't for me. They needed someone to blame I suppose. After the funeral they apologised and very kindly asked me to finish his paintings, try to sell them and keep the money; they didn't want to have any memories of his life abroad.

Lorraine miraculously survived the crash. She had an operation on her spine and was told that she might eventually recover and be able to walk. She had been badly facially scarred and had numerous other injuries but at least she was alive. The problem was that John had been driving with no insurance – so the question was who was going to pay the enormous French hospital charges?

I'm not sure exactly how things turned out, but I heard that the people from the town Lorraine was originally from formed a charity and raised a lot of the money. The local French people from the area where the accident occurred found the rest. She was eventually taken back to England where she spent months convalescing. She'd had her body smashed and her boyfriend was dead. What a tragic end for such a beautiful loving couple.

John Greene

R.I.P

47
Mercedes

BECAUSE of the accident, I'd spent some time with my parents, who were convinced that my life would soon end in similar circumstances to John's. So when I asked them for a short term loan to buy a car in Germany they weren't very forthcoming. Having given the matter some thought and realising that I might overstay my welcome they eventually buckled under the pressure of my constant nagging. It wasn't a lot of money to them but it was the principle: 'If you want to live this crazy existence you're on your own', which was fair enough.

I'd discovered that it was possible to buy very cheap cars in Germany as they had stringent MOT tests called the TUV. If the car failed the test, then *kaput*–it had to be scrapped or exported to third world countries and the like. Because of the salt used on the roads to combat the snow and ice, the chassis underneath would often be very rusty and therefore unsafe to drive... in Germany.

I bought a German newspaper, found a German-speaking friend who looked through the adverts for me. He found a Mercedes for a few hundred pounds, called the owner in Dusseldorf and agreed the price with him.

Two days later I arrived at Herr Kutz and his fraulein's house. The car was Bismark grey, immaculate inside and out, except for the rust below the doors and across the chassis. It was so bad that you could actually stick your finger through it in some places.The vendors weren't that happy that I was intent on driving it to Portugal–they probably had kids, so they were genuinely concerned. I reassured them that I would be OK and that I would get it fixed when I arrived. I explained to them that in the poorer countries of Europe there weren't so many rules and regulations, that they could mend anything and joked about the lack of snow and ice in the Algarve.

I had to get a special oval number plate from the customs which I think was only legal for 1 month, but once I was out of Deutschland it didn't really matter, I was now faced with the long drive to the Algarve. I was very careful not to fall into the same trap that had led to John's death, but on the other hand I wasn't intending on hanging around. Every time I felt my eyelids drooping, I knew it was time to pull over and have a sleep. It was such a pleasure to drive I could go hundreds of miles without stopping. This was a powerful luxury limousine built for wealthy Germans and I loved it.

After two days of almost non-stop driving I had reached Seville. I thought about stopping for the night but as I was so near to the Algarve I had to keep going. The last hundred kilometres was a struggle, as the road was in a terrible state and I was scared that the car was going to fall apart, so I had to take it really slowly. I was soon on the ferry across the river and arrived back completely shattered. Jimmy and Tommy were there to greet me, ready for a fresh start.

48

Letter Spray

WE QUICKLY got ourselves organized so that we could sell in three places at the same time. We would set off each day when we had recovered from the night before. We had three sets of everything we needed so I would drop Jimmy off in one place, Tommy in the next and then I would drive to Albufeira and sit in the garden. Some days we would swap places to make a change, other days we would all go together.

One day Jimmy was in Albufeira and got chatting to an English lady. After hearing the story about John's accident, she offered us a place where we could work on finishing his paintings, as we needed space which we didn't have at home. Her name was Jane MacGregor and she had some empty stables at a place called Quinta de Saudade, a few kilometres west of Albufeira towards Pera. We weren't that au fait with the painting technique, but we had watched John a few times. I always remember his advice that to make them look more artistic try and make as much mess as possible which suited us down to the ground.

John had already drawn out the designs, so all we had to do was follow the lines with white acrylic paint that was squeezed out of an empty mustard pot, then fill in the gaps by randomly splashing water colour paint in roughly the correct places. When they were dry, we had to go over the lines, which were in relief, with an indelible black felt tip pen which gave them a 3D effect, and then spray on a coat of varnish for the final touch. It was quite remarkable how good they looked considering that none of us had an ounce of talent. What was even more amazing is how well they sold.

After a while we had other street sellers working for us on commission, we had most of the best spots in the Algarve covered and once again we were living the life of Reilly. The letter necklaces were selling well, but we couldn't trust other people to sell them as we couldn't control the stock. We didn't know if they had sold Ed, Ana and Jo or had a day of Christophers and Elizabeths. They were all the same price, which we had calculated as an average, so we kept that side of the business for ourselves.

We soon had a bit of a reputation as unscrupulous wheelers and dealers: turning up in a Mercedes, collecting loads of cash up and down the Algarve. Jimmy and Tommy were pretty tough, so we looked the part with our suntans and dark glasses. At the end of a day's trading we would usually end up in Albufeira. We got into a routine of going to Catunas for dinner every night, where we became almost part of the family, then it was down to Sir Harry's, then maybe Zelios bar, then over the road to see Julio, the owner of Snoopy's bar. We usually ended up in Silvia's disco – that's if João the doorman would let us in. It was still early in the season and we were out most nights, so João, after hearing that we spent well, which included a whiskey for him, stopped hassling us and became a good friend.

Benson was getting bigger by the day and getting over-adventurous. Because of our lifestyle, we were unable to give him our full attention. We couldn't leave him at home, so he spent a lot of time travelling and sitting around with us – but if he wanted to be a street dog, he would have to learn the hard way.

Unfortunately, he never made it. We were all together in Albufeira one afternoon when we heard a screech of brakes and then a squeal. He'd been run over and killed by a car. We were so distraught we were ready to murder the driver, that was until he got out of the car... it was João the doorman. Jimmy was still ready to strangle him and at one stage I thought he was going to do it; he was raging, I'd never seen him so wild. Some of the crowd that had formed had to hold him back before he gradually calmed down.

We took Benson's little lifeless body home with us and buried him in our back garden, another one gone. When is this all going to end, I asked myself? It was as though we had a curse on us. Whatever it was – fate, karma, destiny – it struck again within a matter of days in the most bizarre manner.

João was working on the door of Silvia's when he refused entrance to a local off-duty policeman who had had far too much to drink. Having been turned away the policeman protested angrily then stormed off into the night. Later on that evening, he returned to the club – but this time he was armed with his police handgun. He banged his fist noisily on the door, João opened the hatch to see who it was, whereupon the policeman pulled the trigger and shot him through the door, seriously wounding him in the stomach.

João was taken to hospital in Portimão. He'd lost a lot of blood, but he was alive. Two days later we went to visit him. He was sitting up in bed and reasonably cheerful, considering the ordeal he'd been through. We had a laugh and a joke with him. He admitted he'd been driving too fast when he ran over the dog, we accepted his apology and wished him a speedy recovery.

That same afternoon he was given a blood transfusion but collapsed and died shortly afterwards due to complications. A day or two later we went to his funeral, another young man gone to an early grave. I'm not sure what happened to the policeman. I have a feeling that he was transferred but never punished for his crime.

Within a few months I'd lost two dogs, and the two people who were involved were both named John, both young friends of mine and now both of them were dead. It was a horrible coincidence, almost as though the dog world had put a jinx on them.

49

Splashing The Cash

OUR ROUTINE nights out in Albufeira continued. At Catunas we would spend what was often a long wait before the food arrived by passing the time with me giving elementary Portuguese lessons to Jimmy and Tommy and anybody else who wanted to join in. We were all crammed together on wooden benches, literally rubbing shoulders with total strangers, who were more often than not already pissed – or well on their way – so the pre-meal evening's education classes descended into chaos.

First of all, we would choose a theme, for exampIe colours. Then I would ask something like, "What's the word for Blue?" The first to answer correctly would earn a point (we'd started the point system after the failure of the drink-a-glass-of-wine reward had to be abandoned due to one of the contestants throwing up). As too many people got involved, we had to introduce a new rule whereby, before answering the question, you had to tap the wine bottle with a spoon or a fork or whatever came to hand.

As the evening progressed, we would have quick fire rounds of quiz questions – first to five wins.

"Green?" Ding! "Yes, Tommy?"

"Verde." Correct.

"Orange?" Ding!

"Laranja." Tommy again, two-nil.

"Red?"

"Tinto!" No Jimmy, that's only for wine.

Tommy: "He didn't tap the bottle! Points deduction!"

Jimmy: "I haven't got any points."

"Minus-one then," and so on, until other tables were dinging their wine bottles and shouting out the answers.

The tapping on the bottles turned into hitting them harder to try and get the answer in first, with the inevitable breakage with wine spilt everywhere. Fernando, one of the brothers who ran the place, came over with his tongs gripping a piece of red-hot charcoal from the grill to light my cigarette, which was a bit of a party trick of his, and suggested that we should play our silly games elsewhere or he'd drop it down my lap. That brought about an abrupt end to quiz night once and for all.

One night in Catunas we sat with Tom, a Scottish lawyer, and his very attractive blonde wife. He was very loud and brash, dominating the conversation while she sat there looking sexy but bored. After dinner he invited us all up to his villa. Jimmy and Tommy and one or two others from the restaurant took up his invitation. Luckily, I had other plans, so I left them to it.

The evening at Tom's villa began with some serious drinking and ended up with all the male guests taking it in turn to go upstairs and have sex with his wife. Jimmy was apparently awarded a very respectable 9 out of 10 for his performance. I was so glad that I hadn't gone. I liked sex of course, but with someone else's wife and after three or four previous candidates – never in a million years. As Dick used to say so eloquently: "It would be like a worm in a well, Paul."

50
The Smell

OCCASIONALLY we didn't go to work, or out to Albufeira at night. We would have a day off and emulate what almost everybody else did and go to the beach, usually on a Sunday, as Catunas was closed. Sundays would bring out the Montanheiros – which literally translated is 'mountaineers' but colloquially meant village folk from the interior.

On one of our trips to get a bit of fresh air in our lungs we were driving to the nearest beach in Quarteira when we saw a couple hitching a lift in their underwear. Against my better judgement I pulled over and gave them a ride. The man was only wearing white Y-fronts and the woman had matching bra and pants that were probably fashionable in the First World War. It was hard to tell their ages, as neither of them had much in the hair department and when they smiled, which seemed to be all the time, they had about seven teeth between them. Lovely people I'm sure, but they probably hadn't washed since she bought her underwear. The stink of BO was overpowering. (Years ago, I shared a house with a few young men, one of whom was an engineer. He had a terrible case of BO, so bad that when he was out we would invite guests up to his stinking bedroom just so they could proudly say that they had 'done it'.)This couple could have bottled their aroma and developed it into a deadly weapon. A skunk would have been proud of them.

Jimmy, who was in the back of the car with them, stood up and stuck his head out of the sunroof. Tommy had his head out of the window. With one hand holding my nose, I was attempting to drive to the beach as fast as possible before succumbing to the poisonous fumes. We dropped them off, avoiding the ritual kissing and handshaking. We went as far away as possible along the beach from where we had dropped them off. We went straight into the sea to get rid of the lingering smell and enjoyed a lovely day at the beach.

On the way home, just outside Quarteira, there they were again, the same couple, a bit redder than earlier, standing by the road with their thumbs out. As I slowed down to pick them up again, just to annoy Jimmy and Tommy, I could hear them in unison: "Dad, for fuck's sake no!" (They had started calling me Dad as I was a few years older than them, some kind of Liverpudlian or Glaswegian humour.) The stench was the same, but now mixed with Medronho breath which on its own would have probably been banned under the chemical warfare section of the Geneva Convention. They asked us if we could take them home and maybe have dinner with them, (imagine what that would have been like!). We politely declined and dropped them off on the 125 before rushing home and disinfecting the car and ourselves.

51

Hugh Jardon at The Movies

WE WOULD sometimes eat in the village and then spend the evening trying to play pool in a local cafe that was nearly always empty. It was a dark and depressing establishment with an owner to match. He was an old man who wore a pair of specs that looked like two magnifying glasses. All three of us were reasonable pool players but the Portuguese had balls that were bigger than ours and their holes were smaller, if you catch my drift.

We would play 'winner stays on', as there were only three of us, but it took so long to pot each ball we soon got bored with that. Even when the ball was over the pocket it wouldn't drop. We asked the owner if he would like to make up a foursome although none of us wanted to be paired with a myopic pensioner. I lost the toss and my new partner broke the balls and proceeded to give us a master class in how to play the game. We couldn't believe our eyes. He hardly ever missed a shot. He stroked the balls softly across the green baize just hard enough for them to reach the pocket so that they would either go in or block the pocket, instead of smashing them all round the table. I presume he was an ex-champion; he was that good. It just goes to show that you can't judge people by their appearances.

We were in the village one Friday night, in a cafe on the main road trying to have a conversation among ourselves.

Every few seconds a 50cc motorbike would pass by the door. The noise was deafening and extremely annoying. We went outside to try and fathom out where they were all coming from. Someone told us that it was sex film night at the local cinema and all the motorbikes were parked in a garage under the cinema. When the film ended, a few hundred highly-aroused horny young male virgins ran down to the garage and fired up their noisy machines. They mounted their machines, waited their turn to be ejected with the throbbing between their legs and, gripping their helmets, they would race back home before the erotic images escaped their memories, and take matters in hand.

The next Friday (which is aptly sexta-feira in Portuguese) we decided to go along to see what all the fuss was about. It was early June and seriously hot. We were dressed in shorts and T-shirts. The cinema was packed. I kept thinking Bender's ghost would appear at some stage. The film itself was very dated but quite naughty. There was pandemonium when the lights came on, with a stampede for the exit.

Jimmy was the only person still in his seat

"What are you waiting for, it's all over?" I asked him.

"Dad, I've got a stiffy nearly sticking out of me boxers."

"Well put your straw hat over it," suggested Tommy, giggling to himself.

We walked up the aisle towards the door and everybody was pointing and laughing at Jimmy.

I turned round to see what was so amusing.

"Look Dad, no hands!"

Jimmy had his hat balanced on the end of his dick with his hands in the air.

The ushers and security men were not amused and told us that if we wanted to come again we must wear more clothes. Outside, the motorbikes were flying out of the door like a giant wasps' nest that was under attack.

The next Friday we went again, just to wind everybody up. Jimmy was a specialist in that department. It was maybe even hotter than the week before. We had found a few old winter clothes that belonged to the owner of our house. Coats, scarves, gloves and hats – even socks. By the time we arrived at the ticket office dressed for a Siberian winter, with the sweat pouring from us, the officials had seen enough. They gave us a wry smile and politely told us to clear off.

52
Coffee and Cakes

JIMMY and Tommy were basically looking to have as much fun as possible in their lives. They didn't really take anything or anybody seriously, which was difficult to keep up with at times, but I loved their ridiculous attitude to life.

They were guaranteed to cause trouble almost wherever we went. Jimmy was the main culprit – we usually stood back and watched.

The cafes were full of sweetmeats, candies, tarts and cakes – hundreds of varieties. They were usually on view behind a glass counter, row upon row of sugary temptations, a diabetic's nightmare. If you didn't know the name of the one you wanted, you would have to point to it. This involved the assistant, who was normally stressed and in a hurry to serve other customers, bending down with tongs in her hand trying to identify the specific variety of cake that was required. We had even seen some of the local people struggling to obtain their favourites. In a flash, Jimmy had picked up on the fallibility of the identification system and pushed it to its limits.

When it was his turn to be served he would point at the cakes through the glass, then for an excruciating length of time would mess about about chopping and changing which one he wanted, until finally the exasperated lady behind the counter put something on a plate – to then be told that it was the wrong one. By this time the waiting customers had justifiably begun complaining, and there's Jimmy with a huge grin on his face pretending to be shocked at why people were glaring at him. We'd had a go at learning some of the cake names but you can easily make a complete fool of yourself. A 'bolo de côco' is a coconut cake while a 'bolo de cocô' is a shit cake. The moving of the accent from one letter 'o' to the other makes a big difference. A lady friend of mine went into a cafe and asked for a 'queca' instead of a 'queque'. The male assistant and the customers in the cafe started sniggering. She was then asked if she wanted it there and then. She said, "Yes please," with a smile on her face – only to find out that what she had asked for was a shag, not a cake. They know how to laugh at us too.

There are so many ways to have your coffee it's mind-boggling. To avoid upsetting any more customers we always asked for a galão which is simply a white coffee that is served in a tall glass balanced on a saucer with a long spoon stuck in it – which makes it easier to knock over. If you haven't managed to do that and survive the journey to your wobbly table, you'll then need a pair of oven gloves to pick up the glass.

53

The Green Light

UP TO this point we hadn't tried to make the luminous necklaces, as it was still early in the season and we had no idea where to get the light sticks. I went to Lisbon where I eventually found a specialist ship chandlers called Azimute-Aprestos Marítimos that had them. They weren't cheap, and they didn't have many in stock, but it was a start. I looked around for the transparent tubing but every shop I tried had the same as all the others, and what I was looking for didn't exist. The problem was the interior dimension, which had to be as small as possible, otherwise too much liquid was needed. We had to make ten necklaces per tube for a decent profit and with these dimensions that was impossible.

When I got back to our house we decided to have a trial run. The light stick itself was a plastic tube that contained liquid, with a glass vial floating inside it, which in turn contained another liquid. To start the light reaction all you had to do was bend the tube and the glass vial would break, which then mixed the liquids together giving the bright green light. We then had to cut open the tube and pour the contents into a glass receptacle through a tea strainer to filter out the broken glass and then immerse one end of a length of the narrow tube held in the liquid and suck the other end to get the green juice flowing down the tube. When the liquid had nearly reached the open end, the sucker had to quickly stick a stopper in the tube and the person at the glass end did the same.

So we now had a five metre long luminous tube which had to be quickly cut up into necklace sizes. This was very messy as in the process of cutting the tube and inserting a stopper the excess liquid got everywhere. Once that part was completed, the finished article had to be put straight in a freezer, which stopped the chemical reaction until they were taken out at a later date. We had never done anything like this before and,- like most things, practice makes perfect. Let's just say our first few attempts didn't go quite to plan. Each of us was assigned a specific task and somehow we all failed dismally. It all sounded reasonably simple in theory, but in our home-made laboratory almost anything that could possibly go wrong did exactly that.

The tube cracker forgot to break the tube, before pouring out the contents; the sucker pulled the tube out of the glass; the glass full of the precious liquid was knocked over; the sucker got a mouthful of toxic chemicals; someone forgot the tea strainer; all in all, total chaos and money down the drain. The freezer wasn't really cold enough. What we really needed was dry ice, which was something like -80 degrees Centigrade. There wasn't much chance of us finding that in the Algarve, so we had to do the best we could.

To add to our problems, the tube that the Argentinians had sold us had been left out in the sun, or was defective, as the bore varied in dimension and so we had to adapt by having various sizes of wire to block the tube. That's why our generous warm-hearted South American friends had sold it to us. I knew they had somehow ripped us off, but we had at least produced something like the finished article. Things could only get better. We were at the bottom of the learning curve and we eventually had something that we could sell.

54
Pamplona

WE HAD this crazy idea in our heads that we could now conquer the market with our fantastic new luminous business, so we decided to hit the big time. Somewhere where we would be able to sell thousands of them in one go. The famous festival of the running of the bulls in Pamplona was on in a few days in the north of Spain. It would be a long drive but usually there were at least 100,000 visitors at the event, either watching people getting chased by the bulls or actually taking part in what was a seriously dangerous bit of fun. There were deaths and horrible injuries every year.

San Fermin is the official name of the festival, which always begins on the 6th of July. But when we arrived the independence-seeking Basques had started a riot and a lot of visitors were already leaving, which wasn't a great start. There were still thousands of punters milling around and, to our horror, there were lumies hanging around most of their necks.

We started trying to sell but ours weren't as bright as the ones that everyone was wearing, so sales were very slow. We hadn't been there long when some nasty looking characters came over to us and told us to pack up and go. They were selling the lumies as well and we were giving them a bad name. First of all we ignored them, but then one of our Argentinian friends from the Canaries suddenly appeared – the one who had sold us the tube. He was reasonably amicable and told us that we were doing something wrong in the manufacturing process, which was why the light wasn't very bright. He actually put some of the green liquid in his mouth to test the quality.

After that his attitude changed. He reminded us that we had promised him that we were only interested in selling in

Portugal, so we had breached our agreement, and told us that if we didn't disappear there and then he would get his gang and there would be trouble. I had been intending to bring up the matter of the dodgy tube that he had sold us but under the circumstances and after consulting my business partners we agreed that the best policy would be to make a hasty retreat before things turned ugly.

Our venture into the big world of commerce had come to an abrupt halt. Apart from the long journey it was a financial disaster as all the lumies we'd worked so hard to make had to be thrown away. We set off for Portugal totally deflated, with our tails between our legs. Jimmy and Tommy had suggested that having come so far that we should stay the night and have a go at the bull-running.

"What time does that start?" I enquired.

"Eight-o-clock in the morning," they replied in unison.

I was already in a bad mood thanks to our business failure, so I just wanted to go back home.

"If you think I'm waking up at the crack of dawn to get run over by a herd of mad cows you can think again!" I shouted at them.

"OK Dad, keep your hair on, it was just an idea."

Apparently, the festival was cancelled the next day for the first time in forty years. Some leftist Trotskyite had been shot and killed and the ensuing battles with the riot police turned into a mini bloodbath. After our first foray into foreign fields we realised how easy things were where we lived. Big fish in a small pond came to mind.

55

Moving House

BY MID-JULY there were big crowds in Albufeira almost every night. We had mastered the lumie-making process and were selling hundreds of them. We kept them in a deep freeze and took them frozen in ice boxes. Our sales improved if there was a blackout when the electricity went off, which was quite a regular occurrence. Some of the locals even accused us of doing it deliberately – as if!

One of the street sellers was so pleased that somebody had a product that was selling better than our letters and the paintings. He wasn't happy when he found out that we were behind this one too. We were doing so well that we moved into more luxurious surroundings just around the corner. The house belonged to José Madeira Lopes with his wife Solange and their two young children. José, according to him, had been a bit of a lad in Paris as an immigrant and had made enough to buy this huge property. It was a modern house in its own grounds, and not far away down the bottom of the garden he had an out-building with maybe 50 pigs.

Every morning without fail he would set off with his tractor and trailer on his daily trip to Vale de Lobo where he collected the waste from the Dona Filipa hotel restaurant, which they offered to him as he was doing them a favour. So, he was basically feeding his pigs for free. José and his wife were lovely people and we were lucky to find the place. We all had a big modern bedroom to ourselves. They were fascinated with our lifestyle. Where they were hard-working and saving every penny where possible, here were we out all night spending all our cash in restaurants, clubs and bars. They were totally bewildered with our way of life. We spent a few fun barbecue evenings at home with them. We would always end the night with all of us pissed on wine and Medronho. José would give us a lesson in economics and beg us to start saving and invest and stop spending it all. If only we'd listened!

He had a couple of dogs and a sheep that thought it was a dog, as it ran around with them and played with the kids. I thought it was really good of him to keep a sheep as a pet. That was until one afternoon when we came home: its carcass was hanging up on the washing line ready for that evening's dinner!

56

The One-Eared Cão

ON OUR way home after selling the lumies in Albufeira, we got into this stupid habit of putting a luminous necklace on a small sculpture of a concrete dog, which was on a wall of a house in Ferreiras. It became a ritual. One night we had driven past Ferreiras and were well on our way home when Jimmy shouts out in panic:

"Dad, we've forgotten to put the lumie on the one-eared cão (dog)!"

"Well, so what? I'm not driving all the way back just to put a necklace on a concrete dog," I mocked.

"You've got to go back,Dad, it's not far. It's bad karma."

"Oh for fuck's sake, Jimmy, yer off yer heed," Tommy complained.

I stopped the car and had a few words with Jimmy, who was in one of his silly moods, and I couldn't tell if he was serious or not.

"What's the point of going all that way back, and for what?"

"For the dog. People expect it of us. It's why we do all these daft things." Jimmy hadn't finished. "Go on,Dad – just for the crack, then we can have a laugh about it tomorrow".

Fifteen minutes later we had driven all the way back to Ferreiras, just to put a bloody necklace on a concrete dog. On the second attempt at driving home that evening, I started to question my sanity: what was going on with my life? Why am I doing these things? This is not normal behaviour by any stretch of the imagination but... why not be different. It's fun to do crazy things sometimes.

A few nights later we'd picked up a couple of young ladies in Silvia's and convinced them to come home with us. As we drove out of Albufeira, my old friend Bacalhau and two of his muscle-bound amigos saw the two girls in the back of our car. They were sitting in a high-powered Mercedes sports car and they waved their hands telling us to stop. We ignored them and drove on towards Ferreiras. I looked in the mirror and they were right behind us waving frantically for us to stop.

"What shall I do?" I asked my passengers.

"Just keep going – they won't follow us all the way home, surely?"

"Go as fast as you can, we'll probably lose them."

"They're in a sports car, we've got no chance."

"What about the one-eared concrete dog?" I laughed.

"Fuck that, let's get home quick," came the answer from the back.

"What about the karma and all that crap?"

The two girls were having at least second thoughts. "Where are we going? Why are you driving so fast?"

"There's three blokes following us because of you two."

I was getting a bit nervous at the wheel. After many years on these roads I wouldn't say that I was used to the tailgating, but it didn't really bother me anymore. On the other hand, they were only a matter of inches behind us. I couldn't go any faster, just as well probably. My taxi-driving days had taught me to keep calm under pressure with years of having drunks threatening me, throwing up or opening the doors at 70 mph and trying to jump out. All my experience was beginning to kick in. I just hoped that I was ready and prepared for whatever they were going to try. We were racing along the notorious 125 and every time I overtook the car in front, they did the same. I couldn't lose them. Apart from the high speed we were travelling at, I didn't take any risks. Instead of going home I drove all around Almancil in a futile attempt to confuse them, but to no avail.

The two girls were panicking and wouldn't stop crying. "We're going to crash; we're going to be killed!"

Tommy was comforting them and reassured them that all would end well: "That's me Dad, he's sound."

I decided that we would have to go to our house and see what happened, before we finished up having an accident. The last part of the track to José's house was very narrow. It had white walls on either side and two or three nasty bends to negotiate. The first time I tried it slowly at night the width of the car felt as though we could just about squeeze through without scraping the sides. After a few attempts I mastered the art of just missing the walls without having to slow down too much.

On this particular occasion, with these lunatics still seriously close behind me I shot through the bends faster than I'd ever tried before. I just about avoided touching the walls, drove past the gates into the yard where we all jumped out and ran into the house. We waited and waited for them. I for one was pretty scared of what they might do.

The three of them appeared on foot at the gate and walked over to the glass door where they could see us waiting for them. They looked shaken up but were at least smiling. The biggest of the three comes out with, "Who is driving car Emerson Fittipaldi? I would shake your hand but it's shaking on its own."

"We have big crash on wall – car broken, but was fun – where are girls? Are you going to offer us a beer?"

We reluctantly invited them in, wondering where all this was going to end. After everybody had shaken hands the atmosphere became reasonably pleasant, and they had a few beers. A very irate José came into the room. He had been woken up by all the noise. There was a short conversation in Portuguese. José was quite small but hard as nails and from what I understood he told them to get off his property and that they would be getting a bill for wall repairs.

Recently restored

57
Big Mal

ONE EVENING down at the fisherman's beach in Albufeira, our friend Alistair MacGregor (his mother Jane had helped us with the paintings) told us that he was helping out in the GB bar and restaurant for that evening. It was quite up-market and not the kind of place we would normally eat in. When we arrived, there was a long queue outside the door. We couldn't be bothered waiting and chose to try somewhere else, but as we walked past one of the open windows, we spotted an empty table. Seizing the opportunity, we climbed through the window–to the bemusement of the other diners–and sat ourselves down at the table.

Before any of the staff had noticed, Alistair came over and read the riot act; but even he thought it was quite amusing, so he let us keep the table. Instead of keeping it quiet he made an example of us by announcing in a loud voice for all to hear: "OK lads, you've successfully jumped the queue–but next time could you please enter through the door not the window!" There was a lot of disgruntled murmuring, but also a few appreciative giggles in the background.

As the meal progressed, with Alistair as our waiter, everything we asked for was served with some kind of humour involved. He was outsmarting us in every department. When he asked us for our choice of dessert, I asked him for a Sahara. Without batting an eyelid, he left our table having taken down my order. Five minutes later he presented me with a dish full of sand with a cocktail umbrella stuck in the middle: "One Sahara, sir!" "Touché" shouted some of the guests near us, giving Alistair a round of applause.

We had reached the coffee and brandy course when this large man with a hat plonks himself down next to me. "I've been watching you lot, and you certainly know how to annoy everybody. Why don't you come over to my table and join me and my young lady . . . "? It was Malcolm Allison, the football manager well-known for his Fedora, big cigars, boozing and womanising. His petite English girlfriend was absolutely gorgeous, first division material. We sat there in awe as he regaled us with his football stories: as a player at West Ham with the likes of Bobby Moore, as Joe Mercer's assistant where they had won trophy after trophy at Manchester City, and how now he was a manager in his own right. At the time he was with Plymouth Argyle, but was soon to go on to greater things.

We moved on to another bar/club for a few more drinks, where he almost got into a fight–and then after another hour or so he collapsed on the floor, unconscious, completely legless. We were a bit concerned for him and his girlfriend, but she said that these things happen some nights with all the stress of management getting on top of him. We called a taxi for them and said goodbye. In the 1981/1982 season he was back in Portugal and won the league and cup double as Sporting Lisbon's manager and became a much-loved figure for quite a while in Portugal. I liked one of his famous quotes after his team were well beaten: "A lot of hard work went into that defeat."

58

A Day Out In Faro

ONE MORNING, Tommy woke up complaining of a medical problem in his nether regions or, has he put it: "I think I've caught a dose off that wee slut I shagged the other night."

"Well, you'll have to see a doctor then won't you."

"I don't fancy that. I might catch something."

"You already have by the looks of things," Jimmy sniggered.

"What about Jorge the vet?" I joked.

We drove to Faro hospital, which turned out to be even worse than my previous hospital trip a few years before in Portimão. Blood and bodies everywhere, wailing and screaming emanating from the hidden depths of the corridors. The waiting room alone was bad enough with the coughing, sneezing and vomiting.

We eventually got 'served'. As the doctor took Tommy away, I asked him if he spoke any English as I might have to help if not.

"Yes thank you, I'm fluent. I learnt it at school."

They hadn't been gone long when the doctor re-appeared looking a little frustrated. "I can't understand a word of what he's saying, could you please come in and help me?" Tommy was obviously a tad nervous, which seemed to have affected his powers of speech. He had returned to the streets of Glasgow for some strange reason.

"E canny ken a worad I'm saying!" The doctor then asked him what was wrong with him.

"Abin wi a wee lassie, she's given me a dose o the claarp."

"Thank you, Tommy, perhaps Paul you could translate whatever he said into English."

"He thinks he's got gonorrhoea."

"Thank you Paul, if you would like to step outside for a moment while I take a look at the problem. I'll call you back if I need you, so don't disappear."

Tommy looked even more worried. "Dad, I don't want him playing about wi me knob, I just want a jab in me arse."

The doctor, utterly bewildered, looked me up and down. "You're his father?" he asked.

"Do I look like his father?... no it's a term of endearment."

"A what?"

"Look, never mind, just give him the clap injection or whatever, there's people waiting outside who sound like they're dying out there."

Tommy got his injection and could hardly sit down afterwards. We got back in the car and went to the gardens in the centre of Faro where there was a cafe that had the best 'tosta mistas' (cheese and ham toasties). Jimmy got talking to a weirdo from Birmingham. He had travelled extensively in the Algarve. He'd been to, as he put it, "Laygos, Portimayo and Albafuhrer" and was flying out that afternoon from Pharaoh airport.

"It's luvly 'ere, what's it like on the other side of the island?"

"Do you have any idea where you are at all?" I enquired.

"No, not really. I'm usually too stoned to care, if you really want to know."

"Stoned on what?" Tommy asked.

"Hash oil man. I smuggled it in no sweat. I've got a last bit left if you want to try it 'cos I sure ain't risking taking nothing back."

I'd never got involved with drugs of any kind up to that point. For a start, it was obviously illegal with severe penalties – at least prison, probably ten years hard labour. I had no idea; it just wasn't done. We had enough problems as it was with the non-stop drinking and partying. I'd seen it in Ibiza and the state the hippies were in on acid and mescaline. Dick's brother with his heroin habit destroying his life. People jumping out of windows on LSD convinced that they could fly. No thanks, you're not getting me into that stuff. I liked to be in control.

We sat in the Mercedes by the gardens and watched the Brummy from the cafe roll his joint. He smeared the brown oil onto the cigarette paper. The oil was contained in what looked like a tiny bottle of eyedrops. He then put some more drops onto the tobacco. We sat there trying to look inconspicuous with all the windows closed. He lit it up and took a few deep drags and then passed it on first to Jimmy then Tommy then to me. "No thanks, not for me" I said, pushing it away from me.

"Go on,Dad, it won't hurt you." The fumes in the enclosed space had already made me dizzy. Jimmy stuck the joint in my mouth. "Get yer lips round that yer poof." What could I do other than succumb to peer pressure and all that malarkey?

We sat in the smoke-filled car. We could hardly breathe. Slowly we opened the windows to let some fresh air in. We sat there for ages in complete silence. First off everything was a blur and nothing seemed to matter anymore. Things were spinning around in my head, but I wasn't feeling sick just numb. No one spoke for ages until someone said, "What the fuck is he doing?"

"Who?" I asked.

"That bloke in the garden."

I looked over in the direction they were pointing. There was a council worker being observed by, presumably, his foreman, tapping little sticks, a bit bigger than your normal lollipop stick, into the lawn that surrounded the flower beds and the paths.

"What the hell is he doing that for?"

"God knows. He's got hundreds of them in his bag."

Totally stoned we sat there for ages, just looking at him in amazement.

The garden lawn was beginning to look like a military cemetery in miniature. "Dad, go and ask him what he's doing."

"I don't think I am able to walk at the moment; my legs have turned to jelly."

"Go on Dad you'll be alright."

I almost fell out of the car as I made my way slowly towards the gardener. I was making a conscious effort not to do anything that would give the game away – that I was in fact mentally far, far away in an elliptic orbit around the moon. I politely asked the stick man why he was doing what he was doing. He told me. I said, "obrigado" and went back to the car to tell them. When I reached the vehicle, I lent on the roof to repeat the answer to my friends through the open windows.

As I tried to get the words to come out of my mouth it occurred to me that the answer that I had been given was so ridiculous that I couldn't actually say anything, because the whole situation had got the better of me and my hysterical laughing had started.

"Come on, tell us!"

"Stop crying, get a grip!"

I was doubled up in pain from the laughing and what made it worse was it wasn't even funny – but I was 'stoned, man!'

I tried to pull myself together. "He said it was to stop . . . " I broke down again making donkey noises. "People . . . walking on the . . . grass!"

The car doors opened, and Jimmy actually fell in the road holding his stomach with laughter. The other two sat on a bench hugging each other, having convulsions. The man from Birmingham had one of those loud laughs like a hyena; he had lost control of his face and had nasal fluid and tears dripping from his chin – not a pleasant sight on anyone at the best of times. Everyone in a twenty-metre radius came over to see what all the noise was about . . . inconspicuous? . . . not really. One of the bystanders started guffawing not exactly with us but because of us. This set off a chain reaction to the point that everyone around was laughing and nobody knew why. It took us a long time to recover from that episode.

59

Punch-Up At The Beach

ONE AFTERNOON the three of us were driving around trying to make our minds up as to where to go selling. We opted for Praia d'Oura, a few kilometres east of Albufeira. It was getting towards the end of the season, so we didn't expect anyone else to be selling in that spot. When we arrived, there was only one person there and he had taken up the whole area with his paintings. It was Fernando from Vale de Éguas, the communist with the German shepherd who had not only ripped John Greene off but had now copied the idea. We had stopped doing the paintings by then to concentrate on the names and the lumies.

We despised him. Why was John dead and not him? Life isn't fair sometimes. This was the first time I'd seen him again since John's accident. We knew he was around but until that day we had somehow managed to avoid each other.

There is a very steep hill going down to the beach and the official selling place was by the bottom of the road where the taxis and coaches could turn around. I parked the car as near as I could up the hill. We opened the boot, took out our table and all the boxes of letters and strolled down to face him.

Tommy moved two of his works of art to one side to make room for our table. We opened up all the boxes containing the letters all neatly sorted into compartments and I sat down ready for business to begin, while the other two hovered around waiting to see if he would be crazy enough to try anything. Fernando came over to me and in a fit of temper knocked over my table, scattering the letters all over the road.

Jimmy started barking orders: "Dad – get the car quick and chuck everything in the boot. Keep the engine running!"

"Tommy, start smashing all his paintings." Then, addressing Fernando, "You, yer bastard!"

Jimmy was much smaller than Fernando, but he certainly knew how to fight. Him and his younger brother had been two of the leaders of the Everton supporters who had regular battles with rival clubs. Fernando never knew what hit him and in seconds he was rolling on the ground holding a bloody nose screaming in agony. Meanwhile Tommy had jumped on every one of his paintings, destroying everything in his path, and then for good measure took a running leap and kicked Fernando hard in the teeth.

With the noise of all his cries, loads of Portuguese lads from the beach cafe came running towards us.

"Get in the fucking car quick," we all shouted at each other.

My brother David, Jimmy, Me and Tommy

I leapt into the driver's seat and began driving up the hill. I could see Jimmy and Tommy being chased by a noisy mob of angry locals. As it was such a steep hill, the car was still hardly moving. I'd left the back doors open so that Jimmy and Tommy would be able to get in. They soon caught me up and dived into the back with the car accelerating away from the chasing pack. One or two of the fitter ones actually got their hands on the boot but fell by the wayside once we got going.

When Tommy had kicked Fernando in the teeth, he'd come off probably worse than his victim. He had a deep cut in his foot, as he had been wearing flip-flops. He wrapped his foot in a towel and he needed stitches for sure. We drove to Albufeira hospital, which is above the tunnel and opposite the GNR police station. We hadn't been there long when Fernando arrived in an ambulance. He came into the same waiting room, holding his nose which had now swollen up, so it was even bigger than it was before.

I phoned my favourite waiter and old friend Alistair to ask him if he could help as we were in a spot of bother. He soon arrived on the scene, by which time the injured parties had been treated and were now being questioned by the police. Alistair told them what had happened and what had gone on in the past and luckily for us that was the end of the matter. We had to have a police escort to our car as some of the angry mob were still hanging around.

Tommy had had a few stitches in his foot, I presumed Fernando's nose was broken. Jimmy left him with a parting taunt of, "That was for John yer bastard!" That night in Albufeira our 'incident' was the talk of the town. The gossips were having a field day and we weren't very popular, to put it mildly. As one of our 'friends' put it:

"We don't mind you being here having fun, but you can't go around beating Portuguese people up. You're here as our guests and you should remember that."

I think what saved us from further retribution was that nobody knew Fernando particularly well, and the ones that did, disliked him. We had to tread carefully for a while after that.

60
Olive Branch

ONE DAY we were driving around in the countryside when we found ourselves caught up in a long queue of vehicles. After waiting for an eternity, we had almost reached the front. It was obviously some kind of road maintenance that was causing the hold up as the traffic control was being directed by a council worker holding a sign which was green on one side and red on the other. He was letting about ten cars through at a time, which vanished from view round a bend, about three minutes later some cars drove past in the opposite direction.

Finally, it was our turn. We were the last ones to be let through on that turn, and the red/green man gave Jimmy, who was sitting in the back with the window open, a freshly cut branch of an olive tree and said something to him.

"What did he say?" I asked.

"Dad, do you think that overnight I have suddenly mastered the Portuguese language?"

"Maybe it's a peace offering?" Tommy suggested.

I was getting annoyed with them by then. "Look, he must have given it to you for a good reason."

"An olive branch symbolises peace."

"We're not at war with him, we have never laid eyes on him before, what are you going on about?"

Jimmy was sniggering in the back. "He's taking the peace! Get it?"

We carried on driving for a while and came up behind another queue of traffic. When we got close to the front we watched to see if any bits of a tree changed hands. Sure enough, the last car to go through was given a branch. We then watched the cars coming the other way and the last one to come past stopped and gave the sign man a familiar looking piece of foliage. Tommy wasted no time in explaining how it worked.

"I get it now, that's how they know it's the last car – very clever system."

"Thanks Einstein, you know what that means don't you and, by the way, what became of ours Jimmy?"

"I threw it out of the window."

"So the next lot of cars where we were are probably still waiting."

Tommy was more confident: "They'll have sorted it out. Why don't they give you a proper stick with something written on it, like 'hand this in at the other end please', in three or four languages?"

I tried to help keep calm.

"You may not have noticed,Tommy but most people who live here can speak Portuguese."

But I must admit that they were extremely unfortunate to pick Jimmy, possibly the only person on the road that day, who was incapable of one simple task. All it involved was transferring a small piece of tree from the hands of one road person into the safe hands of another.

On the way back we 'branched' off the main road and took a different route in case they were on the look-out for us. It was getting dark. The usual push-bikes and motorbikes without lights were there to contend with. Cars with one headlight, the occasional horse and cart, holes in the road – all part of a normal night's journey. We were cruising along when out of nowhere there was a rock lying in the middle of the road. I only saw it at the last minute, the front wheels just missed it but then there was a loud Bang! It had hit the floor of the car in the back. The rock had smashed the chassis and the road was now visible through a hole in the floor. This was our punishment for messing up the traffic control system.

We kept on driving – and we now had air-conditioning. The next day at Brent's, the mechanic in Almancil, we were told that the car would soon break into two halves as it was splitting apart in the middle. Our vehicle's days were numbered, so we decided to sell it for parts and go back to the UK. The season was virtually over, we'd had an excellent summer business-wise and a lot of fun on the way.

1979

61
Shellfish Behaviour

AT THE end of last season, with the cash from the sale of the Mercedes, I'd bought a newer version of the VW van from Nobu our Japanese friend. Jimmy and Tommy went back to Touro campsite. I was destined for another winter back on the taxis in Bedford – which I found seriously depressing after two years away. I was lucky to get my old job as one of the regular drivers, Peter, dropped dead of a heart attack thus creating a vacancy for me to fill. After that I was stuck with the label, 'Dead Man's Shoes'.

In the spring of that year I met a lovely girl called Germaine. She was very attractive, with long brown curly hair. She'd been living with a well-known tough character and they had a young son together – but they had now split up. She had her own house, so I moved in with her and her son. She herself was a bit of a 'wild child' so she was ready for a bit of an adventure. She agreed a deal with her parents and her 'ex' that the boy could stay with them for the summer while we went back to the Algarve.

Over the winter I'd been in touch with Jimmy and Tommy who had both returned home. We arranged to all meet up again at José's house and do more of the same. By early June we were up and running but now we all had our own transport. It soon became apparent that Germaine didn't get on with the other two and that they didn't much like her either. Then Jimmy's girlfriend from Liverpool came out to stay, who took an instant dislike to me – I don't know why. Tommy said she wanted Jimmy for herself.

Then we had a visit from Jimmy's brother Kidda, who was a giant version of Jimmy but much younger, maybe only 19 at the time. He was a menacing figure and although he wore glasses there was something scary about him. Jimmy didn't really want him there; he was too much to handle. They got into so many arguments that it was ruining the status quo. One afternoon Kidda brought Jimmy home, carrying him like a sack of potatoes over his shoulder. They had got drunk and Kidda had beaten him up after yet another row. They made up the next day but things between all of us would never be the same.

We'd been having some issues with a gang of Brazilians in Praia de Oura, which in those days was just a dirt road and a make-shift tourist market. The South Americans had muscled in on our patch and were selling *heishi* necklaces the same as ours. These necklaces were made from shells and were all the rage. The white band around a brown neck looked stunning and everybody was wearing them.

Kidda took it upon himself one morning to get rid of the Brazilians. He began the day early one morning at the cafe around the corner from our house by ordering a crate of beer and sat there until he had drunk all 24 bottles. He then got in Jimmy's van and went off to sort out our competitors.

The fact that he didn't have a driving licence or any real experience behind the wheel hadn't deterred him. What exactly happened when he arrived there I'm not entirely sure; all I do know was that the next time we went to sell there we were told by the police to leave and never come back.

Tommy had had enough and moved down to the west coast to do his own thing. We split the money up and he left on reasonably good terms. Germaine and I moved out too, a short while later and found a flat in Albufeira. I carried on working with Jimmy but at a safe distance. For some time, we had been trying to get a permit to sell in the street in Albufeira but all the licences were spoken for. The only alternative was to sell through someone else.

We knew Pedro, a young fisherman, who had a licence but all he used to sell were things like shells with 'Algarve' written on them with a felt-tip pen. We hadn't seen him for a long time. He was a bit, let's say 'simple' or 'a couple of sardines short of a basketful'. We put the word round that we were looking for him and eventually we were able to track him down.

We couldn't believe our eyes when he we met up with him. The once scruffy street urchin had been transformed into a man about town. He was wearing what appeared to be the equivalent to an Armani suit, a polo-neck shirt, shiny new shoes, was clean-shaven and even had a trendy haircut.

"Wow, what happened to you?" I asked him innocently.

He just giggled and looked embarrassed. He then confessed that he was basically a rent boy and that some foreigners paid him handsomely for sexual favours. Just for good measure he lifted up his jacket at the rear, bent over a table and gave a very realistic impersonation of someone taking him from behind. He then went on to tell us that he quite liked it and that he didn't need to go fishing anymore or, more importantly, need to sell in the street – so we could have his place. For a moment I was wondering if I should return the favour in some way – but bearing in mind what he had just said I couldn't be arsed.

It was hard to believe what I had heard and the matter of fact way that he talked about it, as if it was a new job he'd just started. He'd learnt a smattering of English despite his intellectual failings. He strongly denied that he was a homosexual and said that he now had a girlfriend to prove it. Some of his friends were doing it as well because they could 'earn' something like the equivalent of a month's money in one night. I thought I'd seen and heard it all up to that point, I hadn't exactly had a sheltered existence, but I'll be buggered if I can remember such a queer affair.

We employed Deca, a young lad from Angola, as our salesperson while we got on with more important things like relaxing on the beach and eating out. We spent quite a lot of time with Nobu who was still doing his wire names. Most of the time we could never really understand what he was saying but he was such a pleasant young man to be with and always the gentleman.

The latest craze at the time was karate and kung-fu. Every male between 15 and 30 seemed to have suddenly become martial arts experts. They were sticking their hands into bags of rice, kicking each other in the face, punching planks of wood, making silly noises like 'Woo waa Hay yah', with their arms flying in all directions. They were all budding Jackie Chans and Bruce Lees, desperate to use their new powers.

As Nobu was Japanese the locals presumed that he was at least a black belt. One night he was alone and a bit drunk waiting to get into a club. The doorman refused him entry and challenged Nobu to attack him so that he could show off his skills. Nobu bowed and turned his back on the man in an attempt to defuse the situation. The doorman karate chopped him in the neck and punched him in the face breaking his jaw.

This time we had to drive to Portimão hospital where the unfortunate João had been operated on. Tommy joined us on the visit – they were the best of friends. His jaw was wired up, he could hardly open his mouth and could only feed himself through a straw. The doctor told him that he could leave the next day and that it would be about six weeks before they could remove the wire. Poor bloke he was painfully thin as it was, there wouldn't be much left of him by the time he had fully recovered. The wire man had been wired up.

If conversation with him had been difficult before, we had now reached the realms of absurdity. The only sounds he came out with were "nnnnyyyynnnng" or the more difficult "shhhkoiko" and "heeeennnuuttttta". He couldn't laugh either; he closed his eyes and stretched his lips as far as he could, exposing his wired-up teeth with an "aaahsoo". From then on, he had to write everything he needed on a pad but at least he was able to get back to work. He quietly told me that it would have been far worse if he had broken his wrist... well, I think that's what he said.

By mid-September Germaine had had enough. She was missing her son; she was homesick and was tired of the Jimmy and girlfriend situation; so, we drove back to England rather prematurely. Not a year to remember. When we got home, she told me that our relationship was over and kicked me out. I was devastated at the time, feeling sorry for myself again. I found it difficult to accept rejection.

The bleak prospect of another stint on the taxis and finding somewhere to live was almost too much to bear. I began to wonder how much longer I could persist in this pursuit of happiness or whatever I was searching for. I was in my element in Portugal – the hot weather, the beaches, dining out, making easy money. I felt at home. Here in Bedford I was a nobody. I had to trust in my belief that I was only temporarily passing through and that I would soon be back on my feet again.

My old friend Mick from school kindly offered to rent me a room in his house. His mother had died some years ago of MS. His father started a new life after years of watching his poor wife slowly deteriorate. He had just found a new lease of life when he was diagnosed with a terminal illness and passed away shortly afterwards, still relatively young. Mick was the oldest of the four children. Because of his mother's disability he was probably the only boy at school that had to make and bring in his own lunch every day. After the death of both his parents he received some inheritance and purchased a property in quite a well-to-do part of the town. His youngest brother was in a famous orchestra and had a promising career ahead of him – but then he became unwell and died of leukaemia in his early twenties. Some families are blighted by tragedy.

I returned to my job as a taxi driver, but this time on the rank at St Peter's or the bus station. It was worse than ever, but I soon became good friends with some of the drivers, which helped me get through the long days.

I had found a new girlfriend. Her name was Louise, she was young, beautiful and highly intelligent. She'd been in the local newspapers as she had contracted meningitis after being raped by a drug addict. She was 17 or 18 and still at the High School studying for her A-Levels. It was big news at the time because it was thought that she was going to die. Somehow, she defied all the odds and made an incredible recovery. She had been in intensive care and there were worries that she might have suffered brain damage, which was possible in these cases, but she had amazed everybody and was well on her way to a full recovery.

When I met her at a local dance she was almost back to normal and had only recently started going out at night again. I overheard some lads saying that she wasn't right in the head, a drug addict and unclean. No one would dance with the poor girl. Despite the way people behaved towards her she had risen above all the gossip – she didn't care, she was enjoying herself, she was simply glad to be alive.

I wasn't interested in the stories. I'd never heard or read anything about her. We started to see each other mainly at the weekends as she was still at school finishing her A-Levels. She had missed a year because of what had happened to her. She was an exceptional student and would soon be going to university. She had her own car so we would meet at her local pub in Bromham. This was to avoid her parents seeing me pick her up in a VW van with only curtains and a mattress in the back.

After we'd been together for a while, I was forced into having dinner with her parents – her mother was curious and wanted to meet me. They were very posh and weren't at all impressed with me or my credentials. That came as a surprise. A wealthy couple watching their only daughter stepping out with her new boyfriend, a 31-year-old long-haired taxi driver with zero prospects. I could imagine the conversation after we'd departed the mansion.

"I say Naomi, future captain of industry that young man – perfect match for our Louise. Let's hope he asks her to marry him, eh what!"

1980

62

Life Threatening

THE MAJORITY of my time between January and March was spent sitting at the taxi rank playing with a puzzle that Louise had given me. She had found it in a craft shop in a local village called Ampthill. There was a leaflet only in Hungarian included in the package and the word Rubik. It must have been one of the first ever to be seen in the UK. I was obsessed with trying to solve it. I had a notepad full of intricate steps and elaborate moves that I had devised. If a passenger got in the back of my taxi while I was in the process of a 23-step manoeuvre I would apologise and discreetly carry on fiddling with it between my legs until I had finished. I dread to think what they must have thought I was doing.

In the middle of March, I had my Eureka! moment. I had the whole puzzle completed except for two pieces that needed swapping around. After a couple of twists, they reappeared, but this time in the correct places. Months later it seemed like everyone owned one – they were on TV, there were even books by mathematicians explaining all the short cuts. I had all sorts of strange people coming to see me asking for help with their cubes.

My other puzzle was with whom, how and when I was going to return to Portugal. My mate Gordon, a colleague on the taxis was game and then a friend of a friend Pat decided he would come along too. Gordon was well-built, the sort of bloke you would expect to see in the middle of a rugby scrum, but he was seriously overweight. Pat was Irish, tall and thin. They both had wicked senses of humour, but they didn't really know each other, so I wasn't sure whether we would all get along.

Louise had a German girlfriend in Munich, so we got in touch with her and in early June the three of us set off for Germany. It had been difficult for me to leave Louise behind because she was special, but it had to be done. We made the same journey as I had made before and bought another rusty, grey Mercedes. Two days later we were in the Algarve. The other two had already fallen out with each other en route when Gordon was driving through Lisbon. We had been struggling to find the correct route onto the bridge. Pat was navigating at the time and threw the map out of the window in frustration. Gordon wasn't happy and this set the tone for the rest of what was to be a short trip.

We found temporary accommodation in Albufeira and we were soon out looking for selling places. Jimmy had arrived earlier in the season and with his girlfriend had most of the best places sewn up. I had a long chat with him about who should sell where and when and I reminded him that it was me that had introduced him to the Algarve – but he wasn't having any of it. We finished up falling out with each other, which was a pity as we had had some great times together.

Pat, Gordon and I found a few places where we could sell without crossing Jimmy's path and things began to improve. We moved into a little house in Guia, a village west of Albufeira. To celebrate our new-found accommodation, we hit the town in buoyant mood. By the time we arrived at the posh restaurant that we had chosen for the evening, Pat and I were so pissed that we ended up singing the menu from the lectern – not to everyone's amusement.

Later on that evening we went to Silvia's club. We were still in great spirits and congratulating ourselves that the future was looking bright for us, despite all the aggravation from Jimmy. I went upstairs to the balcony to observe the dancing below when I felt a tap on my shoulder. It was Jimmy.

"Dad, you better get out of here now – me brother-in-law is in here somewhere looking for you. She hates you so much that she's told her brother to do you in. If he finds you, he'll throw you over that fucking balcony!"

I found Pat and Gordon, told them what had happened, and we legged it out of the club and the town as fast as possible. Jimmy had said that it would be safe to come back in a couple of weeks but to keep well away, as the brother-in-law was seriously dangerous and would stop at nothing. When we got back to the house in Guia, Pat and Gordon were understandably annoyed with me, as I had never mentioned to them that I was involved with all this violence. Our whole world had fallen apart around us in just a matter of minutes.

I tried to explain what had gone on in the past and that this was none of my doing but we were all justifiably scared, so we packed up our belongings and just left, there and then, and began the long drive back home. On the way back we were driving along in the middle of France somewhere when there was a loud bang: a stone had shattered the windscreen. We pulled over. There were thousands of tiny pieces of glass all over the car and ourselves. We were tired and irritable. Gordon was becoming progressively more annoyed with Pat.

When we had cleaned ourselves up and picked up most of the glass from the inside of the car, we set off again. It was cold, windy and the ominous black clouds meant heavy rain was on its way. It was Pat's turn to drive. Gordon was in the passenger seat at the front, well wrapped up, wearing his sunglasses ready for what was going to be a very unpleasant journey. Gordon turned to Pat and warned him: "Drive slowly otherwise we'll freeze to death – and don't do anything to wind me up."

Pat started the engine and in what could have been a scene from a Laurel and Hardy sketch, squirted the windscreen washer liquid all over Gordon's face. Gordon just sat there for a while with the wind blowing in his face. He was big and strong but always very calm. He looked at Pat and simply said, "You stupid boy, – don't you ever do that again, or else!"

We arrived back in England later that day. We had been blown to bits by the lack of a windscreen but had avoided most of the rain.

In Bedford everyone was shocked to see us back home again so soon. After a few days of confusion and indecision Gordon and I agreed that we would give it another go, but somewhere well away from Albufeira. We still had a large amount of stock to sell that we had invested in, apart from the silver letters, so why not? We had the car fixed and a week later the two of us were back in the eastern end of the Algarve in Tavira.

63
Tavira

WE FOUND a cheap room in a place called Residencial Imperial, right on the riverfront overlooking the marketplace and the River Gilão. The rooms in the establishment were very basic and the facilities left a lot to be desired. The plumbing and electrical systems had seen better days. Hot water in the only available bathroom was a bit hit-and-miss and flushing the toilet involved tugging really hard on a long piece of string attached to the cistern high up near the ceiling. I was convinced that sooner or later the whole thing would come off the wall and do someone some serious damage. The flush water would send shockwaves reverberating through the water pipes, making them bang against the wall. If you turned on a light in the kitchen, for example, the hall light would go out. If someone rang the bell outside, that tripped the fuse and all the lights went out.

The lady of the house Maria Ludovina was such a warm and friendly host that we learnt to put up with all the shortcomings of our new home. She gave us the best room at the front but warned us that occasionally we would have to be moved, as the one at the front had been booked for some of the summer. Her husband João was an alcoholic who could barely walk or see properly. When he shuffled around the house, he had to hold onto the furniture to find his way around and stop himself falling over. He had been a tuna fisherman, a very arduous and dangerous profession. He didn't like the daylight; he never left the premises. He would turn off the fuse at night so none of the lights worked. This meant that a trip to the toilet at night would often end in bumping into a total stranger trying to get to grips with the layout of their new surroundings while in total darkness.

Worse still was the man himself. He often got up late into the night staggering around in the dark looking for more of the local 'firewater' that Ludovina had tried to hide from him. Luckily, you could smell the stench of his breath well before knocking into him and maybe exchange a polite "Boa noite" with him in passing. Purely for safety reasons we invested in a torch but even with that I had some scenes that wouldn't have looked out of place in a horror film. First of all, you would hear the creaking of the rotten floorboards, then the torchlight would catch the shadowy outline of a skinny figure, with a bottle attached to its face, murmuring eerie, ghostly sounds. I don't scare easily, but some nights, after a skinful, I must admit that I freaked out once or twice. In the mornings Gordon, I and quite a few other guests would often find ourselves comparing each other's hair-raising events of the previous night's trip across the 'landing from hell'. That poor woman, trying to look after her husband and run what was basically 'Nightmare on Elm Street: The Boarding House'. I really admired her spirit. (Actually it's on Largo Dr.José Pires Padinha which doesn't exactly roll off the tongue.)

The town had a pleasant vibe and people in general were very warm towards us. Tourism hadn't arrived in Tavira and I think that's how they wanted it to stay. The more discerning type of visitors who had ventured off the beaten track were the only foreigners to be seen. I knew all the waiters from the Beira Rio restaurant, so over a period of time they introduced us to many of the local characters. There was no nightlife to speak of, so we had to be content with hanging around the cafes and bars. There was little or no chance of meeting any available young ladies, it was all very old fashioned. I quite liked it once we'd relaxed and settled in. It certainly was nothing like the madness that I was used to before. As Jimmy's mum had put it when he had complained to her about his lack of sex: "If you can't get yer end away in Albufeira you might as well fucking forget it!"

Gordon and I started selling in Vila Real in the daytime and Monte Gordo at night. We took it in turns, as we needed to take a break from each other. Spending too much time together wasn't healthy, so once Gordon had got into the swing of things, I would leave him and spend a day on what must be some of the best beaches you're ever likely to come across. Even the sea was warmer and calmer in the eastern part of the coast. You could literally walk for miles without hardly seeing another human being, even in the height of the season. If these beaches were in Spain, there would have been Benidorms sprouting up everywhere.

After a day's selling and talking to all kinds of tourists, Gordon's accent would change according to who he had met that day. I would arrive to pick him up and ask him how he had got on and he would say, "Ain't sold owt – trooble up mill lad." The next day it would be, "Alright mate, help me up the apples and pears – where's the motor, geezer?" or, "Och aye the noo Jimmy" or "Hi there are you from the States?" He even got me at it in the end. We could spend a whole evening speaking to each other in pidgin Italian, Chinese French, German, Liverpudlian – you name it.

Gordon was an unfortunate name to have in Portugal, as the word "gordo" means 'fat' – so that became his official title. He tolerated most of the abuse, and only once got really angry after he'd had some gin which he had warned me had a strange effect on him. He became touchy about certain subjects that he wouldn't normally care about, so they were never mentioned again, and he kept off the gin.

Guerreiro was the name of the head waiter at the Beira Rio restaurant. He and his wife had recently opened their own place just around the corner, near the centre of town. It was called Ponto de Encontro (the meeting place), so for dinner we alternated between the two. The Beira Rio was now run by the young men that Guerreiro had trained: Eduardo, Vitor, Romba (aka Speedy) and others.

One memorable evening we were invited to present the prizes to the winners of the top members of staff from the *Paga pouco* shops, which were owned by the same person as the Beira Rio restaurant. We sat at the top table with some of the local dignitaries in a church hall. There were a lot of long-winded speeches – thankfully we weren't asked to stand up and say anything. All we had to do was read out a few names which Gordon had been practising in a Cornish accent, just to further confuse everybody. He stood up and with a ridiculous dead-pan expression on his face deliberately read out the names so badly that the prize winners couldn't understand or hear anything, as the noise of the audience's laughter was deafening.

"Miguel António Carvalho" became "Me gwell ant on eeo car val ho." "Claudia Piedade Nascimento – Claw deer pie dad nash cement". After one or two more I was forced to take over. At the end of the proceedings and after more champagne we were both given a standing ovation – by which time Gordon was so drunk that he was starting to look a bit unsteady on his feet. When the event was over Gordon was nowhere to be seen. I presumed that he'd done the sensible thing and gone back to our room.

The hazy walk back into town suddenly seemed too far for me so I 'borrowed' a pushbike that I'd almost fallen over. I freewheeled down the hill towards the Roman bridge that crossed the river in the centre of the town. The road was normally empty, but for some reason all the traffic on both sides of the river was backed up. There was a lot of horn blowing and shouting, which at around midnight in this sleepy town wasn't normal. I weaved my way through all the cars until I finally reached the bridge.

In the middle of the bridge there was a large figure stopping all the traffic. It was Gordon. He was checking everyone's documents. When I arrived he held up a big hand to stop me and just said one word: "Passport."

"What the hell do you think you are doing?"

"Passport."

I couldn't imagine where he had got them from, but he was wearing a hat and had a bag slung over his shoulder to make him look more official. He wasn't allowing any of the cars to pass until he had inspected the driver's car documents. I tried to reason with him.

"Passport!"

"It's me you idiot – the police will be here in a minute."

"Passport!"

Then I thought, oh yes, the police, I'd just nicked someone's bike. I had better dump it before they arrive. When I returned, the traffic was moving, the police weren't there and Gordon had left. I went to our room and found him flat out face down on his bed snoring like a pig. The next morning, he had no recollection of the bridge incident and denied any wrongdoing. Amongst the townspeople he had gained overnight fame or infamy depending on who you spoke to.

"What got into you last night then? I've never seen you in such a state before," I asked him.

"I'll tell you, what got into me was the beer, then the wine, the brandy, the champagne, more wine and then after that I've no idea, it's all a blur. I do have a vague memory of knocking someone's hat off their head and wearing it for a while but that's all."

Another night we went to watch our waiter friends river fishing on the end of a pontoon in the middle of town. I joined in by attaching a beer crate to a rope and threw it off the end of the jetty. The boys soon packed up as the tide was going out and they hadn't caught anything. Just for fun I pulled up my crate from the murky muddy depths and it seemed to be twice as heavy as it was before. I dropped it onto the boards and in the darkness put my hand inside. Shining in the moonlight I saw a huge octopus tentacle wrapping itself around my arm. According to eyewitnesses I ran down the pontoon screaming, "Sea monster! Sea monster!" What did I say about not being scared easily? I had nightmares for days after that – and what was even worse was the lads continually repeating the story to all and sundry every time the word fishing was mentioned.

On the ferry on our way back from one of our trips over to Spain we bumped into Jimmy and his brother Kidda. We had a few beers together but underneath the exchange of pleasantries there was a very tense atmosphere. They had been over the river for the same reason and for a moment I was sure that there was going to be trouble. When the short journey was over, we shook hands and went our separate ways. Gordon and I were both very relieved that we didn't have to see them too often. My friends had now become my enemies and competitors – not fair at all but that's the way it goes sometimes.

Gordon and I stayed for more than three months at the Imperial. Ludovina had become like a second mother to both of us. She did all our washing and tolerated some of our crazy nights. She didn't even complain too much when we threw most of the contents of our room out of a back window.

It had all started when Gordon had asked me to throw over the bottle of orange juice. Taking things a bit too literally, I threw the plastic bottle half full of liquid at him. It just missed his head and flew out of the window which, luckily, was open at the time. He then picked up a book and threw it at me. I chucked it back straight out of the window again. Things got seriously out of hand after that. I don't know why, maybe we had gone stir-crazy. When we'd finished, there were only the two beds and mattresses, a wardrobe and some of our clothes left in the room. Chairs, cupboards, side-tables, even the bedside lights were lying piled on top of each other down an inaccessible shaft.

The next morning, we were ashamed of what we had done and so we should have been. I asked Ludovina to come and inspect the vandalism. She was visibly shocked, and I was expecting the worst: police, expulsion, the end of the line for us probably. She asked me why. I explained that we'd got into a silly fight but that we were friends again. We apologised over and over again and promised to pay for all the damage. She took it all in her stride and even had a little giggle about it afterwards. Just like your mum did when she caught you being naughty; boys will be boys after all. Which was fine, but we were both in our thirties.

I thought we might get a visit from a psychiatrist but instead a man in grey overalls came to see us, with a little boy who climbed down the shaft with a rope. Using a block and tackle they hauled the contents of our room back up to where it belonged. Most of the furniture was reasonably intact, despite the long drop it had experienced. They recovered everything, even the offending bottle of orange. We agreed a price on the damages and took her to the Beira Rio for dinner with some of her family, which was the least we could do considering. Gordon was convinced that we had become rock stars as some of the wilder ones smashed up their hotel rooms on a regular basis.

"It's the stress of being on tour, on the road for months on end in foreign places. It's only natural that you have to unwind at some stage, otherwise you'll go insane," he explained, trying to justify our destructive behaviour.

"We're not quite The Who at the Hilton live in Tavira are we?" I replied sarcastically.

"The who?"

"Don't start!"

We left Tavira in mid-September. We'd enjoyed our stay there, thanks to the hospitality of the lovely people who make the place what it is. If you visit the town nowadays not a lot has changed. There is no traffic allowed to cross the Roman bridge anymore.

1981

64

Back To Square One

WE DROVE back to Bedford and picked up where we had left off. Louise had become a trainee nurse at The London Hospital instead of going to university. She owed her life to the medical profession and this was her way of paying back the debt. I went to visit her at weekends – they were making her life hell by giving her the toughest jobs, but she was so determined to prove herself that nothing was going to stop her achieving her goal.

I was soon back on the taxis, but this time based at the train station, which was almost a promotion. Another driver named Peter collapsed in my car while I was helping him with his crossword. He was taken away in an ambulance and died a few days later, so my sobriquet 'Dead Man's Shoes' was still alive and well. A few days later, in early December, I was sitting at the station in my new taxi that I had just inherited. I was listening to the radio when the terrible news came through that John Lennon had been assassinated in New York.

I'd met the Beatles in 1963 and helped them carry their equipment on stage at the Bedford Granada cinema before getting all four of their autographs. My generation was the 'Swinging Sixties' and to me John Lennon was the greatest. Why on earth would anyone murder him of all people? There are some global events that are so shocking that you will always remember where you were when they happened. This was one of them.

Over the last few years in Bedford I had remained good friends with Dick. He wanted to get away from Bedford and was ready for another trip to Portugal, so that June we set off once again, this time in his white Mark 3 Ford Cortina. We had planned a return to Albufeira but for some bizarre reason we opted for Monte Gordo instead. We rented a small house in town and sold our stuff in Vila Real during the day. At night Monte Gordo came to life for a couple of hours in the form of a street market. We had permission to sell but it wasn't very lucrative.

The town had little going for it except for the casino which was totally out of kilter with the rest of what was, basically, a fishing village without the usual charm that comes with it. Maybe it was the word Monte as in Carlo that made them think the place would attract playboys and millionaires. This was at the other end of the scale, where most of the gamblers were low-rollers from poor regions of Spain roughing it at the huge campsite.

We weren't particularly happy there but at least we were making a living, eating well and having fun. The people here were not as amiable as those in Tavira, which wasn't far away along the coast. It's almost part of Vila Real, which is on the border and strangely soulless – maybe they have an identity crisis brought on by their close proximity to Spain.

At least I was able to buy a copy of The Sunday Times every Monday for the price of a three-course meal. I used to disappear along the beach, far away from the hordes who seemed to enjoy sitting virtually on top of each other. Monte Gordo beach appears to be never-ending, but ninety percent of the sunbathers occupy only a few hundred metres of the same area of sand; safety in numbers maybe. Around one o'clock everyone leaves the beach for lunch. At three o'clock they all come back again and after an hour or so most of them fall asleep.

On one of my beach trips I spotted what looked like a group of naked young women sunbathing not that far away from me but just a bit too far to get a decent ogle. They were obviously well out of the way for a good reason. I was trying to think how I could get a bit closer to them without attracting suspicion or looking like some kind of pervert. It had to be subtle and look casual. Maybe one of them would go in the sea and I could dive in and pretend to drown or something. I considered gradually crawling along the sand on my elbows like the marines do under barbed wire, but that involved dragging a towel, a bag and a newspaper along with me. Then I came up with what I thought was a clever idea.

They were up-wind so I planned to 'accidently' let go of a page of my expensive newspaper when the next gust came along, which, if I managed to release at the precise moment, would flutter off in their general direction. I sat up looking as nonchalant as possible, preparing the middle page of the business section for take-off. When the gust finally arrived, it was more like a tornado that whipped up the sand and ripped practically the whole newspaper out of my grasp. Most of the sports section blew into the sea, the rest went quite high in the air before coming back to earth nowhere near my intended target. I ran down the beach swearing, while flapping my arms in the air trying to catch the torn airborne pieces. There were some crumpled parts that had come into land that I could still salvage. I must have looked like a complete moron – so much for the subtle approach.

But, as they say, 'It's an ill wind that blows nobody any good'; the naked girls were all having kittens while observing my antics. One of them came over to me with a ripped page in her hand. As it turned out they were topless but wearing tiny bikini bottoms pulled up halfway to their armpits. My visitor was English, attractive, petite, with a brown athletic body. She had medium-length hair and was very well-spoken. In a sexy, almost theatrical, voice, she introduced herself as Dee.

"Would you like to come and join us maybe we could all have a read of what's left of your newspaper?"

"How could I refuse? What the hell are you doing in a dump like this?" I replied, turning on the charm.

After I'd been introduced to the other five potential Miss World contestants, Dee sat down with me and gave me the lowdown.

"We're the showgirls at the casino. We dance there most nights. We'll be here for a month, then we move on to Vilamoura. We have to sunbathe almost naked as we can't have any unsightly bikini lines showing through our costumes. We usually walk a long way down the beach to keep out of sight all of the perverts."

"Well I spotted you without too much trouble, not that I'm a Peeping Tom or anything like that," I joked.

Later that evening we met up for Happy Hour cocktails in the bar below their apartment. I realised I was punching well above my weight but finding other British people in a foreign country is a great leveller. The common denominator of being from the same country can be sufficient to start a conversation with someone who you normally wouldn't associate with and vice-versa.

The girls turned out to be great fun and not at all stuck up or snobby. They were sick of the local gigolos trying to get in their pants. For Dick, all his Christmases had come at once – he didn't know where to start. I'd already fallen for Dee, so I told Dick to at least give me the first dibs with her; not that he ever took anything I said very seriously, especially where women were concerned.

The next evening was the girls' night off and we were invited to join them at their apartment for a small gathering after dinner. It might sound strange, but they looked even more attractive made up and with their clothes on. We had made an effort to look presentable, but we still looked scruffy next to the Portuguese and Spanish playboys and the casino regulars in their dinner jackets and fancy suits. We managed to park our Cortina amongst the Porsches, Mercedes and BMWs parked outside.

As the evening progressed the partygoers gradually relaxed and let their hair down and once everyone was a bit pissed nobody cared what you were wearing or what car you were driving. Dick and I had never been the greatest dancers and we looked even worse in the company of professionals. We had the girls in stitches with our performance and that impressed them a lot more than any show of wealth. They were as down to earth as we were, underneath all the glamorous facade.

Bring on the dancing girls... maybe not quite Vegas

I was quite shocked when Dee agreed to come home with me for the night. She wasn't exactly enthusiastic – more 'Ok but not for long and don't get your expectations up too high' but then renewed hope when she said: "I'll just get a few things to bring with me". She wasn't much younger than me and older than the other girls with the exception of the head girl, or 'captain' as they called her. So, having an occasional fling here and there was, I assumed, par for the course.

We had a fantastic night together and she confided in me that, despite the reputation of dancers in general, she and the other girls rarely got involved with anyone as it always became too complicated, or they were faithful to their steady boyfriends at home. They were a team, so when men were involved it could have a disruptive effect on the camaraderie of the group. Having said that, it didn't stop her moving in with me a few days later.

Dick hadn't been so fortunate with the girls but days later he picked up an older Spanish blonde lady who was the head of the Berlitz language school in Lisbon. So, for a while we were both enjoying female company whilst keeping our heads above water in the financial department.

65

Porto:

(Wrong Kind of Fireworks)

TOWARDS the end of June, Dick and I went on a trip to Porto to sell the lumies at the city's annual festival of São João. We drove to Lisbon, bought the lightsticks and then caught a train to Porto. When we arrived, we took a taxi to a cheap hotel in the centre. Dick's precious light-brown leather jacket was covered in oil stains picked up from the boot of the taxi, so he refused to pay the fare. The inevitable heated argument ensued with the driver threatening to call the police if we didn't cough up the cash – so by the time three or four more taxis arrived at the scene we took the sensible option and paid.

Once we were installed in the hotel I went downstairs to the bathroom and had a hot bath. When it was Dick's turn, he was soon back upstairs saying that he had to have a shower instead because the receptionist had taken off the taps of the bath as we were using too much gas and water. After dinner we went for a nightcap in a cafe near the hotel. There was hardly anybody inside what was a very dreary establishment. We ordered a couple of beers and sat down in a little alcove away from the rest of the patrons.

We were minding our own business when a young lady came and sat down next to us and asked if we needed anything from her. Dick jokingly suggested, "Twos up, eh Paul?" knowing full well that I was never going to let that happen. We declined her offer, so she left us but was soon back at our table with a saucer of peanuts, before leaving us in peace. We had two more beers and then asked for the bill.

When the bill arrived, it was about ten times more than I was expecting to pay. I called the man over and politely told him that there had been a mistake. He insisted that the amount was correct because we had had the privilege of extra entertainment and food. When we had stopped laughing, I asked to see the price list which they had to have by law. He refused, so I gave him what I considered to be the right amount. He started shouting at me and wagging his finger at me and mentioned something about the police.

At this point Dick took over. "If he so much as touches you I'll stick one on him, the bastard."

The proprietor looked at me and enquired as to what had been said.

I pointed at the money that I had put on the table and calmly advised him to take it or else.

"Or else what?" he answered in Portuguese.

I introduced him to Dick and slowly drew my fingers across my throat, which I assume he got the gist of. He thought about it for a while then picked up the cash and told us, "Vai para o caralho" (fuck you). Dick knew exactly what that meant but chose to ignore the insult. We had been told that the people from Porto used swear words quite liberally and that we should not be offended and also that they didn't take to outsiders as they were 'desconfiado' (suspicious). After our first day up north, we could certainly vouch for that.

The next day we locked ourselves in our room and began the lumie manufacturing process. We had green liquid, tubes, lightsticks and ice boxes spread all over the room, when the maid asked if we wanted the room cleaning. Dick told her, in Portuguese, to 'Fuck off'.

"If that's the way they talk to each other around here that suits me fine," he said angrily. "We'll sell tonight and then go back to Lisbon. I can't stand the place."

"I also heard that they have a reputation for being tight-fisted so we may have a bad night," I reassured him.

We began selling in the Praça da Liberdade, which is the main square in the centre. I went on one side; Dick went to the other. It was the 23rd of June, which is the eve of São João, the next day being a public holiday in Porto. The first potential buyer came over to me and asked me aggressively:

"Que merda é essa caralho?" (What's this shit, prick?) and then, if that wasn't bad enough, hit me on the head with a plastic hammer that made a squeaky noise. The square soon began to fill with punters and business eventually picked up, but nothing like we had hoped for – we had been told that half a million people attended some years. I never got used to being bashed over the head that night with the plastic hammers, although some of the young girls did it quite gently almost suggestively.

To be fair, it was a great spectacle. The hammer sellers were doing well but there were probably too many of them to be making a fortune. There was a fantastic atmosphere and they certainly knew how to have fun. Dick came over and joined me, as he was getting a load of hassle from the gypsies and other sellers. He hadn't been hammered too badly, as they couldn't reach his head, so they picked on other parts of his body.

When we had finished trading, we took our stuff back to the hotel and then went out to watch the fireworks and join in the celebrations. The rest of the night was spent literally getting hammered. We went back to Lisbon the next day and agreed that we should try some other places and go on tour instead of returning to the Algarve. We wanted to buy the whole stock from the light-stick supplier but there was no chance of them trusting us or giving us credit. We didn't have anything like enough money to do that... so I hatched a plan.

66

The Silver Coast

WE DIDN'T want to have to come back to Lisbon every time we needed to re-stock, as it would be too long a journey to keep repeating. After a bit of research, we picked a few places on a map and asked our supplier to send fifty sticks to each one *poste restante*. This meant that we would only pay for them when we collected them from the post office, so all we had to do was make enough cash in each place to have adequate funds before we arrived at the next one. The idea was sound, and it worked like a treat. We drove along the Costa da Prata, first stopping the night in Ericeira, then to Peniche, on up to São João do Porto. These were principally Portuguese-only holiday resorts that had never seen the lumies before, that's for sure.

We had to put up with all the silly questions, like:

"How long do they last?" Answer – eight hours.

"How can I stop the chemical reaction?" Answer – put them in the freezer.

"What kind of freezer?" Answer – we can recommend any good quality domestic appliance.

"If I buy three, how much discount do I get?" Answer- none.

It was always difficult to get the ball rolling but once a few kids walked about with them on their heads or around their necks we were up and running. We perfected the technique of selling them as slowly as possible at the beginning, to attract a crowd, and then we would reach tipping point, when it seemed that everyone wanted one at the same time.

The problem with the luminous necklaces is that they do only last a few hours, so the next day all that's left is a bit of tube. They are still green but that's all – so we always had to move on after one night's selling, otherwise there would be a lot of dissatisfied customers wanting their money back. I used to try and explain that it was similar to buying an ice- cream. You pay for it, have it, it may not last long, but you've had your pleasure. Tomorrow you can do it all again. Or, as Dick put it so succinctly:

"Sounds like my fucking sex life!"

By the time we arrived in Nazaré we were financially secure for at least another few weeks. Despite our temporary success, Dick was obsessed with feeling that he had become a failure in life and that there was no real hope for either of us. As we were driving along that day, we were stuck behind one of those mobile caravans that selfishly hold up all the traffic for hours on end. Dick noticed that written on the back it had 'Westfalia' in big letters. "You see, there's the proof, I'm a failure." (His surname was West.)

In Nazaré we found a guest house on the seafront, after being pestered on the trip down the hill to the beach by women in traditional dress who seemed to be on every street corner with 'Room to Rent' signs. We learnt that the town was run by the women, who wore seven layers of skirts for some strange reason. The men were too busy working or talking about football in the cafes. The town is famous for its boats fishing in especially dangerous rough seas. Launching the vessels meant fighting against the power of huge waves. This was a challenge in itself and when the brave fishermen returned it took a load of bullocks (or oxen) to pull the fishing boats back out of the sea. As with many old traditions, technology, in the shape of tractors, eventually took over.

We were shown to our room by an odd character, who was so white he looked like he had never been outdoors. It was hard to guess his age – yet another one who would be in a care home in a different modern society, whereas here they looked after their own. There was a double bed and a single bed. As soon as our room attendant had closed the door, Dick dived onto the larger one to claim it before I had a chance. The bed collapsed underneath him as I sat on the smaller version watching the comedy show.

In front of the bed was a dilapidated brown wardrobe nearly as high as the ceiling. Dick pulled the handles on the two heavy doors that opened about halfway up the piece of furniture. The bottom half was a chest of drawers. The weight of the doors as they swung open and the excess force that he had used brought the top half down on top of him, knocking him backwards onto the bed that he had just spent ten minutes repairing.

"Right, that's it! That could have killed a normal person. Let's find somewhere a bit safer."

"We've already paid remember, so that won't be easy," I reminded him, trying to suppress my guffaws.

As Dick stormed out of the room the door handle came off in his hand when he opened it. Outside the door was our weirdo on his knees. He had been peeping through the keyhole. Dick picked him up and grabbed him by the throat.

"Put him down he's a simpleton," I pleaded.

"He's a perv, he needs locking up, this whole place is a madhouse!"

We complained to the management but all we got was the usual shrugging of shoulders, as if everything was perfectly normal. After repairing the furniture and blocking up the keyhole we got on with making the lumies to sell that evening. We sold out quickly that night, so it was a great success and one of the best places we'd ever been to. When we'd finished, we drove up to the top of the cliffs, where we had seen that there was a funfair in town.

There were the usual fairground attractions: dodgems, a carousel, a ferris wheel and dozens of stalls selling snacks, mostly 'farturas', which must be pronounced with care. 'Fart ur arse',as we called them,are hot donuts. They aren't sold in the shape of a normal round donut but in strips. The cook uses a large metal tube with a nozzle to squeeze the mixture in a circular motion into the boiling oil bubbling away in a metal bowl that is perched on a gas burner. In a matter of seconds, it's cooked, carefully pulled out with tongs, covered in sugar and cut up into manageable pieces. They usually have a strong cinnamon flavour. Business was booming, queues of families were patiently waiting for their turn, while their kids leant over the hot bowl which was inches from their faces – an accident waiting to happen if ever I saw one.

Dick had his eye on two pretty young women who were clearly enjoying his attention. They jumped onto a carousel, so we hopped on too. The contraption had swings on ropes attached to mechanical arms. All very tame we thought, until after a few slow laps the arms magically extended, and the speed was suddenly ramped up. Half of the ride was flying over the fairground but the other new, longer, part took us over the edge of the cliff, hundreds of feet above the sea and rocks below. Apart from my driving on certain occasions I'd never seen Dick so scared.

"Tell them to stop it now, I want to get off before a bolt comes loose or something. Get me off this fucking thing quick – I'm not joking!"

It was quite nerve-racking; the G-forces were throwing us about in all directions – but the whole point of the exercise was the thrill and to be frightened. Dick's panicking had ruined his attempt to impress the girls, who ran off giggling at the big tough guy quaking in his boots.

The following day we drove north to Figueira da Foz which is on the coast near the university city of Coimbra. Figueira, as it's known, is a port and a modern-looking resort – not very Portuguese at all. The streets in the centre are all straight in a criss-cross pattern like downtown Lisbon. We couldn't find a proper guest house, so we had to rent a room in a family house just outside the centre.

We were in the process of making the lumies in the afternoon when there was a knock at our bedroom door. The owner wanted to return our passports. The magic liquid formula contains two main chemicals, one of which is hydrogen peroxide. As most blondes know this is a bleach, so after messing about with it for hours on end not wearing gloves, your fingertips turn white. We tried to pretend that we were having a sleep, but he wouldn't go away. I turned the lights off. There was green liquid glowing in patches and spots all over the bed, the carpet and the furniture. I heard a key in the door turning the lock. I switched the lights back on and made the shush noise as the door began to open. Dick quickly laid on the bed 'asleep', I stuck my hand through a small gap in the door to accept the passports but kept my foot jammed against the door so that our landlord wouldn't be able to see what we were up to.

As I grabbed the documents from him all I could hear from the other side of the almost-closed door was "Que horror!" (literally, what horror!). The corridor was quite dark even during the daytime, so my glowing fingers had clearly shocked him. Through the gap in the door I tried to think of an explanation, but he had already had enough and was off back down the hallway, shaking his head and muttering something about crazy foreigners.

Dick said I should have worn the rubber gloves that we had bought, but which had turned out to be too slippery to use.

"Who wears rubber gloves when they are on holiday for goodness sake?" I asked.

"He probably thought you were giving me an enema when he saw all the tubes and the funnel," Dick suggested.

We must have come across as an odd pair that's for sure. He watched us like a hawk. Every time we went to the bathroom he was peering through the door at the end of the hall; even as we left for dinner carrying two heavy ice boxes, there he was, spying on us. He probably thought that the boxes contained body parts, very suspicious behaviour. I bet he was in our room nosing around as soon as we were out of sight.

After another good night's work, we only had a few lumies left over, so we packed up and had a few drinks before going back to our lodgings. Our landlord had asked us to try and be quiet on our return as they liked to go to bed early. It must have been well after midnight by the time we found the house and the alcohol had already slightly impaired our judgement. The harder we tried to be quiet, the noisier we became. Stupid childish giggling had set in and then our uncontrollable pig imitations started with loud snorting noises. Dick couldn't get the key to turn the lock. We quickly checked to make sure we were at the right house.

Dick whispered, "I can't open it, there must be a trick to it."

"Let me have a go you idiot, before you wake everybody. You probably have to shove the door at the same time."

At the precise moment that I tried the lock, while putting my full force behind the door, the landlord – who must have woken up with all the kerfuffle -suddenly opened it from the inside. I fell through the opening and onto his feet, throwing cold water, ice and the luminous contents of my picnic box (which I'd forgotten to close properly) all over him and his hallway. A woman, presumably his wife, and one or two other people in nightwear appeared, one armed with a stick, probably thinking that the man was being attacked; which wasn't far from the truth.

When things had calmed down and everybody had stopped shouting, we set about mopping up the mess that I had made. Our landlord wasn't happy with his now wet, luminous, pyjamas although actually they looked quite fetching. At least he let us sleep in his house that night, which was very generous of him under the circumstances. I gave him some extra escudos when we left and apologised for the 'accident'. In the meantime, Dick had had one of his laughing fits. He just wouldn't let it go. The sight of me lying on the floor after flying through the door and showering that poor man with ice and water had all been too much for him. He wouldn't let me forget about it.

" 'Let me have a go you idiot,' huh... wait until I tell your dancing friends!"

67

Monte Gordo Or Bust!

I HAD a pleasant surprise on my return. Dee (*above*) and the girls were still in town, as there had been a mix-up with their agent over their schedule. We had paid the rent for our house for another month, so everything was back to how we had left things – except that when we went to sell in the street that night we found someone had moved our table that we had put in place before we had gone for dinner. As we hadn't been there for a while the other sellers had wrongly presumed that we had left for good.

After dinner we parked our car in front of our official position to sort things out. Dick got out of the car with a baseball bat that he had hidden under the driver's seat. He then calmly proceeded to move all the other tables out of our spot and put ours back in its rightful place. As our competitors started to complain, Dick smashed the baseball bat down hard on our table and stared at the crowd of bemused street-sellers. At the top of his voice he shouted, "If anyone ever moves this table again, they'll get this wrapped round their head", pointing at the bat.

Funnily enough, after that we never had any problems with our selling position. In fact, our neighbours very generously gave us more room than we were used to. Dick had gained respect with most of the locals because of his show of strength. They all wanted to be his friend and shake his hand. A few nights later, while we were selling, he caught a black lad, who was with a big group of mates, stealing a piece of jewellery. Dick grabbed him, held him up with one hand then hung him up on some railings as he emptied his victim's pockets. None of his friends came to help him. Dick's reputation had spread far and wide.

I resumed where I had left off with Dee. I had been worried that in my absence she might have been seduced by one of her many admirers. Dick and I went to see the show in the Casino. I was expecting evening dress to be *de rigueur* but casual dress was acceptable. The show usually started around two in the morning, by which time most people had gone to bed, which meant most of the seats were empty nearly every night.

The girls' act was basically a singing and dancing cabaret, where they mimed well-known songs while performing high-kicking routines in skimpy outfits. It was also quite humorous in parts, with audience participation if anybody in attendance was brave enough to have a go. It was all a waste of their time really, but the casino was obliged to provide some form of entertainment. The girls weren't paid a lot, but they were dancing, which was what they loved doing, while enjoying a low-budget version of a glamorous lifestyle.

At the end of August, the girls finally moved to the more popular casino at Vilamoura, where their show was watched by decent-sized crowds almost every night. Dick went up to Lisbon to be with Pilar his Spanish lover and I moved in with Dee and the girls in their spacious apartment near the casino.

68

Festival do Avante

DICK DISCOVERED that there was a huge event in Lisbon that weekend called the 'Festival do Avante', also known as the communist festival. I went up on the train and moved into the upstairs part of the Berlitz language school where Pilar was the director. We spent the whole day making the lumies, as we had been warned that the event would be packed. We drove up one of the fabled seven hills of Lisbon, called Alto da Ajuda, where the festival was being held. The stunning view of Lisbon from up there had already made the trip worthwhile.

The festival lasted three days and nights, which meant that there would be no respite for us: making lumies all day and then selling them all evening. We could have done with some help, but we didn't know anyone that we could trust with our secret manufacturing process. On a normal night's trading we made and sold about two hundred – now we were faced with a target of a thousand a day. By Sunday night we were totally exhausted but we still had enough energy to count all the money, which amounted to something like two thousand pounds, which in those days wasn't bad for three days hard graft.

We couldn't get permission to sell inside the festival, as any form of capitalism in the midst of thousands of hardcore Bolsheviks, Marxists and Leninists probably wouldn't have gone down that well with the Politburo. Having said that, one of the stands inside was making a real fortune selling Yasser Arafat-style black-and-white scarves. It looked like almost everyone was wearing one. It was probably the PLO funding their organisation, as a lot of communist countries were represented at the event. Although Palestine wasn't officially considered a state, the

Avante committee probably recognised and accepted them as a potential future fully paid-up member.

While we were selling, we were constantly being terrorised by the Lisbon waifs and strays. It was very dark outside the huge gathering, which was good for our business as the lumies looked brighter, but it made things difficult for us security-wise. We were constantly being hassled and jostled by all sorts of dodgy individuals. We were very uncomfortable and feeling vulnerable as a lot of escudos were changing hands in large crowds with no sign of any police presence.

Inevitably, I suppose, it had to happen and on Friday, the first night, it did. We both wore ex-army or navy shirts as they had large front pockets, which we used as our version of a cash register. Coins in a bum – bag, twenty notes shirt left pocket, fifties right pocket, everything larger in even bigger bomber jacket inside pockets. Despite the heat we had to wear jackets with lots of storage room, not just for cash but for easy access to the necklace connectors. We refused to change anything larger than a thousand note, as it attracted too much attention fumbling around in the dark with all sorts of reprobates hanging around.

Instead of picking on me, the obvious soft option, Dick's twenty-note shirt pocket was torn off his chest, scattering the notes all over the ground. In the ensuing melee Dick held on to his attacker's foot, while trying to break his ankle. Unfortunately, Dick finished up with just a black shoe in his hand. Meanwhile, all around us it was mayhem on the ground under our feet, as kids were fighting over the cash. I couldn't believe it when some of them actually gave the notes they had found straight back to us. We didn't lose a lot but that was a warning. The next two nights we paid a few of the older boys to help us. We put them on the frontline, so they took the cash and handed it over to us to check or to change. They were dealing with their own kind, so not only did we avoid the language problem, we were out of the firing line too.

When the three days were finally over, we treated our helpers to a slap-up dinner in a restaurant nearby, close to where they lived, and paid them what must have seemed to them to be a small fortune. They showed us the area where they were from and all I can say is that I would never have dreamt of going anywhere near the place if I hadn't have been with them. We were crazy considering all the cash we were carrying but we felt strangely at ease in their company. Some of their friends and relatives who we were introduced to in a cafe that the Michelin Guide would have rated a couple of notches below seedy, looked like out-of-work pirates. Skinny with mad staring eyes, tattoos, earrings.I'd never seen women like it.

We arrived safely back at our night school and, as I previously mentioned, checked our bank balance so to speak, and crashed out.

A day or two later, when we had just about recovered, Dick and I had a long chat about the coming days and agreed it was a perfect time to go our own ways. We would finish on a high. He was going to drive his car back after spending a few days with Pilar. I was happy for him to take our stuff back to Bedford, while I was planning to be with my dancing girl at least until the season had finished for them.

I stayed in the apartment in Vilamoura with the girls until the end of September when their contract was terminated. The head girl of their group, Christine, was living with a Portuguese playboy who had his yacht in the marina, the Porsche in the garage and, of course, a penthouse. He'd made his fortune from buying and selling land and property in the Algarve where business was booming. His first name was Joaquim, but he preferred to be known as Quim (pronounced Kim in Portuguese). He'd recently expanded his business to London, but what he hadn't realised was that his shortened name in English was the same word as an intimate part of a lady's anatomy. By the time he had had his company registered, the logo and business cards printed etc. it was too late. He tried to carry on, but the amount of abuse he received was too much for him, especially when his board meetings would end with certain members of staff saying, "Goodbye then, see you next Tuesday."

When the girls flew back to the UK, Quim offered me a lift back to London in his Porsche 928 Turbo, which made the trip a lot quicker than usual and more exciting too, watching him overtake anything that got in his way. He spent a lot of the journey telling me about his yacht and his love of the sea. We took the ferry from Bilbao to Portsmouth. It was a rough crossing and Quim, like most of the passengers, spent most of the trip in bed in their cabins feeling seasick. After dinner I watched a film in the cinema and by the end of the movie, I was the only one still there. My theory is that if you have a few drinks first, you become unsteady on your feet and become a bit dizzy which counteracts the swaying and up and down motion of the ship. If you can get into the swing of things, it's almost as though you're on dry land. However, when we did reach Blighty and *terra firma,* I felt nauseous and struggled to walk straight.

My first port of call (the ferry had had a nautical effect on me) was to visit my parents. They lived in a modern house but in Old Stevenage, which was slightly more up-market than the new town but not by much. They were,of course,glad to see that their prodigal son had returned and,once again,virtually empty-handed. After a few weeks my parents had understandably had enough of my idleness and told me to go back to Bedford, get a job and do something with my life. They said that I'd upset their routine. I was annoyed with them at the time, but it was exactly what I needed: a kick up the backside.

I returned to Bedford, found a flat, got back on the taxis and gradually settled in for what was to be another long hard depressing winter.

1982

69

Rank Indiscipline

I WENT to visit Dee in Kensington, where she lived with her parents in a property owned by the Queen. Her father was the Queen's accountant. We went for a stroll past Kensington Palace, the heavily guarded Israeli embassy and then on to Harrods to see how the other half shop. This wasn't a world where I belonged, and I could sense that Dee could see how uncomfortable I felt. Possibly because of the change of environment, things weren't the same between us as they were in Portugal.

Back on the taxi rank I was surprised but glad to see that there were two new drivers, Guy and Tim. I knew both of them well. The pair of them were very handsome, fresh-faced, young men who were both former pupils of my old school. They were almost ten years younger than me, but unlike yours truly had that public-schoolboy look about them.

Their attractive girlfriends were both the daughters of Mr Randall, who owned a large electronics factory in town. He'd already bought his girls a house and a car each. Tim was hoping to be selected as a trainee Royal Navy helicopter pilot. He was taxi driving to earn some pocket money and was already on something like his fifteenth job since he had left school, He fancied himself as a boy racer and so he regularly tried out his rally driving techniques on his Vauxhall Victor taxi.

The three of us all worked for the same boss, Mr Deegan, who only employed us at the time because he was struggling to find some steady professionals. We were all assigned numbered call signs on the radio: I was 112, Guy 71 and Tim 145. A West Indian driver was 222 or, as he called himself, 'Orl de toos'.

Tim had discovered that when his car was in reverse, the mileage numbers went backwards too. We all worked on a percentage, based on odometer readings. When things were quiet, we would save Tim's place in the queue on the rank while he drove up and down De Parys Avenue (where I used to live when I was at school) in reverse. By the end of the day when he handed in his figures, he had knocked off so many miles that his car was averaging about 10 MPG. He got away with it for a while until an old lady called head office to report that she had seen one of our taxis not only speeding through her village but being driven backwards.

He was eventually accepted by the Royal Navy at a cost of £250,000 to the taxpayer. We gave him a big send-off, as we didn't expect to see him for a few years. Three days later he was back. He didn't like it and missed the dog.

Guy worked a lot more hours than most of us and was studying at art college at night and was hoping to get a place on a degree course starting in September. He was determined to do well in life, and it showed. We both worked the weekend evening shifts as that was where the money was to be made; but picking up drunks from pubs and the rank was always a risky business. Bedford, like many towns at night on weekends, could be a dangerous place to be walking the streets.

I once picked up four big lads who wanted to go to different addresses all over town. They were bragging amongst themselves that they weren't intending to pay and that I might get a slap if I wasn't careful. I was scared but angry at the same time so I drove as fast as I could down the high street. We nearly took off when we went over the hump on the town bridge and there was total silence in the back of the cab until we arrived at the first drop-off point. They all got out looking a bit pale, paid the fare plus a tip and even said thank you.

There was a long queue at the rank once the pubs had closed, so for us there were a few hours when it was non-stop action. One night, Guy drove up to the rank and a gang of punks jumped into his car. As he was about to set off, the back door opened and one by one each of his passengers were thrown onto the pavement. A very angry Dick West jumped in the front: "Fucking queue jumpers."

Guy's first words were, "I'm a friend of Paul's."

Every morning during the week I had to pick up a severely handicapped girl and drive a fair distance across country and drop her off at a special school. I hated getting up early at the best of times. My ethos has always been 'get up when you wake up', sleep is good for you, the body needs rest and it will tell you when you're ready to start another day. But I needed the money so there I was scraping the ice off the windscreen at 7.30 every bloody morning just to earn a crust. When I arrived at the house, the girl's father would wheel her out to the car and tell me to "drive carefully, we wouldn't want anything to happen to her would we!"

She was about 10 or 11, she never spoke to me – maybe she wasn't able to. I never asked. She seemed to be completely oblivious to what was going on in the world, so after a few sensible trips I speeded things up a bit. I may have misdiagnosed her reactions but I'm sure I saw a flicker of a smile when we almost slid off a bend once. That winter brought a lot of snow and ice, so driving conditions were appalling at times, which made the journey more interesting. At the same time, I was trying to concentrate on the radio. I was totally enthralled listening to the latest news bulletins on the BBC about the Falklands conflict.

This wasn't the only time that I had been involved in mental health transport. The year before, I had to start the day on a school run by picking up Sandra, a carer, who had to be present in case one of the patients attacked me. I was more concerned about her than the kids. She was well past her sell-by-date, a chain smoker and over-friendly. Once she was in the car, we then had to pick up three kids. The first two were reasonably well behaved but the third one was a young Pakistani boy who sat in the front with a plastic plate which was his version of the steering wheel. He made all the gear-changing noises, while simultaneously rocking backwards and forwards in the front seat.

The front seat had taken so much punishment from him that one morning, en route to the Bromham mental hospital, he finally broke the back of his seat and was left lying prostrate on his now collapsible seat. The other two children started screaming and fitting. Sandra and I were also in fits, but of laughter. When we arrived at the hospital to hand over our patients everyone in the car was crying for one reason or another. When the nurses opened the passenger door and saw the boy lying there flat out their immediate reaction was that he was dead. It was only when they noticed that we were actually laughing and that the boy was now alive and sobbing that they saw the funny side of things.

Out of the blue Dee called to tell me that she was going back to Portugal for the summer on a six-month contract and that she was now the captain. She came up to Bedford on the bus from London. When I arrived to pick her up the other drivers' eyes were all out on stalks, I had to whisk her away quickly before anybody's eyes popped out of their sockets. I was embarrassed having to take her back to my hovel of a bedsit, although she'd probably seen worse on her travels.

My landlady wasn't happy, as she had recently started flirting with me since the tenant on the top floor who she had been giving extra room service to had been evicted. After a thorough investigation she had been able to solve the mystery of why her lounge windows were often covered in yellow streaks. She had discovered that her upstairs lover was pissing in a bottle and pouring the contents out of the window because he couldn't be bothered to walk down two flights of stairs in the middle of the night. When Dee had to leave the next day, she must have returned to Kensington suitably impressed.

In the meantime, Guy had split-up with his girlfriend of many years and was looking for a new challenge. He'd been to Portugal before on holiday and on work trips for his pottery business. I asked him if he fancied a trip to Portugal with me and he accepted my offer. He had a green Cortina estate that we could use that he called 'Tina'. We had plenty of spare time to plan our trip while we were sitting in our taxis waiting for customers to turn up. We got so involved one afternoon that I sat with him in his car while he took a fare on a short trip. Halfway to our destination, the boss called my number through on the radio.

"112, position please."

"Goldington Road."

"Pick-up near you, 28 Castle Road. How long?"

"Quite a while probably."

"And why is that?"

"I'm not actually in a car at the moment."

"71, position please."

"Goldington Road."

"Can you do that Castle Road job?"

"That's a negative, fish on board."

"Is 112 in your vehicle?"

"Roger."

"Am I to understand that you are both in one car with a paying passenger?"

"Roger."

"I don't suppose 145 is in there with you as well is he?"

"That's a negative."

After a moment of radio silence, Deegan was obviously pulling his hair out by now, came back on the radio.

"112 call me on a landline. 71 do likewise, preferably after you have dropped off."

We both got a bollocking for what he called joy riding and told us in no uncertain terms that our long-term future with the firm was in serious doubt, which was ironic as we were about to hand in our notices.

70

The Final Frontier

IN MID-JUNE I was on my way to Portugal for the very last time. I didn't know it then obviously, but this was it, there was no going back. I was alone as Guy had to finish his college course before coming down to join me. Besides the luminous necklaces we had invested in a large quantity of Donald Duck and Mickey Mouse silver balloons. We'd spotted similar balloons at the royal wedding of Charles and Diana on TV and I'd never seen them in Portugal so I had a feeling that they would complement the lumies We had had a few miles of plastic tubing made to measure and enough light-sticks to last us for a while. We also had the new lumies which were ready-made and came in long tubes. All you had to do was take them out of the tube and crack them. They were a great improvement, no work involved, no ice needed – but they weren't cheap.

The car was packed to the roof by the time I set off. We had invested a small fortune, so I had a lot of responsibility, which was constantly weighing on my mind as I was driving through France then Spain. I had chosen a border crossing in the north of Portugal as I was heading for the São João festival in Porto again. I picked a place on the map that was off the beaten track where I would hopefully pass through unnoticed.

When I had almost reached the border, I stopped the car to hide everything as best as I could under all my bags and other belongings. I had a roadside wash and brush-up, put on some clean clothes to make myself look presentable, in the unlikely event that I would be stopped. I was knackered from the long drive, so I double-checked that everything was to hand: passport, car documents etc. I didn't want to do anything suspicious that might attract their attention.

The final stretch of road was dead straight, with no traffic visible in either direction. As the customs building came into view, I could see a small group of border guards all staring at me, shaking their heads slowly in unison. Unperturbed, I put on my best smiley face as they asked me to get out of the car. I knew there was something amiss, but I couldn't quite put my finger on it until I suddenly realised what I had done: I'd driven that last few hundred metres on the wrong side of the road, in full view of the police and the customs officers.

My days as a smuggler and criminal mastermind were almost over before I'd got started. I had the same feeling as I had had as a novice teenage shoplifter when I was caught red-handed on my first outing. I had hidden a giant bar of Cadbury's Fruit and Nut under my school jacket when the old lady in the newspaper shop had turned her back on us for a second. When she turned around the chocolate, encased in silver paper, crashed to the floor with a bang, while I was left looking rather flushed holding the empty wrapper (an obvious design flaw). Mick handed back the cigarettes that he had taken, as she was threatening to call the police. She said that we were a disgrace to the good name of our school, which sounded vaguely familiar.

The customs officials didn't seem to want to get their hands soiled, as they told me to empty the vehicle – which I did, except for the balloons which were laying flat in the place where the spare wheel was supposed to be. They weren't bothered about the tubing but the light sticks and the green tubes containing the new lumies were the problem. I would have to pay the import duty, plus a fine for not declaring them. They instructed me to leave everything at the border and drive to Porto because this was far too complicated for them to assess the correct classification. I asked them if there was another way, we could sort this out, or a phone call maybe to HQ? Unfortunately not. They sent me on my way, sarcastically recommending that I keep to the right-hand side of the road.

The drive to Porto didn't look far on the map but it took me at least five hours, trying to negotiate what seemed like never-ending bends on dangerous mountain roads and witnessing some of the worst driving I'd ever encountered. I'd just driven all the way through France and Spain without incident and now I was having near-misses two or three times an hour. By the time I arrived at the customs building I was a nervous wreck. I spent the rest of the afternoon arguing the toss with customs brokers as to the correct classification of a light stick. I'd taken some samples with me for demonstration purposes, so when I broke one to show them how it worked, they literally saw the light. It wasn't a candle or electric or a flare but a safety device. I paid the duty, which was a lot less than I was expecting, and was told to go straight back to the border where I would pay a small fine and my stuff would be returned.

Normally I quite enjoyed driving but I was far too tired to attempt the return journey, so I splashed out on a hotel for the night. I awoke the next morning slightly refreshed and returned to the border. The guards were all smiles. They apologised for the inconvenience caused and explained that they were only doing their job. I gave them all a light stick each and set off once again. I chose to take a different route. I couldn't face that trip for a third time, and anything would be an improvement on that road. How wrong could I have been? I even managed to get lost in the fog and heavy rain. I was in a part of Portugal called Trás-os-Montes which means beyond the mountains; behind the times would be more apt. Remote but fascinating. I promised myself to return one day for a stress -free visit.

71
An Ice Surprise

IN PORTO I met up with a couple from Bedford, Paul and Enid who were travelling around in their Mini. This wasn't, of course, a coincidence. Paul used to be a radio controller on the taxis, and we'd often talked about Portugal in the past. He'd said he would join me and, true to his word, there he was. We sold well in São João and then drove down to Lisbon and booked ourselves into the Hotel Internacional in the centre of the city. I didn't know at the time, but this hotel was to become almost a second home to me. My room on the third floor was at the front with a balcony and an impressive view of Rossio, the main square in Lisbon. My assistants were two floors below, which I had already thought might come in handy later.

We had a few days to prepare for our next event. One of the main ingredients that I needed was dry ice, which is frozen carbon dioxide. It was available to buy at the petrochemical plant on the outskirts of Lisbon by the river Tagus. The site was a massive industrial landscape with metal towers and giant tubes with steam and smoke billowing out into the atmosphere. It was quite a daunting experience, like a day trip to Chernobyl (which was still in one piece at the time). I was escorted by security to Sector Z, where I met the icemen. They gave me a warm welcome which I hadn't been expecting, considering the nature of their trade. I had an enormous ice box made from six- inch thick polystyrene which just about fitted in the car. I'd been told beforehand that I would be served only if I had the correct receptacle.

The ice wasn't cheap, but it was essential for our state-of-the art cold storage process. It was around -80C and had no residue, unlike normal ice. The ice itself looked like compressed snow and was poured out of a tube in cylindrical pellets the size of cigarettes, controlled by the icemen. I had paid by the kilo, but they gave me extra when I waved a reasonably large escudo note in front of them. Under ideal conditions this ice would last three or four days as it gradually sublimated into the gaseous state as it mixed with air. It was vital to keep the lid on the box for as long as possible.

Back at the hotel I very carefully transferred a small quantity of the ice from the mother lode into picnic boxes using industrial gauntlets since this stuff could give you frostbite in no time at all. I had all sorts of wicked ideas of what I could do with it but then I remembered I wasn't at school anymore. I was two floors above my assistants and the tube needed to have a drop for the liquid to run down, so it was obvious what had to be done. I was the sucker on top and the other Paul was down below, with his rod in his hand ready to stick it in quickly when the moment arrived. We agreed on our codenames before we started. I dropped the first line of tubing over the balcony and called out:

"Romeo, Romeo, wherefore art thou Romeo?"

"I'm down here you twat, there's no need to shout," came the reply.

This system worked well but took far too long, so we started getting a bit carried away by using multiple tubing ejection from above. I hadn't noticed at first, but a small crowd had gathered on the opposite side of the busy road, fascinated by the green lines running down the side of a hotel. Down below, Paul got into a bit of a panic and missed one of the tubes, which was now dripping luminous green liquid onto the pavement – and one or two of the heads of passers-by, who would probably have woken up the next morning with blond highlights in their hair.

There was a knock on my door. I presumed it was Enid, so without thinking I shouted, "Come in." It was the receptionist. He looked inside my room, which by now resembled a chemical laboratory. He politely reminded me that the room was to be used for sleeping in and would I please respect that. He left shaking his head in disbelief, just as Enid arrived from downstairs with rolls of lit-up tubes.

The Festa do Avante was held in the same place as before but this year, for some reason, it was on in the first weekend in July. We found people to assist us over the three days but didn't do as well as the year before because there was a lot of rain, which didn't exactly help an outdoor festival. But we had done reasonably well, plus we had the cash from Porto, so things were looking good.

Guy arrived at Lisbon airport and joined me at the hotel. The other two were going to a music festival in the northernmost part of the country, by the sea near the Spanish border. We arranged to meet them there and sell the new lumies. We had two weeks to get there, so we stopped in a few places along the way to try our luck. We revisited Nazaré, so for a laugh we booked into the same place that Dick and I had stayed in the year before. Nothing had changed of course. I warned Guy about the Peeping Tom and the dangerous furniture. In the morning we strolled along the seafront, found a cafe and sat ourselves down at the counter next to a hardy-looking bunch of individuals.

We couldn't help notice that, instead of the normal espresso café, they were all drinking Nescafe. They had some kind of special technique that had probably been handed down over many generations where they poured the contents of the little red sachet, added some sugar and a drop or two of hot water, then stirred it furiously for what seemed a lifetime, poured on more hot water, before swallowing it in one go. I asked what the purpose of all this was and was told "espuma", or to make it frothy. Guy and I had to have a go and deliberately messed about, taking the piss with the contents flying all over the counter. Our attempt at humour had upset some of the customers by the looks that we were getting, so we literally had to leg it out of town before they got their hands on us.

Two weeks on we eventually arrived unscathed at the Vilar de Mouros festival where U2, The Stranglers, Echo and the Bunnymen *et al* were performing over the next week or so. As usual, we couldn't get permission to sell inside but we did quite well outside, where we could hear the music, but had to miss the live entertainment. By the time we left we had enough money to re-invest, so we made a phone call to the factory in France and placed an order for more light sticks and lumies.

72

Daylight Robbery

WE TOOK the long drive back to Lisbon and arrived many hours later, ready to collapse. The next morning, we had to change most of our hard-earned escudos into French francs, as in a few days' time we would have to go to the post office in Bayonne just over the Spanish border to collect our goods. We were put in touch with a backstreet money changer who gave a better rate than the banks and didn't ask questions. We stashed our francs into a black briefcase which we hid in the car.

We now needed a gas bottle for our new silver balloon enterprise. This was far more complicated than we had expected, as we had to apply for a licence to transport hydrogen. Just as well, probably. We passed that test and then drove down to the same petrochemical plant by the Tagus where we were taken to Sector F and bought our first bottle of hydrogen. Helium, which is inert and therefore didn't explode, was seven times the price, so we didn't have much choice really. The gypsies always used it, so why not us? The bottle was heavy, about five feet long and took two people to lift it into the car. Fortunately for us it just fitted in nicely, with the screw top part almost next to our heads. We both smoked cigarettes (SG Gigante) at the time, so lighting up next to a potential hydrogen bomb was obviously not very sensible. With a few kilos of dry ice added to the equation we were well on our way to nuclear capability.

On our drive back by the river passing the docks and hundreds of containers Guy suddenly spotted a schooner, which was one of the entrants in that year's Tall Ships race. A good friend of his was crewing on it, so he ran down to have a look while I parked the car. When I caught up with him, he asked me if I had brought the case with the money in it. I hadn't given it another thought, so we both went straight back to the car to fetch it. We were back at the car in minutes. It was locked but the briefcase containing the money was gone and with it our travelling backgammon board, which looked like a carrying case. Nothing else had been touched.

We found a policeman and took him to the car. He then met up with the car park attendant, who I noticed had a thick wire ring hanging from his belt with dozens of different car keys on it. I was convinced he was the culprit, or something to do with the theft. I wondered if we had been followed from where we changed the money. We even had a gas bottle in the car, which would have put most thieves off. At the police station we wasted ages filling in reports, but we never saw our cash again.

We went back to the hotel and sat on our beds in shock, completely demoralised. All that work and planning gone to waste because of one silly mistake. At least we didn't blame each other or row about it, we just felt that we didn't deserve to be punished so cruelly. We'd been knocked back, but we were determined to get over it and make a quick recovery. That afternoon we drove to a fair in Setubal not far south of Lisbon. We found a spot where we could put our table, someone let us plug into their electricity supply for the heat-sealing machine that kept the gas from escaping from the balloon and we were up and running.

We had our two examples under Perspex so customers could choose which character they wanted. We soon learnt the names of 'Rato Mickey' and 'Pato Donald'. As with the lumies, they were visible in the sense that everyone could see when you had bought one, so the kids were soon saying, "I want one!" We sold so many that we ran out of gas, leaving a lot of disappointed customers behind. The next day we invested in two bottles and made another small fortune, enough to embark on our trip to France. We changed all our money again – this time with a different currency exchange dealer – and kept it with us at all times.

We took the sleeper train from Lisbon to Paris – it could have been called the Trans Iberian Express... they missed a trick there. The dining car felt like we were in the 1920s with its linen tablecloths, posh silverware and waiters in bow ties. There's something romantic or nostalgic about dining on an international train journey. We stuffed ourselves over dinner as we travelled through the mountains of northern Portugal, admiring the view. I'm almost certain I caught a glimpse of Hercule Poirot somewhere along the corridor. At the Irun/Hendaye border the wheels came off... then were replaced with some different ones, something about the gauges being incompatible, apparently. We disembarked at Bayonne and after some language difficulties found 'La Poste'. Inside the building our problems continued, until we came across a member of a very rare species... a Frenchman that could speak English. He did everything for us and if it wasn't for him, we might have missed the return train.

Now loaded up with contraband, we had an anxious wait to see if we could pass through the Spanish and then, later at night, the Portuguese customs checks. We had another episode of the 'Wheeltappers' and Shunters' Social Club' to sit through before we crossed over the border, which gave us more time to distribute our bags all over the train in other travellers' carriages. We'd just ask people to keep an eye on the bag while we found our seats. The idea was that if a bag was confiscated nobody knew who it belonged to, so although we might lose it, at least we wouldn't be arrested.

In the end there wasn't a problem. The only worry was the Portuguese ticket collector on the train. He was the same one going back as we'd had going there, so he couldn't understand why we had made such a long journey only to then go back an hour or two later. If Hercule had been on the return journey we would have been in big trouble. The Portuguese border was crossed in the middle of the night. My 'Do Not Disturb' sign didn't stop the police waking me up, shouting "Passport!"

(Just for a minute I thought I was back in Tavira with Gordon.) Apart from being disturbed, we suffered no more inconvenience and were soon back at the hotel in Lisbon.

The receptionist had become a good friend by now and he even let us store stuff in his backroom when we went away for a few days. He always asked us about our travels and where we had been the night before. When we said France he just laughed and said something about British humour.

73

The Fall Guy

THROUGH all this period I had kept in touch with Dee. I couldn't wait to see her again. We drove down to the Algarve and found her in Vilamoura with her troupe of dancing girls, staying in two apartments near the casino. We carried on where we had left off and she moved in with me, while poor old Guy had to suffer the inconvenience of sharing with the other four young ladies: Jackie, Bippy, Fiona and Kim. From then on, we were nearly always together. They even came selling with us sometimes when they weren't busy.

We often went to see the show and on numerous occasions Guy had to go on stage with them. There was one part where Dee had to call on a member of the audience to participate; if nobody would do it, Guy was the stand-in – I wasn't allowed to thankfully. In another song Jackie had to imitate calling someone on the phone using her hand and Guy would be on the receiving end trying his best to make his hand look like a phone. One night before the show he unplugged the phone in the apartment and put it in his pocket. Sure enough, that night he was called up to do the phone scene, when he whipped it out (the phone) to pretend to answer the call. The girls and the audience were falling about with laughter. Jackie was miming the song, so by the time she had recovered her composure she was completely out of sync.

Jackie was a very witty blonde Londoner. One of her previous jobs was in a circus where she was an acrobat and the human cannonball who was shot out of a large gun and, if all went well, landed on a safety net. She got fired from that job. The year before, when our millionaire friend Quim had been trying to impress the girls by showing off his luxury apartment overlooking the river estuary in Lisbon, he finished by asking rhetorically, "Where else in the world would you find a place like this?" Jackie thought about it for a moment and came out with the classic put-down: "Next door?"

Most nights, before the girls went on stage, we usually had to endure a performance by a third-rate singing act that the casino had found at the bottom of the talent barrel.

One ageing Portuguese artist was so bad it was embarrassing and excruciating to watch. It was so bad that there was hardly any applause after each song. We felt for him. Dee described our reaction as cruel and cynical when both of us stood up and gave him a standing ovation when we erroneously guessed that he had finished. When he did come to a halt, we were up on our feet again shouting, "Encore, encore!" – which got the rest of the audience to join in with their false appreciation. After that we became his unofficial fan club for a while. I even kept his signed photograph.

Later on in the summer, when the girls moved to Monte Gordo casino, he was there again but was replaced by a Welsh lady soprano,who was even more painful to listen to. Guy had a severe case of the runs early one morning, when he had to make an emergency visit to use the facilities belonging to one of the beach cafes. It was one of those toilets with no seat, no lock on the door and no toilet paper. The cafe was just opening as Guy flew through the door and ran straight out the back to the bathroom. He just made it in time but there was nothing that he could use to wipe his backside with. He looked in his pockets but all he could find was a wad of twenty escudo notes. Out of sheer desperation he had to use two or three of them to clean himself and then threw them in the plastic basket that was provided for this purpose, as you weren't supposed to put paper down the toilet because of blockages.

Afterwards he'd been sitting outside the cafe for a while when Dee and some of the girls turned up for breakfast. He gave them a quick rundown on what had just happened, when suddenly he had to go again; this time he took some tissues with him. When he'd finished, he noticed that the soiled twenty notes had gone but that the basket hadn't been emptied. He told the girls to avoid any twenty notes that might be in their change.

Later that night when we were all having a drink in the plush casino bar, the parsimonious Welsh soprano was complaining that her apartment in Vilamoura didn't have a sea view and that it if she wanted one it would cost her an extra twenty escudos. Dee laughed and shouted over to her for all to hear, "That's nothing, Guy uses them to wipe his arse on!"

74

Fair Enough

DURING August and the first half of September we travelled all over the Algarve, working and having fun with the girls. We then turned our attention back to the annual fairs that were held on saints' days in different towns and cities. We were backwards and forwards to Lisbon for gas bottles and ice. Guy flew to England a few times for more balloons; we went to France again on the train and once in the car.

On that trip I practised how to ask, 'where is the station?' in French, as we knew the way to the post office from there. We arrived in Bayonne early in the morning when there was a dense fog hanging over the town, making it almost impossible to drive or find anybody. I spotted a young man and went over to him and said, "Bonjour monsieur, ou est la gare silver plate?" He mumbled something in French and went on his way. I went back to the car and Guy asked me what he said.

"Funnily enough, I didn't understand a word he said, as you might have guessed considering that je ne parles français seulement un petit peu – which is the other phrase I had learnt," I answered.

"Well that's come in useful, hasn't it," Guy replied. "Try someone else then, get them to point in the general direction."

"I don't think the last one understood my accent. Maybe he just didn't know, or was it the thick frog?"

I had a go with a young woman, if you know what I mean.

"Bonjour madame, ou est la gare?"

"Le bus, ou le train?"

"Oui."

"Non, non, non le bus ou le train?" She looked at me as though she was speaking to a moron.

I started pointing in different directions: "La gare, la gare, parles anglais?"

"Non, merde, au revoir stupide!"

We found the place in the end and arrived back safely without any hassle at the borders.

We had now become part of the fair circuit and had got to know a few people, including some of the gypsies. They had made friends with us despite the fact that we had virtually destroyed their rubber balloon business. They weren't angry, more in awe. Ours were a lot more expensive but they were new, shiny, foreign and lasted for ages. The gypsies were smart: they wanted to know where to get them from, they even lent us gas bottles and drove to Lisbon for us to get more in their vans. They were handy people to know on a fairground, especially when there were no available selling places. They would always help us find a spot.

In most places the fair was held in a field outside the town with an enormous fairground, a circus, restaurants, cafes, fartura-caravans and hundreds of market stalls. In Vila Franca de Xira we were given a place inside a pavilion which was perfect for balloons as there was no wind or rain to contend with. We sold hundreds every day. In most other places we had to ask one of the 'feirantes' (the market people) if we could plug into their supply. Most of them said no for one reason or another, so it was never easy.

Our next fair was in an amazing town called Elvas, in the Alentejo very close to the Spanish border near Badajoz. They were both former fortress towns, Elvas is a star shaped fort and the old town is still surrounded by the walls. When you drive in you pass under an archway and enter another world. The fair was just outside the town and being near Spain meant that we were expecting a lot of visitors from their wealthier Iberian cousins. We'd brought four gas bottles with us in anticipation. The only people at the fair that looked easily approachable were selling personalised T-shirts with your face printed on, using film cameras and a computer digital print out. Back in those days, in the middle of a field in the Alentejo this was back to the future material.

I was convinced that the team that was running the show had to be foreigners like ourselves. We asked the young man if he spoke any English – he just laughed and said, "Of course." We had a pleasant chat with him about our electricity dilemma and he told us to go and speak to his sister, as she was the boss. Guy went over to the young lady, and I couldn't help but notice how smiley and bubbly she was. Guy asked her:

"Would you mind if I stick my plug in your socket?"

I thought she was going to say something like, 'Anytime you like ,handsome!' but all she said was that it would be OK and warned us that they were having a lot of problems with the current situation. The electricity supply wasn't constant enough for their technology to function properly. Their computer was enormous by today's standards and took up nearly all the space in their VW van.

As it turned out, they were all Portuguese except the boss's boyfriend Richard, who was an Australian ageing hippy surf dude. He had this hang-dog miserable face but, as is often the case, was great fun to be with once you knew him. We all needed some form of accommodation and the only place that we could find was a 'Casa de Hóspedes', which means guest-house – more like doss house in this case. The dividing 'walls' inside weren't paper-thin, they were just paper. Guy and I shared a bare room with two beds, a sink and a tap – which weren't that close to each other. To have a wash, there was an empty, rusty baked bean type can that you filled up with cold water to do your ablutions. There were maybe two or three toilets for about 30 guests so there was always a long wait in a queue.

We had dinner together that night and gradually got to know each other. The young lady's name was Rica and her brother was called João. They were from Sintra, a mystical place near the coast just west of Lisbon. We'd all had a long day, so we were looking forward to a good night's sleep. I'd almost nodded off when the guests from upstairs arrived. It was the men from the bullfight known as the 'Forcados', the tough and incredibly brave team of men that jump onto the bull's head and attempt to immobilise the poor animal after the other lot on horses have stuck lances in it. The leader jumps on first and tries to hold on, while the rest of them, except the tail man, jump on top of him. They wear old-fashioned boy's clothing, with tight pants and green Noddy hats on their shoulders. I'm not making this up.

To practise their art, and risk life and limb while having a head-on collision with half a ton of charging bull, I assumed that part of their training was to get as pissed as possible before kick-off. After work, I expect they carried on drinking, because judging by the singing and cheering going on upstairs, they had started practising on each other. They were stamping around so loud up there that I began to wonder if they had brought one of the bulls back with them.

I was complaining about the noise and the lack of amenities to Richard over coffee the next morning, when he summed it up very accurately with, "Look,sport, you don't get a colour TV for 200 scoobies a night, cobber." The fair was a great success for them and for us. We took it in turns to have dinner with either Rica or Richard. At night, after we had finished work, we would all go and unwind in Eric's bar, which was a very trendy spot considering where we were. It even had an old GPO red telephone box inside.

When the fair was over, we arranged to meet up with them at the next fair in Faro. Before that we went back to the Algarve, to Vila Real and then on to Tavira,where we caught up with our old friends from the restaurant. The more places we visited, the more *feirantes* (stallholders) we got acquainted with, as we were a novelty to them and were probably the only foreigners on the circuit. There was an old blind gypsy lady, who wore the typical long traditional skirt that scrapes on the ground. She had thick black sunglasses and sold a kind of almanac called the 'Borda D'água'. We always stopped and gave her some money, as basically she was begging. Guy was having a chat with her one afternoon behind one of the restaurants. As she walked away, he noticed that there was a wet patch on the dry ground where she had been standing. She had been urinating while in mid-conversation.

One of the fair attractions was the Smallest Man in the World. To see him and one or two other bizarre specimens you paid the entrance fee and went behind a thick curtain into a small tent. There he was, lying down inside a box with a big head and a child's body. In reality, he was normal size, as we'd seen him around. It was all done with mirrors. There was a stuffed sheep with two heads, another one with five legs, a huge and definitely alive black man who was the monster from the African jungle, or something ridiculous. It was as though we were back in Victorian days.

In Faro we met Rica, João, Richard and Rica's son Nuno, who was about three years old. She had married a Portuguese man when she was very young, but things hadn't worked out and, by the amount of arguments that she had with Richard every day, it didn't look as though they were getting on too well either. I expect the stress of the travelling life and looking after a child was taking a toll on their relationship. When the fair ended, Rica told us that the next time we were in Lisbon, or if we ever needed any kind of help, to come and visit her. She had been brought up in a palace in Sintra with maids and servants. Her grandmother had had eighteen children – two had died, but her father was one of sixteen brothers and sisters. I couldn't help wondering why she was living this lifestyle – it just didn't make sense.

Guy and I stayed in the Algarve with the girls while selling at the fairs in Silves, Portimao and finally Lagos in late November. We didn't do so well, as the weather had deteriorated which meant the fairgrounds had turned into fields of mud. It was a hard life when it was cold and wet. I admired these fair people and what they went through to make a living. In Lagos, Guy was having a look round when a familiar voice shouted his name – it was the blind lady waving to him across the road. So, clearly, she could see after all. She asked us not to tell anyone as it was a secret and gave us the index finger over the lips sign – or else we'd be cursed.

75
Up North

WE FOLLOWED the girls to the north of the country's casinos, first to Figuera de Foz and then to Espinho, just south of Porto. The winter up there was cold and windy. The sea was rough,and there was very little to do during the day. At night we sometimes drove to Porto and toured the clubs trying to sell the luminous necklaces. We had tried this in Lisbon and Cascais with a certain degree of success. However, part of the problem was the word 'boite',which could mean a night club, a disco or a strip club, so we never quite knew what we were getting involved with.

We had bought a suit each, to smarten ourselves up, (*that's me suited and booted above)* as some of the casinos had a dress code and there was no getting past the doormen in the clubs unless you were well dressed. We started in Cascais and visited as many clubs as we could in one night. I did the talking, Guy carried the tube and, when asked, did the demonstration if we were lucky enough to meet the owners. In nearly every place we visited, the management were happy to listen to us and almost without fail offered us a whisky 'com gelo e castelo' (with ice and fizzy water). By the time we were into double figures we didn't really know what we were doing anymore. I'd just about lost my ability to speak English, let alone any Portuguese. When it came to Guy's turn to show how the product worked and impress the owner, he somehow managed to throw half of them at him and dropped the rest on the floor. By the time we staggered back to our hotel we had visited seventeen different establishments.

In one of the clubs in Porto they purchased some and invited us to have a drink and enjoy the show. Inside it was very dark, with rows of seats like a private cinema. Two girls emerged from behind the curtains wearing nothing but our luminous necklaces – some around their huge breasts and more at the top of their thighs. They came straight over to us and suggestively wiggled their bits in our faces; it was probably their way of saying thank you. The owner hinted that we could have some 'extras' later if we were interested. We politely declined.

A wealthy local businessman had his eyes on at least one of the dancing girls, but Bippy was his favourite. He used to take us all out for dinner two or three nights a week. He would pick up the girls in one or two of his seven luxury cars and we would follow him in our car, usually to Porto. He was in the shoe business and was known as 'Tony from Porto'. His right-hand man was 'Maravilha' (Mr Wonderful). He had a shoe factory in the city, copied designs from Italian magazines, then sold them on the markets.

Guy was driving along in the centre of Porto following behind his Porsche one wet and windy night when he lost control for a second and scraped against a car coming in the opposite direction. The road was at a different height to the tramline, which Guy hadn't noticed at first, and which caused him to swerve. The other driver jumped out of his car ranting and raving. Tony came over, told him to shut up, gave him a wad of cash and off we went as though nothing had happened.

Guy and I went to watch the show in the Espinho casino one night. This place was what I had expected of a casino, with its sumptuous table-lit dining room surrounding the stage. When we had finished eating, the waiter asked us if we would like a whisky with our coffees. After he twisted my arm, we reluctantly accepted. When he returned to our table, instead of pouring a measure into our glasses he said, "Help yourselves", and left the full bottle on our table. We couldn't believe our luck – maybe he knew we were with the girls, so we were entitled to some extra privileges. The northerners had a reputation for being mean but after meeting Tony and now this I was beginning to question the veracity of this story.

We drank far too much of the bottle, but – as they say – never look a gift horse in the mouth. When we asked the waiter if we could pay, he came over to us with a ruler and a felt tip pen to measure the amount still left in the bottle and presented us with a massive bill. That put us in our places, thinking we were entitled to special treatment. We were greedy nobodies hoisted with our own petard.

76

Disaster Strikes

DECEMBER is not the time to be in Monte Gordo – a bit like most of the year – but Dee and Co. needed the work, so there we were again. One of our fair friends had been in touch and had ordered three thousand balloons that he was taking with him to Madeira. We didn't do wholesale, but for that many we could still make enough for a quick killing. He put ten bottles of gas on the ferry to the island ready for the festivities over the New Year period when Madeira has one of the biggest fireworks displays in the world.

Guy flew back to England with two empty suitcases and would be back in Lisbon in a few days' time with the goods. By sheer coincidence we received a phone call for Miss Wood, which was Dee's surname, saying that their next month's contract would be in Madeira. So, it looked like we would all be going, as New Year's Eve would be great for the lumies.

(I had this recurring dream where I'd turned into a West Indian and would arrange to meet my young lady in the pine forest nearby, yet when I arrived, I could never find her. I knew she was there somewhere; the problem was that "I couldn't see Dee Wood for de trees".)

When we were in Vilamoura, the girls bought Guy a traditional knitted jumper for his birthday, which was subsequently stolen from their dressing room.

Guy and I had earlier given Dee a portable radio cassette player, which we used to record a mock news report on tape capturing the moment the thief was caught. On the BBC news today… 'A criminal has been apprehended this morning after a spate of robberies in the Vilamoura area. The suspect confessed immediately when he was stopped in a road block and the police had said to him... Pull-over'.

A few days later, I received a distressing phone call from Guy. He'd been stopped and searched at the customs in Lisbon airport, along with all the other passengers on the plane. It was coming up to Christmas and people were bringing back fur coats and the like. He tried his best to talk his way out of it by saying the goods were for a party, but they confiscated the lot and told him that he would have to go to court if he wanted to get them back. We had heard about Portuguese courts and how long the process could take – years probably.

I left for Lisbon the next day, having promised Dee that I would try to get to Madeira. I met Guy, who was with Rica at a customs broker. She was trying to pull a few strings but without much luck. We went back to Sintra, together with Richard in their VW van and then on to a place called Varzea de Sintra, a small village just outside Sintra. They had a rented house and a barn next door, where Guy and I could stay while we tried to sort out our problem.

77

A Mad Era

WE SPENT Christmas in Sintra at our new residence and then began making plans for a trip to Madeira. The weather was good, so we set up a lumie production line outside in the yard. Guy and Rica were filling the tubes in a ruin next door, as there was a staircase which they could use for the dropping process. The rest of us were doing the messy part of cutting and blocking. Guy and I were flying to Madeira on New Year's Eve and Rica and family were going to try Lisbon.

We boarded the plane with our ice boxes as hand luggage with what looked like smoke pouring out of them – imagine trying that nowadays! Dee and the girls were already there but we couldn't stay with them that night as there was a problem with the accommodation. There was a spectacular pyrotechnic display over the harbour, with the cruise ships' horns blaring out at midnight to add to the excitement. We sold all the lumies we had bought with us, celebrated the New Year in style at a nightclub and then, as we couldn't find anywhere to stay, finished up in a place called the Pousada dos Vinhaticos, somewhere in the middle of the island, in what appeared to be a hikers' hotel.

At hangover breakfast, half the guests were dressed-up as though they were about to climb the Matterhorn, the other half were ramblers with waterproof jackets, climbing boots, woolly socks and hats, gloves, rucksacks, supplies and wads of maps, Madeira was supposed to be a warm winter destination. We had a look at some of the walks on offer and opted for a hike up to Pico Ruivo. We were still dressed in the same clothes as we'd worn at the nightclub – we'd left the rest of our stuff at the girls' hotel. When we went outside, we were shocked to find that we were surrounded by steep mountains.

We set off on walk number eleven – or whatever it was – all the walks had numbers, and we had a pamphlet that we had picked up at the reception which showed us the way. The first hour or so wasn't too bad, but then the path started climbing and all we could see ahead of us were never-ending steep steps. Superman Guy was flying up them like an Olympic athlete, but I was well behind, struggling to keep up. Conditions got worse the further we climbed. At one point, we were fighting our way through undergrowth and branches while crossing the side of a rock face.

Spot the white slip-on climbing shoes

Over the edge was a terrifying view of the valley below – definitely not for the faint-hearted: one false move and that would be the end of you. I was beginning to regret ever agreeing to such a ridiculous expedition, especially wearing my white slip-on shoes. We were halfway up what was beginning to feel like Mount Everest when some professionals crossed our path on their way down. They were Americans.

"My God what the Hell are you guys doing dressed like that on walk eleven? You're gonna die when you get up there!"

"Is it much further?" I asked wearily.

"You better turn around before it's too late. The weather conditions are extremely unpredictable – you're lucky to have got this far. It's nearly two thousand metres high at the top!"

"That's nearly twice the height of Snowden, what a way to spend New Year's Day," I laughed in despair.

The Yanks went on their way down, we carried on up, as it was a pleasant sunny day and there was no sign of any bad weather approaching.

We drank water from natural springs but had nothing to eat. I'd convinced myself that there would probably be a cafe at the top. By late afternoon, Pico Ruivo was in sight. When we finally made it to the summit we couldn't take in the fantastic view as it was nearly dark, freezing cold, wet and foggy. We followed a path to a car park, but it was empty – and no cafe of course. We set off down the only road, whistling some marching songs to keep our spirits up. I was about as exhausted as you can possibly be and still be able to move, while Sir Edmund Hillary continued to stride ahead up front.

Eventually we came across a village with a restaurant and rooms to rent. Funnily enough we were the only guests. The old couple that ran the place served us a hot stew, which at that moment tasted like the best meal I'd ever had. I couldn't recall a time when I had ever been so hungry. They asked us where we had come from and where our car was. I could see by the look on their faces that our story was, at best, improbable.

Upstairs our bedroom was dank and musty, even the sheets were damp. There was a one-bar electric heater, which I put in my bed in an attempt to dry it out – not exactly health and safety, but the steam coming off the bedclothes was proof of just how wet the beds were. We put newspapers in the beds and kept our clothes on and, despite the conditions, we had a good night's sleep. In the morning we ate breakfast then walked all the way back down the mountain, this time along the roads and the levadas until we reached the capital Funchal in the early evening, which was where we had started from two days before.

We met up with the girls, who had moved into an apartment and were booked in for a month. When they asked us where we'd been for two days we just said climbing up and down a six-thousand-foot mountain.

A week later, Guy flew back with all our loot to Lisbon and then on to Sintra. He and Rica tried in vain to recover the balloons from the customs and the courts. I enjoyed the rest of the month in Madeira, doing most of the levada walks in the process. These are man-made channels which carry the water down the mountains. There's a path that always runs along beside them and, armed with a guidebook, you can cover most of the island. For sheer excitement, the walk from near the top of the island at Pico Arieiro to where we'd climbed, Pico Ruivo, is unbeatable. It takes from six to eight hours there and back, depending how fast you walk and what the weather is like. The last time I went up there, the locals were playing a game where you built a snowman on the bonnet of your car and then drove back down to see how far you could get before it melted or slid off. Which just goes to show you how lucky we were with the weather that day.

I loved my time in Madeira. I even designed what I thought was a fool proof gambling system on the roulette tables – luckily Guy had taken most of the money with him, so I didn't lose too much. It's weird how my ingenious method had worked in training. I'd even bought a mini roulette wheel. What an idiot. One afternoon, I had tea and cakes at the famously posh Reid's Palace hotel, which was another quick way of getting rid of plenty of cash. A captain of one of the cruise liners in port had invited the girls to join him and was doing his best to impress them when he looked me up and down and asked me what line of business I was in, to which I replied:

"Market trader."

"Stock Exchange, finance, that kind of thing?" he asked.

"No, I sell novelty items at fairs and festivals – and yourself?"

"I work for Cunard."

"So do I, on rare occasions... anyway you shouldn't swear in front of the ladies."

"What are you talking about?"

"You said fucking hard!"

"No, Cunard, the shipping lines. I'm a captain."

Dee and the girls held their hands over their mouths, trying in vain to suppress their giggles.

"I do apologise, genuine misunderstanding," I said, trying to keep a straight face.

I went back to Sintra to join Guy. We were at a bit of a loss as to what to do next, or where to go. While I'd been away he'd been thoroughly enjoying himself partying and getting to know the Sintrense as the people from Sintra were called. Apparently Sintra high society consisted of half-a-dozen wealthy families, all with loads of children who were now grown up, or well on their way. Some of the families had suffered financially after the revolution and were now finding themselves having to face difficult times.

Rica and Richard cooked most nights, so we usually all had dinner together. One night after we'd eaten, we sat around a card table and Rica introduced us to a game called 'King'. It's a tad complicated at first but once you get into it, and I did with a vengeance, you could find yourself hooked on it. Guy, on the other hand, was so confused by the rules that he threw his cards on the log fire out of sheer frustration.

The next day it was my turn to be upset. Dee came over from Lisbon to tell me she was off to Japan for six months and then probably on to Las Vegas. She had always told me that her dancing came first in her life and that one day our romance would be over. I hadn't been expecting it to happen so soon but realistically I knew that day had to come eventually. I was devastated. I tried all I could to stop her going, but her mind was made up. She was so excited about it, I could see what it meant to her, but I just felt so miserable because we'd probably never see each other again, so I couldn't join in with her enthusiasm.

We had a very tearful farewell and promised to keep in touch.

Guy and I actually did some hard work for two weeks when we did some earth-moving for Barry and Alvaro, an openly gay couple who had recently bought a *palacete* in Colares, near Sintra. We had the pleasure of watching the Adonis that was Guy in his Wellington boots and tight shorts.

There were a couple of bars in the Vila de Sintra we often frequented, where Rica's friends and brothers used to hang out. The young men didn't exactly welcome us with open arms although some of the ladies, however, were very friendly towards us. I was still pining for Dee, so I wasn't at all interested in getting involved in another relationship in the near future. However, a few drinks later, and some irresistible feminine charm, I found myself in the front of our car with one of the local girls. I was reluctant to have sex with her. She looked very sweet and innocent, but things got out of hand as usual. We had started to make love when I asked her:

"Are you on the pill or something?"

"Don't worry, you won't make me pregnant," she said.

"How can you be so sure?"

"Because I'm already two months pregnant, but I'm having an abortion next week!"

"Oh, that's alright then," I answered sarcastically, wondering what the hell I'd got myself into.

I was at the house one morning, when Richard packed up all his stuff and left. He'd told me that he and Rica hadn't been getting on well for a while, so he had no choice but to leave her and the young boy. He was a broken man. They had even been to Australia together and met his parents, but it wasn't to be. He was in more pain a few days later, when he turned up at a football match that we were involved in. He was in goal when I kicked a wet muddy football so hard at him that he never saw it coming. It hit him in the middle of his chest and knocked him over, leaving a perfect imprint of a football on his clean white T-shirt. It looked like one of their computer printouts.

It wasn't long after that when Guy and Rica got it on together. The young lady who I'd met sorted herself out and moved in with me, then another one of her girlfriends gave me a gorgeous black and white puppy. It looked like we might be staying here for a while.

To Be

Continued...

Printed in Great Britain
by Amazon

46630683R00185